بِسْمِ اللهِ الرَّحْمٰنِ الرَّحِيْمِ

Praise for *Secrets of Divine Love*

"The fragrance of the Beloved permeates every passage of this magnificent book, gently opening the gates of the heart and inviting the reader into a direct experience of that which the author so beautifully evokes. Whether you identify as a Muslim whose faith has perhaps grown weary or as someone who would like to taste of the essence of a tradition you do not understand, *Secrets of Divine Love* is a masterful map of the landscape of the soul on its journey home to the One who both transcends and dwells within all that is."

—MIRABAI STARR

Author of *God of Love: A Guide to the Heart of Judaism, Christianity and Islam* and *Wild Mercy: Living the Fierce & Tender Wisdom of the Women Mystics*

"A. Helwa's book, *Secrets of Divine Love*, is a magnificent accomplishment. So often we are asked where and how one accesses the inner heart of the Islamic tradition—here it is! Helwa does a beautiful job of taking us, no matter what our faith background, through the Qur'an, teachings of the Prophet, Rumi, and other mystical luminaries. She does so with gentleness, kindness, never preachy, and always inviting. *Secrets of Divine Love* is a beautiful book, and a major contribution. I wholeheartedly recommended it for spiritual seekers of all paths!"

—OMID SAFI

Professor of Middle Eastern Studies at Duke University and author of *Radical Love: Teachings from the Islamic Mystical Tradition*

"Here is a manifesto to Love, love of God, God's love for us, love for ourselves and all of creation, a manifesto to hope and a manifesto against despair. Helwa draws on diverse literary sources and the wisdom of many authors to illustrate universal spiritual teachings . . . Her prose is captivating, poetic and oozing with the passion and vitality that she herself embodies . . . For the reader this book breathes the spark of life into us and plants in us a longing to experience these truths for ourselves."

—NURA LAIRD

MEd, Professor at the University of Sufism, Chair of the Department of Spiritual Peacemaking, Mediator, Sufi healer and Counselor

"I am simply entranced by Helwa's metaphors and insights. The bulk of her sentences are poetry in motion and studded with pearls of wisdom. Fragrant with beauty. Many of the sentences are musical. You can rap with them. Enchanting! The creative way Helwa has integrated her heart knowledge into her understanding of Islam is stunning."

—IMAM JAMAL RAHMAN

Author of *Spiritual Gems of Islam: Insights & Practices from the Qur'an, Hadith, Rumi & Muslim Teaching Stories to Enlighten the Heart & Mind*

"*Secrets of Divine Love* is the product of A. Helwa's earnest search for truth and meaning. It is also her invitation to us, the readers, to see what she has seen. This is a fascinating book that offers various profound insights and a vision of Islam—and indeed the Divine—that many readers will surely find enlightening and uplifting."

—MOHAMMAD KHALIL

Professor of Islamic Studies at Michigan State University

"*Secrets of Divine Love* opens with one word: 'Love.' This word appears and reappears, until the reader comes to understand only a fraction of the ways that God pours His light on them. Helwa guides the reader through a spiritual journey, highlighting aspects of Islamic spirituality, practices, and tenets of the faith. This book serves as a contemporary primer on Islam, and blends passages from the Qur'an with reflection and discussion prompts for the reader. One regularly is flushed with examples of God's compassion, kindness, forgiveness, patience, and comfort. This is simply a wonderful book, written with care and precision, weaving us into God's beautiful tapestry."

—DR. NAZITA LAJEVARDI

"*Secrets of Divine Love* remedies my deepest existential dread by reminding me of my inherent worth as a being that is unconditionally loved. It pulls from common as well as less known sources, providing evidence to quell the mind and soothe the heart. The carefully curated content strikes deep emotional chords. I find myself irresistibly falling in love with God and Islam."

—MAHYA SHAMAI
Multidisciplinary Artist

"*Secrets of Divine Love* is a gem! It's relatable and readable for those of us who consider ourselves 'faithful,' those of us struggling to feel so, and everyone in between. In the language of sweetness and compassion, Helwa walks us through the journey of connection back to the love of Allah."

—LEILA ENTEZAM
LMFT, MBA, Emotional Intelligence Thought Leader

"The author's work has a special way of speaking to the heart. This reading offers exceptional spiritual nuances on the core of Islamic belief and practices. More than ever, we are in need of content like this that shines a luminous light on a faith that is frequently misunderstood."

—SEYED MAHDI AL-QASWINI
Educator at Islamic Educational Center of Orange County

"A marvelous book that gives a sound grasp of this great religion and nourishment to the heart we deeply need. This book is a source of majesty and beauty."

—DR. FAWZIA AL-RAWI
Author of *Divine Names: The 99 Healing Names of the One Love* and
Founder of the Center for Feminine Spirituality and Sufism

SECRETS OF DIVINE LOVE

A Spiritual Journey into the Heart of Islam

A. HELWA

Naulit
PUBLISHING

*"My Lord! Cause me to enter whatever I may do sincerely
and cause me to leave it sincerely and grant me supporting
authority from Your presence."*

QUR'AN 17:80

*In the name of Allah, the Lord of Mercy, the Bestower of Mercy.
All praise and glory belongs to Allah, Lord of the worlds.
The Lord of Mercy, the Bestower of Mercy.
Master of the Day of Judgment.
You alone we worship; You alone we ask for help.
Guide us to the straight path.
The way of those on whom You have bestowed Your grace,
Not of those who earned Your anger nor of those who went astray.*

QUR'AN 1:1-7

Acknowledgements

In the name of Allah, whose love made this book possible. Blessings be upon the Prophet Muhammad ﷺ, whose gentle mercy has taught me how to walk in faith. I am deeply grateful to all the prophets, whose examples help guide me on the path of divine love. To Sidi, who taught me how to hear the music of my soul. To my mother, whose softness and prayers changed the course of my destiny. To my father, who embodies what it means to be a sincere and generous servant of God. To Amir, whose kind heart and sweet soul teaches me how to love. To my grandfather, whose spiritual stories fill the pages of this book. To my family, who have always unconditionally supported me. To my soul friends, whose wisdom and love uplifts and inspires me. To my spiritual community and in particular my teachers who taught me how to love God and experience His unending peace. To the hundreds of thousands of kind souls in our beautiful online community, who taught me what it means to be vulnerable and sincere. To my editors and designers, for guiding this book towards its greatest potential. And in the loving memory of Esmat, who embodied what it means to be joyful, kind, and selfless. I dedicate this book to all of you and to all the spiritual seekers seeking the path of divine love and truth. All praise to God.

ALHAMDULLILAH

CONTENTS

*"In the name of Allah,
the Lord of Mercy, the
Bestower of Mercy."*

QUR'AN 1:1

INTRODUCTION

Love. It is the reason there is something instead of nothing. It is from the soil of love that all of existence blossoms into being. Love is why we are here. Love is why you are holding these words in your hands, speaking them on your tongue, or hearing them with your ears. This book did not call you or find you because of who I am, but because of how loving God is.

The words I will offer you are not new, but I do believe many of these teachings of love and mercy have been forgotten. Islam does not have to change, we just need to return to the spiritual heart and soul of its timeless message of love, mercy, peace, freedom, justice, and unity.

Although this book is about Islamic spirituality and practices, I believe God is bigger than any one religion or philosophy. I choose Islam as my faith, but I offer you these words from the Qur'an not to change you, but to remind you how much you are loved by God. I believe that just as wisdom teachings from other faiths have enriched my relationship with God, the deeper dimensions of Islam may also inspire you, regardless of what path you choose to walk. I pray these words awaken your heart to fall deeper in love with Allah, God, Elohim, Yahweh or whatever you choose to call the supreme eternal Being, who has infinite names, but only one essence.

No one has the power to truly change a heart. I believe only God can decide what path we will walk on this spaciously beautiful Earth. God is intentional and nothing happens by accident. I am a snowflake in the sun, soon to dissolve back into the earth that once formed me, but God and His words are eternal and unchanging.

I am happy you found this book, and my deep prayer is that through its words you find forgotten pieces of yourself. You are a palace of hidden gems and the greatest treasure you could ever find is already within you. Gold will melt, money will burn, but you carry the everlasting and mysterious breath of God inside of you and that can never be taken away.

Your connection with God is innate, because it is His love that brought you to life and His love that keeps you alive. If you are seeking to reignite the deep connection you already have with your Lord, then my prayer is that this book returns you to the path of divine love.

Secrets of Divine Love was written for the longing heart, for the one who is searching for something they have not been able to find. For the one who sometimes spirals into hopelessness and cannot help but feel too imperfect for a perfect God to love. This book is for the one who is at the edge of their faith, who has experienced religion as a harsh winter instead of the life-bearing spring it was sent to be by God.

Whether you are on the path of Islam or just seeking to know God, *Secrets of Divine Love* uses the language of spirituality to transform your relationship with God, yourself, and the world around you. Beyond offering heartfelt perspectives on Islamic theology, *Secrets of Divine Love* walks you through practical exercises that inspire love, strengthen faith, and increase reliance on and intimacy with God. By drawing upon the inspirational words of the Qur'an and the Prophet Muhammad ﷺ, delving into spiritual poetry, and learning through stories from the world's greatest spiritual masters, this book seeks to connect the heart of the reader to God.

Secrets of Divine Love takes you on a journey through the mysterious nature of God and His unconditional mercy and love for you. It then delves into who you are and how the Qur'an can be used as a map for manifesting your greatest potential. By unveiling the spiritual secrets that are hidden in the heart of Islam's pillars, principles and practices, this book calls you to contemplate the divine beauty that is imbedded in every atom of existence. *Secrets of Divine Love* is a reminder that no matter who you are God's love is like a healing balm that can mend your soul and reignite the spark of faith within you.

Awakening to faith is not a one-time event, but a continuously unfolding reality. The journey of faith is not a race, but a marathon of love that each person walks at a different pace. Although each person's experience of God is unique to them, in writing this book I felt guided to share my story with you, as a testimony that God's love and mercy has the power to change every heart it touches.

My Journey from Fear to Love

I was born Muslim, but growing up I was never taught how to love and be loved by God. Eventually, as a teenager, I gave up praying, and for the next decade I wandered in search of something that would fill the emptiness of my soul. I visited mosques around the world, lived in a monastery, had spiritual experiences meditating with Buddhist monks, studied Taoism and Kabbalah, but I still couldn't find the inner peace I was seeking.

In my early twenties, I was traveling through a small town in Turkey called Cappadocia, when the divine spark of faith reignited within me like lightning. All it took was my eyes to fall upon a woman who was drowned in her worship of God. I watched her pray in an old seventeenth-century animal barn, as if nothing in the world existed but her divine Lover.

She did not robotically repeat words of prayer like a formula; rather, every word she uttered came with a silent "I love you, my beloved Lord." Her words were like synchronized dancers swimming in unison in the ocean of love that poured out of her. She was the first person I had ever seen in my life that not only prayed but she herself became the prayer.

I knew instantly that she had everything my soul had been seeking, but I still had no idea exactly what it was or how I would reach it. I was perplexed as to how I could suddenly feel at home in a strange land I had never known. It was not until many years later that I came to understand that our real homes are not the houses we grow up in, but our real homes, the home of our souls are built from the brick and mortar of divine praise.

I know now that the beauty that I witnessed in Turkey was not just a woman in love with God, but God's unconditional love pouring upon her. It was the fragrance of this divine love that awakened the sleeping lion of faith within me.

Once the oil lamp of my heart was lit again, the dominoes began to fall—until I fell into the presence of an imam from the holy mosque of Al-Aqsa in Jerusalem, who would teach me how to water the seeds of love and faith within me. It was through the guidance of this elderly Palestinian man—whom I would affectionately call "Sidi"—that my life would forever change.

Sidi was a master of the spiritual sciences of Islam and the first teacher I ever had that called me to God through the door of His love. Sidi told us, "Know, my beloved, that the love is eternal between Allah and His creation and the electric circuitry of His love flows through everything. If not for this, nothing would move that moves; nothing would live that lives. Every planet in its orbit and every cell in its course is a witness to the love of Allah and a sign of His wisdom. Keep this love inside you and love with it all the time, because the moment you lose it, you lose yourself; you lose Him." The deeper I dived into the Qur'an, the heart of the prophets, and the teachings of the countless sages of Islamic history, the more I found that love had always been at the soul of Islam—it was only my heart that had been blind to the experience of it.

As I began seeking more deeply—fasting, praying, and meditating upon God's words—I started to touch places inside my heart that I had never known existed. Slowly, my hardened heart softened, restoring my spiritual vision. The outer shell of who I thought I was started to break as the mask of my ego began to melt away, unveiling a spirit I had felt from time to time, but had never fully embraced.

As I started to feel the joy of my authentic self—which I later would come to know as the *fitra* or primordial goodness that exists at the core of all people—I felt called to write about it. But it was not until a few years ago that the call became so loud I could no longer ignore it. The message was clear: write a book about the loving heart of Islam. Although the guidance was straightforward, the voices of doubt in my mind fanned the flames of my insecurity, making me feel unworthy of what I felt God was asking of me.

"I Am Not Good Enough"

I felt like I hardly knew anything about Islam and the voice of "I am not good enough" started to dance in my mind like a billion butterflies flapping in unison to the soundtrack of my anxiety. I kept turning to God and saying, "I am not worthy of this task," saying it over and over again until one day my heart heard God whisper back, *I know you are not good enough. This is exactly why I have chosen you. Remove yourself even more from this. This is not something you will do, it is something I will do through you.*

It suddenly became clear to me that the whole purpose of faith is not to be "good enough" before we begin on the path to God, but to come with all our deficiencies to God, knowing that only He can fill in our gaps through His mercy.

I realize now that what God calls us to do in His name is not based on our current ability, but on what is possible through our greatest God-given potential. When I turned from facing my limited capacity to facing the infinite greatness of God, my anxiety dissolved like clouds in the presence of His light. Like the staff of Moses, this epiphany struck the Red Sea of fear within me, unveiling a path through the limitations I had created.

In this moment, I was ready to be molded. I felt like clay in the hands of the Maker. I trusted that God would make a way for me—not because of who I am, but because of how merciful and loving He is.

The Powerful Prayer of a Stranger

One evening, after spending hours researching and writing, God opened the ears of my heart to hear the prayer of a boy or girl somewhere in the world who asked Him for something that I was written to deliver. It's hard to explain, but it felt like God was showing me that this book is more than just words on paper. This book is a finger pointing to a living God who cares and compassionately listens to every single prayer we make. In that moment, I felt humility wash over me. I had spent thousands of hours of my life contemplating and finally putting into words this book, all as a means of answering *one* sincere prayer. I thought to myself:

> *Who is this person? Who is the one who owns such a*
> *beautiful heart to make such a powerful prayer?*

Whoever you are, I am certain you will find this book one day, and when you do I want you to know that God loves you. Your prayer meant so much to God that He brought dozens of people together, dedicating their lives to creating this work to answer your sincere calling. I often think of you and how this book belongs to you. After all, it was your love and longing that put into motion something that is beyond me.

I am not a writer. I am a dreamer and lover of God. These words found their place on the page because God wrote it to be that way.

Alhamdullilah, All Praise Belongs to God

If something in this book brings inspiration to your life, please do not credit me. I am just a flower-picker; I am not the one who planted these ideas. If you feel the stir of life inside of you, it is because of all that God has already planted within *you*. If you come across a mistake in these words, know that my humanity is to blame.

This book is meant to remind you of all that you already are and always have been, to remind you that you matter, that God loves you unconditionally, that you have been created intentionally with a divine purpose, and that you already have all that you need to awaken your heart and soul on the path to God. Place your trust in the Divine and let Him lead you back into the embrace of His everlasting love.

In love and light,

A. Helwa

"A pure heart, open to the Light, will be filled with the elixir of Truth."

RUMI

READING WITH AN
OPEN HEART

When we open our hearts to the light of God the answers to our most bewildering questions begin to blossom. It is my hope that through reading this book with an open heart you will have an *experience* of God, instead of simply acquiring new information about God.

There are many techniques and experiences that summon the opening of the spiritual heart. One of the ways of doing this is by taking a few deep breaths, placing your hand on your chest, and following your breath down to your heart. This may be followed by setting the intention to listen and read these words not just from your mind but with the eyes and ears of your heart.

Even if our doubts span an entire ocean, the light of God's wisdom can rise beyond the furthest horizons and illuminate our hearts with contentment. My deep prayer is that this book will give you a taste of this.

A Few Things to Consider

Although this book will walk you through major concepts of Islamic spirituality, it is not a textbook on Islam. Instead of emphasizing every aspect of a Muslim's spiritual practice, it highlights inspirational and practical insights from the Qur'an and Islamic tradition.

However, before we jump into the ocean of divine love, there are a few stylistic things that I would like to further clarify to avoid any confusion.

1. I use Allah and God interchangeably as a means of articulating to the English speaker that God, the one transcendent omnipresent reality, and Allah are one and the same. Although in Arabic the word *Allah* has many connotations that the English word "God" does not have, it felt important to use both, since the majority of Muslims are not born Arabic speakers. Also, since Allah transcends all language, I will often speak metaphorically in expressing different aspects of His holy qualities by using symbols and metaphors.

2. After the words "Prophet Muhammad," "Prophet," or "Muhammad" you will find the following Arabic symbol, ﷺ, which stands for *salla Allahu 'alayhi wa-sallam* and translates to "Peace and blessings be upon him." This emblem is included in the text because Allah says in the Qur'an to send blessings upon the Prophet ﷺ every time his name is mentioned. As the Qur'an says, "Allah and His angels shower blessings upon the Prophet. Oh you who believe, send blessings on him and salute him with worthy greetings of peace" (33:56). In a sense, when we send blessings upon the Prophet ﷺ we are following the sacred path (*sunnah*) of Allah and His angels.

3. Outside of reciting the words of the Qur'an, whenever the Prophet Muhammad ﷺ spoke, his words were referred to as *Hadith*. These "Prophetic sayings" paired with the written observations of the Prophet's ﷺ daily practices make up the *sunnah* or "example of the Prophetic way." After the Qur'an, one of the major means of guidance for Muslims is the *sunnah* of the Prophet ﷺ, as emulated and preserved by his family

and most righteous companions. Although there are many volumes of certified Hadiths, there are also fabricated Hadiths that over time have been falsely attributed to the Prophet ﷺ. The Hadiths quoted in this book were carefully chosen from reputable sources, reiterate principles that are at the core of the message of the Qur'an, and are cited in the endnotes as a point of reference for further study.

4. The translations of the Qur'an I use are taken from the work of a large body of translators, some of which include the following: Muhammad Asad, Muhammad Sarwar, Yusuf Ali, A.J. Arberry, Mohsin Khan, Muhammad Pickthall, Yahya Emerick, and Laleh Bakhtiar. I also have been influenced by translations by Dr. Hossein Nasr and the team behind *The Study Qur'an,* and the famous *Sahih International* translation by American converts Emily Assami, Amatullah Bantley, and Mary Kennedy. I have also occasionally made grammatical corrections to the nineteenth-century English translations, to make the text more approachable for the modern-day English speaker.

5. Whenever there is a direct reference to a particular revelation of the Qur'an you will find the sentence followed by two numbers separated by a colon, i.e. (57:4). The first number, in this case "57," refers to the chapter *(surah)*; the second number after the colon, in this case "4," refers to the verse *(ayah)* within the 57th chapter. A citation of (1:5-7) simply means that the quoted text is from the first chapter as denoted by the "1" and is referring to verses 5 through 7. I have also put these numbers after my own sentences that were inspired by a particular verse in the Qur'an.

6. When I use the word "mystics" in the text I am referring to spiritual masters in the Islamic tradition that delved past the literalism of the religion and into the realm of the heart. A mystic is not someone who ignored the rules of the Qur'an

and prophetic tradition, but someone who sought to learn the esoteric teachings of the faith from a place of love and joy. In fact, most of the utterances of Muslim mystics are directly inspired by the Qur'an and the Prophet ﷺ, or inspired by the family of the Prophet ﷺ and his closest companions.

7. I rely heavily on the profound wisdom of the seventh-century Islamic sage Ali ibn Talib, affectionately known by many as Imam Ali. The spiritual master Imam Ali, may Allah be pleased with him and grant him peace, was the cousin and son-in-law of the Prophet ﷺ and the first person after the wife of the Prophet ﷺ to convert to Islam. The Prophet Muhammad ﷺ said of Imam Ali, "I am the city of knowledge and Ali is its gate."[1] Imam Ali is known to be a symbol of unification and peace, as Sunnis, Shias, and Sufis follow his guidance and adore his examples of bravery, leadership, and spiritual knowledge. I also rely on the beautiful contemplations of the Islamic theologian and poet Jalaluddin Rumi, whose most famous book, *The Mathnawi,* is a poetic masterpiece that was directly inspired by the Qur'an.

8. When words in Arabic could not properly be translated into English, I put the Arabic transliteration of the word in parenthesis as a point of reference.

9. Many of the quotes, spiritual stories, and teaching parables I have included in this book are not cited, as they are oral stories that have been passed down through different cultures and religions. I am forever grateful to all of my friends, teachers, and especially my grandfather, for taking the time to share these priceless stories with me so that I could in turn share them with you.

10. At the end of each chapter you will find a "reflection," designed to help you apply teachings from the chapter into your daily life. These sections felt important to include because the Qur'an describes the acquiring of knowledge without internalizing

that wisdom and putting it into practice like that of "a donkey carrying books" (62:5). The ultimate purpose of these practices is to promote active reading of the text, in which the reader not only intellectually understands the material, but also absorbs and incorporates it into how they practice their faith. Before approaching these practices, it is recommended to set an intention or to do two cycles (*rakah*) of ritual prayer (*salat*), because when we are intentional and spiritually mindful our experience of the practices will become more meaningful and profound. Some practices are suggested to be done every day for a week, while others are need-based. Allow yourself to be drawn to whichever practices awaken and inspire your heart.

*Intra*faith: Celebrating Our Spiritual Similarities

This book will not delve into the history and evolution of Islamic theology, but it does seek to create a bridge—not just between Islam and other faiths through universal spiritual truths, but also between various Muslims who practice differently from one another.

There are, generally speaking, two major schools of thought within Islam: Sunni Muslims, who make up about 80-85 percent of the Muslims; Shia Muslims, who are about 10–13 percent of the Muslim population worldwide; and a handful of other spiritual perspectives within Islam, many of which identify with Sufism.² Although Sufi Muslims generally consider themselves to be either Sunni or Shia, they tend to focus on the inner dimensions of Islam. Nevertheless, the differences between Sunni and Shia are predominately historical disagreements that trickled down over time into theological differences.

I have found that in Muslim circles it is often easier to build bridges with people of different faiths than it is to build a connection with someone who is a Muslim, but practices differently than we do. There are many myths and misperceptions that perpetuate, due to the lack of engagement between the different schools of thought.

The purpose of this book is not to engage in historical debates, but rather to offer an inspiring, uplifting, and spiritual take on the beliefs, practices, and principles that millions of Muslims share. As believers, we can always find common ground through our mutual longing for God.

> *"Hold firmly to the rope of Allah all together and do not become divided."*
>
> QUR'AN 3:103

Often, when it comes to interfaith or *intra*faith we talk about "being tolerant" of different religious views and theology, but the Qur'an calls us to be more than tolerant, it calls us toward open-hearted connection.[3] The Qur'an calls us to know one another and to find ways to make room for each other's experience, without compromising or sacrificing the singularity and supreme nature of God (58:11).

When we judge someone solely based on a label, which means different things to different people, we lose the opportunity to get to know that person for who they actually are. As the Qur'an says, "Oh humankind, indeed We have created you from male and female and made you nations and tribes that you may know one another. The most noble of you in the sight of Allah is the most righteous of you" (49:13). We may not always agree on the interpretation of certain historical events or theological points, but in order to abide by this verse of the Qur'an we have to step out of our comfort zone and get to know all people, without discrimination.

I'm not saying that we should ignore our differences; but rather, that it is important to remember that how someone actually experiences and manifests their faith says much more about their relationship with Allah than a label does. It is arrogant to assume that we know everything about someone or their faith based on an article we read online or a sermon we heard. Plus, the truth will never have a chance to blossom if we keep cutting people out of our lives or religion that we do not agree with. After all, only God can see into a person's heart, so only God can say who has genuine faith in their hearts. It is not up to us to make that decision.

History has shown us the great strides that both the family of the Prophet ﷺ and the most righteous amongst his companions made to establish and preserve unity through the different conflicts the early Muslim community had to traverse. May we follow in the righteous examples left behind by those our Prophet ﷺ loved. May we strive to create bridges where there are walls and work toward establishing peace on this Earth. May we answer the call of God and live the best life we can by holding tight to the Qur'an and the examples of the Prophet ﷺ, and humbly sharing our faith through acts of kindness, love, and mercy toward all humankind.

I believe that *intra*faith communication or bridge-building within the Muslim community is not just possible, but can easily be done when we focus on our shared moral principles, use the Qur'an as our compass, and take the Prophet Muhammad ﷺ as our guide. To be as inclusive as possible, this book will focus on the five pillars that Sunni Muslims follow, as these core principles are all also included within the Shia doctrines of the Roots of Religion (*usool-ad-deen*) and the Branches of Religion (*furo-ad-deen*). The book will be centered around the following universal truths of the Islamic faith: witnessing God's singularity and Muhammad's ﷺ prophethood (*shahadah*), ritualistic prayer (*salat*), fasting (*sawm*), the poor alms-tax (*zakat*), and the pilgrimage to Mecca (*Hajj*).

Although this book will not specifically discuss the additional practices and tenets that are staples in the Shia branch of Islam, it feels important for the sake of *intra*faith awareness to share some of them here. Alongside the five core principles that all Muslims embrace, many Shia Muslims consider the following beliefs and tenets cornerstones of how they experience their faith: belief in divine justice (*'adl*), belief in the Day of Judgment and resurrection (*mi'ad*), belief in guidance (*imamah*). There is also an emphasis on enjoining what is good (*amr-bil-ma'roof*), forbidding the wrong (*nahi-anil-munkar*), paying an additional wealth tax for the needy of 20 percent (*khums*), striving for the sake of Allah with yourself and your wealth (*jihad*), loving the believers and friends of Allah (*tawalla*), disassociating from those who do not honor the path of goodness that the Prophet ﷺ paved (*tabarra*).

Many of these principles are based directly on verses of the Qur'an and so they are universally followed by many Muslims, even if they are not always interpreted and conceptualized in the same way. Although there are differences between Sunni, Shia, and Sufi Muslims, there are also many spiritual similarities that can uplift and inspire both Muslims and sincere seekers of all spiritual paths.

Sunni, Shia, and Sufi Imams

To assure you that this book is in alignment with the deeper meanings of the Qur'an and the prophetic tradition, I sought out the editorial help of several imams or religious authority figures. As an act of unification, I sought help from Sunni, Shia, and Sufi imams. My hope was that if imams from different backgrounds certified the book as theologically sound, then this book can serve to be a meeting place between these three perspectives within Islam.

"Surely the believers are brothers so make peace between your two brothers and remain conscious of God so that you might be graced with His Mercy"

QUR'AN 49:10

This book does not make a statement as to which path is more or less correct, but rather just seeks to remind the Muslim community that the Qur'an and the Prophet ﷺ are our common ground, and if God wills we can use His incredible revelation and messenger as a bridge of understanding and love amongst one another.

I Am Muslim.

For the many who have asked whether I am Sunni or Shia or Sufi, I answer "I am Muslim." The Prophet Muhammad ﷺ was a Muslim. His family members, such as Imam Ali, were Muslim. His righteous companions called themselves Muslim. His daughter, the beloved Fatima Zahra, was a Muslim. As a follower of the traditions of the Prophet ﷺ, as a follower of the family of the Prophet ﷺ, as a follower of the righteous companions of the Prophet ﷺ, and as a student of incredible teachers and the friends of God, I cannot call myself anything other than Muslim.

I love all the sincere and righteous people whom my Prophet ﷺ truly loved. I love all the people in the world who are trying their hardest to be kinder, to be more loving, and to become the best versions of themselves. I love those who are struggling, who are trying to find their way, who are trying to find their faith and have not yet reached the peace they seek. If the Creator of the universe saw you as worthy enough to have been created, then how can I not love you? How can I not love what love Himself created? I respect your freedom to choose whatever spiritual path you feel called to and I love your sacred soul regardless of whether I agree with your choice or not. When I look at you, all I see is the beauty of Allah's creativity and love.

If you are Sunni, you are welcome here.
If you are Shia, you are welcome here.
If you are Sufi, you are welcome here.
If you are from any other religion or philosophy, you are welcome here.
If you are still trying to figure it all out, you are also welcome here.

As someone once beautifully said, "Come as you are, to Islam as it is." The purpose of this book is not to change Islam, but rather to reframe how it is experienced by offering an inspirational take on classical Islamic theology.

I am a Muslim who knows what it feels like to be lost and then guided back to love. I read through hundreds of books, spent thousands of hours listening to lectures, and travelled the world interviewing masters of mysticism and religion to write this book for the person who feels lost and can't seem to find what they are seeking. The spiritual secrets tucked in between the pages of this book are little clues and signposts of how to return to the One—who we sometimes lose sight of, but who never loses sight of us.

"Say: He is Allah, the One! Allah, the Self-Sufficient. He neither gives birth nor is born, and there is none comparable to Him."

QUR'AN 112:1-4

"He is Allah, none has the right to be worshipped but He, Knower of the unseen and the seen. He is The Universally Merciful, The Singularly Compassionate. He is Allah, none has the right to be worshipped but He; The King, The Holy, The Giver of Peace, The Giver of Security, the Guardian over all, The All-Mighty, The Compeller, The Supreme. Glory be to Allah above all that they associate as partners with Him. He is Allah. The Creator of All, The Maker, The Former of the image. His are the most beautiful names. All that is in the heavens and the earth glorifies Him, and He is The All-Mighty, The Wise."

QUR'AN 59:22-24

1

ALLAH: THE ORIGIN OF LOVE

Allah is the Creator of the universe and the light of the heavens and the earth. He is the one absolute, transcendent Reality that unites all differences in the ocean of His love. He is the light that inspires flowers to bloom. He is the breath of love behind the wind that undresses the trees in winter and adorns them with blossoms in spring. He is the power causing mountains to rise. He is the artist painting color into the cones of your eyes. He is the life behind all of nature. He is the One who squeezes a seed to create a tree, the One whose love changes stones into gold. "It is Allah who brought you out of your mothers' wombs knowing nothing, and gave you hearing and sight and minds, so that you might be thankful" (16:78). Allah is the creator of every scientific law, He is the One "who gave everything its form and function" and then guided it into the embrace of His perfect plan (20:50).

Allah is *As-Samad,* which does not just mean "self-sufficient," but comes from a root that means "solid, impenetrable, non-hollow."[1] Allah is the One with no holes, no parts, no separation. Where Allah is metaphorically whole, we are nothing but holes. We are made of atoms, which are 99.99999 percent made of empty space.[2] In essence, when we reach for anything in existence other than Allah, we are reaching for emptiness. Nothing in this world can fill us because everything in this existence is also made of empty atoms. It is only when we reach for God that we are spiritually filled and content because He is *Al-Ahad,* the one, the complete, the indivisible essence that transcends numbers or parts.

Allah is the forger of time, the molder of space, the weaver of souls, the turner of hearts, the One who creates everything in stages yet is beyond the limits of time. Life is created from His breath, the cosmos forms from the vibration of His speech, and love is birthed from the womb of His mercy. He is the One who said, "Be!" to the vast nothingness, and existence sprouted into being. His words inspire light to break the darkness of nothing into the dawn of life.

When the sun sets, when the stars become shy, when the moon hides behind clouds, He is the light that never dies. He is not the universe, He is the breath behind the expansion of space and time. God is not what the eyes see, but He is that which gives seeing to your eyes. He is not what hands can touch, He is that which inspires you to reach. God is the power behind all movement for "All in the heavens and the earth call upon Him, at every interval He is acting" (55:29). He is the One who "created everything in pairs" (51:49), so that you would come to realize that He alone is one. He is the One who is independent and yet everything is dependent upon Him. God is the One that never dies, but deals death; the One that was never created, but creates life; the One that never gives birth, but "knows what is in the wombs" (31:34).

> *He is the One that has no beginning, but that everything begins from; the One with no end, but that everything returns to.*

God did not just create you, He perpetually re-creates and sustains you (10:4). He wraps His love like the arms of a galaxy around every soul who comes and seeks; He sings your cells into harmony and drums your heart into a beat. He is the One that created you from water and earth

(23:12), the One that preferred you to His angels (7:11), the One that planted a reflection of His entire universe into the soil of your spirit. Everything in existence is between His fingers of mercy.[3] "He knows all that enters the earth, all that comes out of it, all that descends from the sky and all that ascends to it. He is All-Merciful and All-Forgiving" (34:2).

Whether you are in a plane in the sky, in the heart of a desert, or in the depths of a sea where no light can reach, God is with you. Everyone else may leave, everything else may break, but Allah will forever be your most faithful and intimate friend.

Allah is the inspiration at the heart of every lover, the beauty behind the song of a nightingale, the mathematician behind the symmetrical perfection in the fractals of nature, and the light reflected in the heart of the Prophet Muhammad ﷺ. It is through God's majesty that the words of Jesus raised the dead (5:110). It is through His power that the Red Sea was parted for Moses (20:77-78). Even though we are often not aware of it, God is always blessing us with His miracles and answering our prayers.

You do not need cell towers to reach God, you just need to plug into your heart because "He is with you wherever you are" (57:4), from the closest atom to the farthest star. God's love makes the ocean shy with its depth and His mercy makes room for every sinner that comes repentant to His door.[4] When the world goes to sleep, God is the One who is awake with you. God sees the tears you hide with smiles and He embraces the pain you think no one would understand. "Not even an atom's weight in the heavens or the earth remains hidden from Him" (34:3). As one unnamed mystic poetically said, "God sees the black ant on a black stone in the darkest night, so how could He not see the pain of a faithful seeker?"[5]

Allah sees you and everything else in existence with His perfect vision. The Qur'an says, "And with Him are the keys of the unseen treasures—none knows them but He; and He knows what is in the land and the sea. Not even a leaf falls without His knowledge, nor a grain in the darkness of the earth, or anything green nor dry but (it is all) in a clear book" (6:59). Tell me, if a single leaf cannot fall on the entire Earth without God's knowledge, how could your heart break without His healing presence embracing you?

"God sends hope in the most desperate moments. Don't forget,
the heaviest rain comes out of the darkest clouds."

RUMI

God's mercy is greater than your sins or circumstances. His compassionate love embraces the cactus parts of you that you swear no one could hug. His grace celebrates the parts of you that nobody claps for. God loved you before you were even created, before you even knew of Him. As the Qur'an says, "It is He who sent down tranquility into the hearts of the believers, that they may add faith to their faith for to Allah belong the forces of the heavens and the earth and Allah is full of Knowledge and Wisdom" (48:4).

The Mystery of "Allah"

There are countless veils between us and God, but no veils between Him and us.[6] The veils we experience between us and God are often created from misperceptions formed during our childhood that result in a distorted vision of reality. When something happens to us, good or bad, as human beings we are inclined to frame that experience with an interpretation. How we interpret events in our life will in turn affect how we see our reality. Since our interpretations come from us and are totally subjective, if they were changed, it would change how we saw the world and God. Our experience of the world has little to do with what happens to us and everything to do with how we subconsciously or consciously choose to interpret our experiences.

Therefore, our interpretations and beliefs associated with them become a barrier to fully witnessing God. Nothing, however, is veiled from God's perception. God has no blind spots or boundaries. We are not veiled due to God's distance from us, but veiled due to His proximity.[7] Just as the life that gives us breath is so close to us that we cannot see it or touch it, the Qur'an declares that despite the transcendence of His essence, God is closer to us than our "jugular vein" (50:16).

God's love is intimately woven within every beat of our hearts. In fact, the Arabic word for God, *Allah,* begins with an "Ahh" sound, which in theories of sacred sound is the sound of manifestation, the sound we allegedly make when our hearts open. Symbolically, this sound represents the human being bursting forth from the nothingness of silence into manifested existence through God's speech.

The word "Allah" can be seen as the same singular God that is referred to in the Torah in Hebrew as *Elohim*, or spoken by Jesus in Aramaic as the strikingly similar *Allaha*. Allah is neither female nor male, for He is beyond anything in creation and transcends all the limits that the human mind can create. Since in Arabic there is not a gender-neutral pronoun such as "it," Allah uses *huwa* or "He" in reference to Himself because in Arabic the male gender form is inclusive of the female, not exclusive.

You will also find in the Qur'an that Allah speaks in the first-person plural, referring to Himself as "We." This does not imply that God is more than one; rather, in Arabic and many other languages this denotes majesty, i.e. the "royal We" that kings use when referring to their subjects. For example, a king may say, "*We* have decreed the following order" even if he is referring only to himself. Some commentators have also suggested that when Allah says, "We created" He is pointing to how He ordered the angels to create, all together. Regardless, when God uses the word "We" in the Qur'an, He often then uses a singular word to refer to Himself, as a means of reiterating His oneness.[8]

Allah is the meeting point of all duality and differences, for He is a singular reality. Some scholars say the word "Allah" is a proper name God has given Himself and thus the word cannot be linguistically broken down. Other scholars say the word "Allah" is derived from *ilah*, which in Arabic means "god"; and that when the definite article *al* is added to *ilah* it creates *al-ilah*, and translates to "The God."

Regardless of the linguistic origin of the word, Allah is that which unites *yes* with *no,* for in His singularity all duality is mysteriously united. Allah is both the bridge between the unseen and seen realms and the meeting point between existence and nonexistence. However, paradoxically, Allah is also the ground of polarity, both fully the manifestation of the inner (*Al-Batin*) and fully the manifestation of the outer (*Az-Zahir*).

"God is outside of things, but not in the sense of being
alien to them; and He is inside of things, but not in the
sense of being identical with them."

IMAM ALI

It is as a result of these seemingly contradicting statements that
Allah is, by definition, that which breaks the mind. As the mystics
say, "Only God can know God" because "there is none comparable to
Him" (112:4). Therefore, by definition, Allah has no opposites, and
since the human mind understands the world through association and
comparison, it is rendered incapable of understanding a singular God
who cannot be divided into parts and is unlike any other thing known
to man.

"Vision does not encompass Him; He encompasses
vision. He is above all comprehension, yet is
acquainted with all things."

QUR'AN 6:103

We cannot express Allah's eternal and transcendent nature with
mortal tongues. We cannot shove infinity into the finite arms of 26
letters. This is why the follower of the Prophet Muhammad ﷺ, Abu
Bakr, said, "Our inability to understand God is our understanding of
God." Our inability to comprehend God's infinite nature does not mean
we cannot have a relationship with God; rather, it means our experience
of God begins through admitting our ignorance before His all-encompassing knowledge.

It is only from a place of humility that we can begin to experience
a connection with God. Like the famous novelist Leo Tolstoy said in
War and Peace, "All we can know is that we know nothing. And that's
the height of human wisdom." It is only when we put our ego aside and
see the limited nature of our intellect that we can begin to walk on the
path of faith. As Rumi beautifully says, "Sell your cleverness and buy
bewilderment"—for at the end of all you know is the beginning of your
journey to Allah.

The Divine Door Is Always Open

Allah is not an old man in the sky; He is not Zeus sitting in a cloud waiting to punish you. Allah is not Santa Claus, with a naughty list from which you cannot be redeemed. Allah is the Creator of the cosmos, the One whose mercy embraces all things, whose love embraces all hearts, whose *hands* heal all wounds, whose *face* is everywhere you turn—for He is with you wherever you are.

> *"Take one step toward Me, I will take ten steps toward you. Walk toward Me, I will run toward you."*[9]
>
> ALLAH

We may be slow in repentance, but God is swift in His mercy, generosity, forgiveness, and grace. The following interaction between two great mystical masters beautifully articulates God's mercy:

> The eighth-century sage Salih of Qaswin said to his students, "Keep knocking on the door of Allah and never stop, for by His mercy, Allah will eventually open His door for those who sincerely seek Him." The mystic Rabia Al-Adawiyya overheard this statement as she was walking by the mosque and said, "Oh Salih, who said Allah's door is closed to begin with?"

Rabia understood that Allah's love is not dependent on our actions, but that it is His love that inspires us to knock to begin with. Like the sun draws the plants to turn their face in submission to its light, God calls us to turn to Him so that we may grow through Him. Allah is the One whose speech lifts the dead from their graves, the One who can part the seas with a staff, the One who uses your hopeless situations as a platform to perform His next miracle. He is the One that transforms your mess into a message, the One that transforms your trials into a triumph, the One who takes the victim and makes them a victor (30:5). God is with you in the beginning, in the end, and in every moment in between. This is why the beloved grandson of the Prophet ﷺ, Imam

Hussein, said, "Oh Allah, What did he find who lost You and what did he lose who found You?"

We do not worship God because God needs it, we worship God because *we* need it. Prayer is not you reaching out for God, it is you responding to God, who first reached out to you. It is only when our seedling hearts submit to God's light that we can harvest the hidden fruits of love that He planted within our spirit. As the Qur'an says, "Whoever strives, strives only for his own soul, for Allah is entirely independent of all worlds" (29:06). No matter how many hundreds of millions of steps we take away from God, it takes just a single thought to return.

As Rumi says, "Each moment contains a hundred messages from God. To every cry of, 'Oh God.' He answers a hundred times, 'I am here.'" Do not ever think that because you cannot see God that He cannot see you. "Do not lose heart or grieve" (3:139), because even in the depths of your darkest nights your Lord is with you always, saying, "I am near" (2:186).

He is only one, yet we always forget Him; whereas He has billions upon billions of creatures and never forgets a single one of us. God's love has no fences or borders. His love has no conditions. His love is not in a faraway Heaven, but with you in the holiness of this very moment.

Whereas we break our promises a thousand times, God is always faithful.

It is only through knowing how much God loves us that we can break free from our anxiety and fear around the uncontrollable and unknown future. The more we trust God's perfect wisdom, the more harmony we begin to feel in our lives. The all-encompassing peace that comes from relying entirely on God is beautifully illustrated in the following Japanese story:

A samurai and the love of his life had just gotten married and were traveling by boat to their honeymoon, when a huge storm hit. The samurai's wife began to tremble with fear; there was no shore in sight and their boat looked like it would capsize at any moment. When she ran to find her husband, she found him peacefully looking out at the sea, as if the sun was out and the waves were calm. She ran up to him and yelled, "How can you be so calm when we are about to die! Do you not value your life?" When the samurai heard her say this, he pulled out his sword and put it to his wife's neck. His wife started laughing. He said, "Why are you laughing? Are you not afraid?" She said, "Because I know you love me and would never hurt me." The samurai smiled and said, "Well, I too am in the hands of the One who loves me, so how can I be afraid?"

When we realize that Allah loves us beyond what can be fathomed and that He always knows what is best for us, our fear of the unknown transforms into faith. After all, as the Qur'an says, "To Him belong the keys of the heavens and the earth" (39:63). When we surrender to God's will even when things do not go as planned, we are still grateful, because we know that God's plan will always be greater than our greatest dreams. So long as we remain chained to this world and everything in it, including our own desires, we can never truly feel liberated. It is only in trusting the Divine and becoming a servant of Allah that the soul experiences true freedom.

Ar-Rahman and *Ar-Rahim*: The Spiritual Secrets of God's Mercy

> *"Call upon Allah or call upon the Most Merciful (Ar-Rahman), by whatever name you call upon Him, to Him belong the most beautiful names."*
>
> QUR'AN 17:110

Allah calls us toward Himself through boundless mercy and grace, which embraces all of creation without discrimination. This divine compassion transcends time and space, providing for the good, the bad and everything in between. In the 114 chapters of the Qur'an, 114 times Allah says *Bismillahi Ar-Rahman Ar-Rahim,* which can be translated as "In the name of God, the Lord of Mercy, the Bestower of Mercy."[10] In Arabic, these words do not just denote mercy, but also carry the qualities of love, forgiveness, aid, compassion, passion, assistance, protection, concern, tenderness, and forgiveness.

Ar-Rahman and Ar-Rahim are both derived from the verb rahima, which refers to "being merciful, loving, and caring in a way that benefits the object of the affection." In other words, God is making us, the creation, the emphasis of His infinite grace and most loving qualities. While Ar-Rahim is seen as God's qualities of love and mercy in action, Ar-Rahman is God's nature of mercy, love, and grace. Ar-Rahim is a specified form of mercy that is given to those who open their hearts to God, longing for the light of His love, whereas Ar-Rahman shines upon all of creation without discrimination.

Both Ar-Rahim and Ar-Rahman originate from the Arabic word rahm meaning "womb." This implies that we can only experience the truth of God's message from the all-embracing womb of His mercy, love, compassion, and grace.

> Ar-Rahman is seen as the mother of all the divine names, for
> it is through the all-encompassing womb of God's Rahman
> that the universe was manifested into being.

In Arabic, the word Rahman is known as a sigatul mubaalagha or hyperbole, which refers to a word that is excessive and extraordinary. For example, a'tash is a word you would use to say you are thirsty, but the form a'tshan means you are desperately thirsty. Another example would be the word ghadhib, which is used to say you are angry, but the form ghadhban means you are infuriated with anger. In this case, rahma means mercy, but the form Rahman is an extreme, infinite form of mercy that is beyond what can be understood by the human mind. Some grammarians also have said that the word Rahman linguistically implies that it is happening in the here and now.[11] In other words, Allah is loving, caring, and merciful not just in a general sense, but in this very moment right now.[12]

Allah emphasizes His name, The Most Merciful (Ar-Rahman), over His name, The Most Loving (Al-Wadud) because Rahman is all-encompassing and present in all places and times. Love is not separate from but enfolded into the meaning of *Rahman.*

> *"Limitless is your Lord in His Mercy"*
>
> QUR'AN 6:147

Allah's *Rahman* is like the sky, it covers everything in existence, including us and the worst of our sins. We were created from Allah's mercy, and the Qur'an was sent like a ladder from Heaven to Earth, so that we could get closer to the Divine. Allah has opened the door for us; it is up to us whether we walk into the palace of His mercy and love.

The Importance of Divine Justice

It is important to understand that God's mercy and justice go hand in hand. The word for justice in Arabic is *'adl,* which at its root means "to proportion, to create symmetry, to be equitable." In other words, harmony and balance are dependent on justice. Jewish mystics metaphorically describe God's justice as scolding hot water that, if poured on its own into a clay vessel, would break it. God's mercy is described as freezing cold water; if poured on its own into a clay vessel, it would also break it. But if you pour them together, a neutralizing balance is created, preventing the vessel from breaking.

The clay vessel in this story is a metaphor for the human heart, which is unable to contain only God's mercy or only God's justice. If God was only merciful there would be chaos on Earth because there would be no accountability; however, if God was only just there would be no one on Earth because no human being is perfect. As the Qur'an says, "If God were to punish people for their deeds immediately, not one creature would have survived on Earth. However, He has given them a respite for an appointed time and when their term comes to an end, let it be known that God watches over His servants" (35:45). It is in bringing together God's justice and mercy that the possibility for harmony is created.

God's Mercy Gives Us More Than We Deserve

If justice is giving you what you deserve, then mercy is when you are given more than you deserve or could ever earn. By virtue of His infinite generosity, Allah is always looking to multiply the rewards for our good deeds, and minimize our wrongs. As the Qur'an says, "Whoever brings a good deed, he shall have ten like it, and whoever brings an evil deed, he shall be recompensed only with the like of it; and they shall not be dealt with unjustly" (6:160). Despite the countless displays of God's unending mercy, some people still proclaim that God is unjust. However, God by His very definition cannot be unjust to us.

> *Justice is when you get exactly what you deserve, but what can we earn in relationship to a God who needs nothing and gives us everything? Can you pray enough to the One who gave you a tongue, a mouth, a body and an existence? How can God be unjust if He takes something from you, when He is the owner of everything in existence including you?*

God is not unjust, it is we who are unjust. We are the ones who withhold from God what He already owns. As the Qur'an says, it is we who have "wronged ourselves" with choices that we have made (7:23). It is not God who oppresses us. God makes this clear when He says, "Oh My servants! I have forbidden oppression for Myself, and I have made it forbidden amongst you, so do not oppress one another."[13]

We must remember that everything we do, say, or give to Allah already belongs to Him. God doesn't owe us a single thing and yet He constantly gives to us, breathes life into us, loves and cares for us, not because of who we are, but because of how merciful and loving He is.

Allah Is Love

Allah is the origin and cause of love. Allah never stops loving you, because His love is eternal and has no beginning or end. Love is not something Allah does, love is something Allah is.

You cannot separate love from God any more than you can
separate water from the ocean.

We can respond to Allah's love by loving and worshiping Him, but our unwillingness to honor Allah does not affect His divine qualities, as Allah is entirely "independent of all creatures" (3:97). Whereas the human being can be kind, God *is* Kindness (*Ar-Ra'uf*); where we can be merciful, God *is* Mercy (*Ar-Rahman*). God is not just peaceful, He *is* Peace (*As-Salam*). God's loving qualities do not change in response to our choices because God is not reactive. He is the cause of everything in existence.[14]

The Prophet ﷺ explains that if every single human on Earth reached the height of spiritual piety—or if they were all the worst in existence—it would not add or take away anything from Allah's sovereignty. The Prophet ﷺ continues to say that if Allah chose to fulfill the prayer of every single human being at once, it would not decrease what Allah has "any more than a needle decreases what is in the ocean when it is put into it."[15] As the twentieth-century theologian, C.S. Lewis said, "A man can no more diminish God's glory by refusing to worship Him than a lunatic can put out the sun by scribbling the word 'darkness' on the walls of his cell."

Allah's love for us never diminishes. What changes is our ability to be receptive to divine love. In fact, the word "hate" does not exist in the Qur'an in relation to Allah. The English translations of "God hates" can more accurately be translated as "God does not love," which implies that our experience of Allah is always on the spectrum of love.[16] The variation in this spectrum occurs not because Allah is withholding from us, but because of our forgetfulness and the veils that result from our misperceptions, false identities, and sins. Just as the sun doesn't stop shining if we close our eyes, when we sin it is not that God hates us, but rather we who are closed off from experiencing His love.[17]

"Moonlight floods the whole sky from horizon to horizon;
How much it can fill your room depends on its windows."
RUMI

Allah loves and provides for whom He wills "without accounting" (3:37), so if we feel limitations, they exist in the containment of our receiving and not in the outpouring of His giving.

Some linguists say that the word Allah is based on the word *wa-liha,* which translates to a love that is so passionate and ecstatic that it completely transcends the senses.[18] This implies that to know God we have to surrender our minds, everything we are, and everything we know in exchange for love, because self-surrender to divine love is the only path to God. Unlike the angels, we have been given the gift of not only knowing of love, but becoming it. Since Allah is the origin of all love, to know Him you must drown in the essence of love. To know Him you must be empty of yourself entirely, for love leaves no witnesses. How can there be two with the One? We must stop trying to understand with our limiting minds what the heart already knows. As Rumi says, "I looked in Temples, Churches, and Mosques. But I found the Divine in my heart." In this poem, Rumi reminds us that God is most brilliantly reflected in the mirror of the spiritual heart, which is the seat of consciousness.

God Transcends the Human Mind

God is limitless. It is our vision of God that is limited to the qualities we seek in the world and reflect within our own existence. Since we see the world through the filter of how we see ourselves, we come to know God through His qualities that we actualize through Him within our own being.

Allah says, "I am as My servant thinks I am"[19] because we see Allah not as He is but through the lens of our finite mind. If we tune into God's love, mercy, compassion, and kindness, then we draw those qualities out of existence and see God through those faces. The Creator meets us with the qualities we meet His creation with. Therefore, next time, instead of only praying for justice when others wrong you, consider praying for Allah's mercy upon them as well.

*"Be merciful to those on the Earth and the One above the
heavens will have mercy upon you."*[20]

PROPHET MUHAMMAD ﷺ

Although we are given the gift as human beings to be a reflection of
God on Earth, our experience of a divine name is still infinitely different
from God. For example, we can only understand the quality of God's
all-encompassing sight (*Al-Basir*) in relationship to our own ability to see,
but God's vision is completely incomprehensible. As Imam Ali says, "He
sees even when there is none to be looked at from among His creation."
Allah sees all things in existence without eyes, without the need for light,
corneas, colors, or irises. Allah sees without the need for contrast or
duality. He sees sound, smell, and love. Whereas our hearing requires an
eardrum and air for sound to travel through, Allah's hearing (*As-Sami'*)
is beyond sound waves. Whereas our life is dependent on a beating heart
and a working brain, Allah has no beginning or end. Allah lit the candle
of our mortal existence, but the light of His Being, is beyond existence.
Allah's qualities are beyond human words.

*"Whatever you think concerning Allah—know that He is
different from that!"*

IBN ATA ALLAH AL-ISKANDARI, 13TH-CENTURY MYSTIC

The life of Allah reaches beyond breaths, beyond what can be captured by mortal hands or calculated by human brains. As Rumi says, "The
language of God is silence, all else is poor translation." Whereas words
limit the interpretation of God to the confines of human language, silence
carries infinite possibilities.

As the teacher of Rumi, the mystic Shams Tabrizi, said, "Intellect takes
you to the door, but it doesn't take you into the house." Despite all divinely
sent prophets constantly calling humankind to not seek God solely with
the mind, human beings have never stopped searching for a God they can
touch and see directly. Islam does not ignore this inclination, but rather
uses the same rational thought to challenge it.

A mystic master was once asked, "How can I see God?" The master told the questioner, "Look at the sun." The seeker looked toward the sun, but after a few seconds squinted in pain and said, "I can't, it's burning my eyes." The master then replied, "You can't even look at the sun without going blind and you want to see the Creator of the sun?"

The seeker then asked, "Then tell me, great master, where is God?" The master asked the seeker, "Do you know where in the galaxy the Earth is orbiting in this moment? Do you even know where you are to ask where the One who created place resides? When we cannot even place ourselves, relative to the universe, how can we attempt to place a formless God in relationship to an existence He completely transcends?"

When our eyes cannot see themselves, or our teeth cannot bite themselves, when we cannot even fully experience our own senses, how can we expect to be able to fully experience the One who created those senses? The human mind will always venture to limit God's omnipresent, transcendent, and mysterious nature into a form or formula that can be understood. Rumi metaphorically remarks on this inclination through the following poem: "The truth was a mirror in the hands of God. It fell, and broke into pieces. Everybody took a piece of it, and they looked at it and thought they had the truth."

There are no images or idols in Islam, so that man doesn't limit God to a form. Nonetheless, true monotheism is not just belief in a single God, but the ability to see a reflection of God in everything for everything is infused and animated through the love of God. The Qur'an speaks to God's infinite and incomprehensible knowledge by declaring the following:

> "And if all the trees in the earth were pens and the sea with
> seven more seas to help it were ink the words of Allah could
> not be exhausted. Allah is Exalted in Might and Wise."

QUR'AN 31:27

How the Universe Points to God

Since the universe has a beginning, and something that has a beginning cannot come from nothing, it is rational to assume that the universe has a Creator.[21] The ancient Bedouins would say that just as camel droppings in the desert would tell them that camels passed by, and footsteps in the sand were proof that a creature had walked by, the Earth's many valleys, mountains, oceans, and constellations point to the existence of a Creator. As the Qur'an says, "Then do they not look at the camels—how they are created? And at the sky—how it is raised? And at the mountains—how they are erected? And at the earth—how it is spread out?" (88:17-20).

When we look at a book, a plane, building, or even a wristwatch, we see a sign of intelligence far beyond the scope of chance. Our planet is specifically designed to harbor life with such precision that it is beyond the grasp of probability that out of chaos and pure randomness such order would arise. The possibility of life lies in astonishingly narrow parameters.

> *Our life depends on the proximity of the Earth to the sun, the tilt of the Earth and the speed at which it revolves, the amount of oxygen in the air, the existence of our atmosphere, the thickness of the Earth's crust, and countless other equations that in some cases must be as precise as 120 decimal places.[22]*

In fact, the constants within the equations of science are so fine-tuned that the world-renowned theoretical physicist Stephen Hawking said in his book *A Brief History of Time* that "The laws of science, as we know them at present, contain many fundamental numbers, like the size of the electric charge of the electron and the ratio of the masses of the proton and the electron…the remarkable fact is that the values of these numbers seem to have been very finely adjusted to make possible the development of life."[23]

As brilliant and awe-inspiring as the discoveries of science can be, they can only ever speak to *how* things work in our universe, while God addresses *why* things exist. Nonetheless, science can be seen as a great ally of faith, because the scientific method, which was pioneered by Muslim physicist Ibn Al-Haytham, helps to unveil the power and wisdom of God that is hidden within the created world, through the God-given intellect of man. However, the intellect of man can only go so far in explaining the world we live in. The following quote beautifully articulates this notion:

"The first gulp from the glass of natural sciences will turn you into an atheist, but at the bottom of the glass God is waiting for you."

WERNER HEISENBERG, PIONEER OF QUANTUM PHYSICS

It was not until the twentieth century that the scientific community confirmed certain claims made by the Qur'an more than 1,400 years ago. For example, the Qur'an speaks about water being the core substance of all living things (21:30), the human embryonic development (23:12-14), the universe not being static but expanding (51:47), and the sun and the moon having their own individual orbits (21:33).

Nonetheless, it is important to understand that since scientists cannot account for every single variable in a given experiment, science can only make predictions and suggest theories about the universe and the created world. Whereas belief in God is seen as an innate natural inclination of every human being, science is traditionally based in speculation and cannot prove something with 100 percent certainty.[24] In the Qur'an, Allah constantly calls us to contemplate and reflect upon the natural world, but we must be careful to not make our intellect an idol before God. The universe having an origin, the fine-tuned nature of existence, and scientific accuracies within the Qur'an are powerful truths to contemplate, but belief in God is not something we acquire merely through reading or intellectual understanding.

The Qur'an states that belief in God has been placed in the heart of every single human being; you do not have to find God, you just have to be receptive to His truth, with an open mind and humble heart.

"God guides to Himself whoever turns to Him."

QUR'AN 13:27

Sincere submission is the only path to God. If we seek God through arrogance, through thinking we are superior because of our knowledge, success, or wealth, we will not only be veiled from the signs of God, but we will find justification for our disbelief. This is because arrogance leads to spiritual blindness and creates separation and heirarchy. As a result, the arrogant cannot reach God because He can only be known through the door of oneness. As God Himself says, "I will turn away from My signs those who are arrogant upon the Earth without right; and if they should see every sign, they will not believe in it. And if they see the way of consciousness, they will not adopt it as a way; but if they see the way of error, they will adopt it as a way. That is because they have denied Our signs and they were heedless of them" (7:146).

It is not information in the form of words that results in belief, but rather the truth of faith is unveiled when we open the eyes of our heart through humility to the light of God. The light of the truth is hidden within the words of revelation and divine signs reflected in the creation and is accessed through gratitude and humble reverence of God. It is through divine grace and the fostering of gratitude and humility that our vision is widened making us receptive to receive the divine inspiration behind the many miracles of God that already surround us.

After all, we live on a planet graced with seas and trees, floating in space around a ball of fire that creates the day, and a moon that creates the waves—and still some days we say God does not exist. The Qur'an asks, "Who provides for you from the sky and the earth? Who is it that has power over hearing and sight? And who is it that brings out the living from the dead and the dead from the living? And who is it that rules and regulates all affairs? They will say, 'Allah.' Then say, 'Will you not then be mindful of Him?'" (10:31)

> *If every book has an author, and every building has an architect, then how can we look at all this intricate perfection and say that it has no Creator?*

As the Qur'an says, "It is He who has created seven heavens, one above the other. You cannot see any fault in the creation of the Universally Merciful. Look again: Do you see any fault?" (67:03). The Qur'an calls us to contemplate natural phenomena, so that through observing the intricate mystery of creation we can logically conclude that such precision is not an outcome of random chance. The greatest evidence of God is not in what the eyes can capture, but in what completely bewilders and transcends the eyes. Just as we cannot directly see black holes in space, but have evidence of their existence due to how their gravity affects the surrounding matter and light, we cannot see Allah, but the greatest evidence of His existence is our existence. From nothing, nothing comes. After all, 0 + 0 + 0 will never give you one (52:35-36).

> *Mystics throughout time have said that they believe in God*
> *like they believe in light, not because they can see light, but*
> *because through it they see everything else.*

Who Created God?

It's important not to fall into the trap of thinking, *If God created the universe then who created God?* because that results in infinite regress.[25] We must understand that God and the universe are vastly different. From the vantage point of our physical reality, time, matter, and space are seen as a continuum in that they came into existence simultaneously. If you had matter but not space where would you put the matter? If you had matter but not time, when would you place it? Since time, matter, and space were all seemingly created together, whatever created the universe must, by definition, transcend all limitations of the created world of forms. The Qur'an depicts this perfectly, because Allah describes Himself as One who is beyond time, space, and any forms or limitations for "Allah has power over all things" (24:45). Since God is eternal and has no beginning, then we can reason that He would have no Creator, because there was no moment in which God was not present to have been created. Thus, He alone is the uncreated Creator, without Him nothing would have been created.

How to Have an Intimate Connection with God

In a world that is constantly changing, it is comforting to know that our God is the same today as He was yesterday and will be tomorrow. In accepting God's essence as being undifferentiated, infinite, and unlike anything in creation, we must not make the mistake of thinking that God is too big or transcendent to have an intimate relationship with a being as small as ourselves.

The question then becomes, how can we have a relationship with a God who cannot be known, seen, or touched directly? We cannot know God as He is, but we can experience His qualities indirectly through the creations He chose to create. Similar to what happens when white light hits a prism and spreads out to unveil the color spectrum, when the light of the name Allah pierces the dense prism of creation, it manifests into the spectrum of divine names. Like white light that carries all colors within its singularity, the name Allah carries the infinite divine names within its oneness. However, since singularity, unity, and oneness cannot entirely be comprehended by the human mind, Allah reflected His singularity into the multiplicity of creation through the manifestation of His divine names. Everything in creation is created from a unique recipe of Allah's names.

Similar to how all physical matter is broken apart into chemical elements that are organized into a periodic table, the divine names form a table in the spiritual dimension that allows us to experience an infinite God, one name at a time.

Allah describes Himself numerous times in the Qur'an with seemingly conflicting names. He introduces Himself as The Living (*Al-Hayy*), The Most Kind (*Ar-Ra'uf*), and The Infinitely Generous (*Al-Karim*). He also introduces Himself as The Bringer of Death (*Al-Mumit*), The Reducer (*Al-Khaafid*), and The Dishonorer (*Al-Mudhil*). Allah's names are not contradictory, but rather complement one another.

Allah is The Expander (*Al-Basit*), the One who opens our hearts to the light of grace; and He is The Constrictor (*Al-Qabid*), the One who closes the doors that would lead us astray. He is The Avenger (*Al-Muntaqim*), the One who confronts our egos and seeks to balance the scales of injustice through accountability. He is The Great Forgiver (*Al-Ghaffur*), the One who covers our sins with the veil of His perfection and protects us from the consequences of our choices. He is The Harmer (*Ad-Darr*), the One who severs the bonds we have made with self-destructive desires. He is The Beneficial (*An-Nafi'*), the One who shines upon the seeds of faith within us, helping us blossom into the greatest possible version of ourselves.

The qualities of Allah can be generally categorized as either a *Jamal* or *Jalal* quality. *Jamal*, or Allah's qualities of beauty, most often correspond to the ease that comes from His blessings. *Jalal*, or Allah's qualities of majesty, relate to the difficulty and pain we experience as Allah purifies and polishes the mirror of our hearts. Although many people struggle with the *Jalal* faces of God, they are necessary on the path of spiritual progress. Just as the human being cannot see in pure light or pure darkness, but light and dark must blend and interlace for vision to awaken, the *Jamal* and *Jalal* complement each other on the path of knowing and experiencing God.

> "*Say: Lord, Owner of the Kingdom, You give authority to whomever You want and take it away from whomever You want. You honor whom You will and You humble whom You will. In Your hands is all virtue and You have power over all things. You cause the day to enter into the night and the night to enter into the day. You cause the living to come out of the dead and the dead to come out of the living. You give sustenance to whomever You want without measure.*"
>
> QUR'AN 3:26-27

The qualities of God perfectly balance one another. Just as when we break a bone, the doctor may have to break the bone again to set it, sometimes Allah may choose to break aspects of our ego through His *Jalal* qualities, to create the conditions for healing through His *Jamal* qualities. It can also be said that the qualities of Allah's *Jalal* polish the heart so that the qualities of His *Jamal* can be reflected. We may have a preference toward ease, but in the spiritual sense there is no difference between *Jamal* and *Jalal* because both represent a face of God.

It's important to remember that we do not only experience Allah's qualities on the spiritual plane, but they are also manifested in all of physical creation. We can see Allah's power (*Al-Jabbar*) reflected in the ocean, we can feel His mercy (*Ar-Rahman*) through the rain, we can experience His love (*Al-Wadud*) through a mother holding her child, we can see His majesty (*Al-Jalil*)[26] reflected in the stars, we can see His gentleness (*Al-Latif*) in the petals of a rose. Every time we see, we experience an element of God's infinite sight (*Al-Basir*). Every time we hear, we experience the quality of God's all-encompassing hearing (*Al-Sami'*). In birth, we see God's quality of life (*Al-Hayy*) and in death we witness God's power to take life (*Al-Mumit*). From inside of us to the farthest edges of the universe we see infinite faces of God's grace, painted with the colors of His names, in every atom that He chose to create.[27] Just as every artist is reflected in their artworks but is not the artwork itself, God is reflected in what He creates, but is not limited by His creation.

> *"To God belongs the east and the west, wherever you turn*
> *there is the face of God."*
>
> QUR'AN 2:115

Here the word "face" does not mean God has a face like a human being because God is formless and beyond time and space; the word "face" in this verse is metaphorical and refers to God's essence (*adh-dhat*) and how it is mysteriously reflected in all of creation. Allah's omnipresence in all things is reiterated when the Qur'an says, "He is the First and the Last, and the Outward and the Inward and He has knowledge of everything" (57:03).

At any moment, what we experience in this world of forms is a three-dimensional reflection of God's names, projected through the mirror of our existence. Essentially, human beings and everything else in creation, both seen and unseen, exist as a reflection of God's qualities in the mirror of the universe. If, for a single moment, Allah turned away the face of His mercy from the mirror of this world, everything would disappear because nothing would exist without Him continually sustaining it. Allah is *Al-Hayy,* The Living, the One who inspires all life into being. Allah is *Al-Qayyum,* The Self-Subsisting, the One everything is dependent on.

We are not God, just as the image in a mirror is not the one facing it, but like a mirror our existence points to the Divine. Similar to how the sun rises upon a horizon, but is not part of the horizon, God's light is reflected in creation, but is not owned by the creation. Every tree, child, star, galaxy, and atom carries a reflection of God's qualities beneath the limitation of its form. Since everything originates from Allah and everything returns to Allah, there is nothing that is ultimately separate from the knowledge and love of Allah, for all of creation is completely dependent and sustained by Allah.

> *"Nothing I say can explain to you divine love, yet all of creation cannot seem to stop talking about it."*
>
> RUMI

Just as love cannot be seen or truly known, but is undeniably felt, we can experience our Lord in places our mind could never travel or comprehend. Seek out these "placeless" places, where the unknown resides. Reflect upon the mysteries of life, travel into spaces with no familiar ground, venture into realms where worldly compasses fail to lead you, walk into the quantum world, where laws of science seemingly fail to work, and feel the vulnerability of your ignorance.

Lean into the divinity that is hidden within everything. Break every wall of known knowledge; do not seek to know, seek to be in awe of the infinite nature of God. This is where you can experience your Lord; this is where you can be most aware that you will never know Allah as He truly is, and yet every moment of every day it is His breath that is mysteriously creating the life inside of you.

My Lord, help me surrender all that I am, so that I can receive all that You seek to give me. Allah, help me to lay down the burden of doubt and to walk freely in faith, trusting that Your plans for me will always be greater than my greatest dreams. Allah, forgive me for the mistakes I have made and the mistakes I will make. My Lord, please remind me that Your goodness will always be greater than my faults, and that Your love will always be greater than my shame. Oh Allah, shine Your light upon me, so that my eyes can awaken to Your truth and so that my heart can be illuminated by the reflection of Your beauty. In Your sublime Names I pray, Ameen.

Reflection: The Mystery of Breath

When we connect with our breath, we are mysteriously connecting with the divine spirit that God blew into us. The following practice is a simple but profound way of bringing God-consciousness to your breath:

- Notice your breath. Allow yourself to breathe naturally.
- Witness how you are not breathing, but rather you are being breathed.
- Observe your breath, as if you're watching the coming and going of waves upon the ocean shore. Inhale…*hold*…Exhale…*hold*…Inhale…*hold*…Exhale.
- Do not manage how long or deep your breaths are.
- As you naturally breathe in through your nose, let your tongue rise to the roof of your mouth, allowing your breath to say, "Al." As you exhale through your mouth let your tongue drop down allowing your outward breath to say, "lah." For the next 3–5 minutes, sit in silent reflection, saying *Al-lah* with your breath.
- Notice how you feel before and after these practices.

Reflection: Everywhere You Look Is the Face of Allah

When we are in a constant state of witnessing God, we are actualizing what it means to be truly human. As previously mentioned, the Qur'an directly speaks of Allah's omnipresence when it says, "Wherever you turn, there is the face of Allah" (2:115). The Prophet ﷺ says, "Allah has ninety-nine names and whoever preserves them will enter Paradise."[28] In other words, when we learn, reflect, and embody divine qualities we become closer to the Divine. Although we cannot know God's essence, we can always experience the reflections of God's qualities. The following exercise can be a helpful way of learning how to do this:

- Grab a notebook and a pen and take a walk out in nature. You can go to the beach, the desert, mountains, forest, jungles, river, lake, or wherever else on Earth that calls to you.

- Allow your heart to choose something around you to meditate on or to just simply notice. It can be the waves at the ocean, a tree, a mountain, an animal, a flower, a sand dune, a shell, or even a stone.

- Take a moment to write down certain qualities that you witness in this natural object. Is it majestic, beautiful, soft, strong, kind-looking, or intricate? Can it move? Can it create life or take life? If it could speak, what would it say? Really listen. Write down whatever comes up for you.

- Go to the appendix, to "The 99 Divine Names of Allah" section, and pick out the names of Allah that most closely relate to the descriptions you wrote down. For example, if you described a flower as living, delicate, and beautiful, the correlating divine names could be The Living (*Al-Hayy*), The Subtle (*Al-Latif*), and The Shaper of Beauty (*Al-Musawwir*).

- Once you have found the correlating divine names, spend 3–5 minutes repeating each name, while you witness the object that carries a reflection of these names. For example, to witness the quality of God's kindness, you could chant *Ya Allah*, in combination with the name of God *Ar-Ra'uf* which means "The Most Kind." In this case, the chant would be: *Ya Allah, Ya Ra'uf.* The word *Ya* denotes pleading and is used when you are yearning for one's attention. A close translation for *Ya Allah* would be "Oh Allah."

- After you have repeated the different names, take a moment and contemplate the reality that everything in existence is held together by the qualities of God.

- What comes up for you when you reflect on this truth? How would you look at the world differently if you saw everything as a reflection of God?

"We have indeed created man
in the best of molds."

QUR'AN 95:04

"I have not created the invisible
beings and humankind except
to worship Me."

QUR'AN 51:56

2

WHO ARE YOU?

You are an intentional creation of a perfect God. You are not a product of chance or luck. As the Qur'an says, "We did not create the heavens and the earth and everything between them playfully" (21:16). There is no accidental life. Allah wrote your story with the pen of mercy, poured His love into every cell that dances and twirls inside of you, and blew His spirit into your mold of clay, making you a bridge between Heaven and Earth (15:29). Like a gentle breeze, God breathes the light of His love within your soil of dirt, bringing to life what was once dead earth (30:19).

You are far more beautiful than mirrors can sing about, you are far too intricate for language to weave into words, because you are the product of a divine love that is so holy and infinite that finite hands fall short in painting your truth. The love of God purposely overflowed to create you and everything in existence.

> *"The God who made the stars, the seas, the mountains and its peaks, the universe and its galaxies felt this world would be incomplete without you and without me. Do you see how you are a puzzle piece in the whole—how without you here, there would be a hole? Your body is*

*not just a clay tent that you live in, it's a piece of the
universe you have been given. You are not a small star,
you are a reflection of the entire cosmos. Can you hear
the big bang in your heart? Eighty times a minute God
knocks on the doors of your chest, to remind you that
He has never left, and that He is closer to you than
the jugular vein in your neck (50:16). Every moment is
divinely blessed, for this very moment God is blowing
the breath of life through eight billion different human
chests. You are not just star dust and dirt, you are a
reflection of God's beauty on Earth. You are not this
mortal body that death will one day take. You are an
everlasting spirit held in the mortal embrace of clay.
You are not a human being meant to be spiritual, you
are a spiritual being living this human being miracle."*

ARU BARZAK, POET

Who You Are to God

You are not just the sum of your success, subtracted by your failures. Your worth is not just an equation of how much you can offer to
the world. Your value does not just come from what you give, say, or
do; there is more to you than just output. The sun doesn't have to run
laps around the horizon, the days do not have to pass to purchase your
worth, you are not worth it in some future plane. You are not worthy
only in the innocence of your past because it is not what you have done
or do that makes you worthy. Your worth does not come just by your
doing, it comes through the perfect God who created you.

Stop calculating your worth with finite numbers when you were
created by an infinite God who brought you to life with an everlasting
spirit of light. Stop dividing who you are by the denominator of other
people's opinions. Remember, infinity divided by any number is still
infinite. Remember forever cannot be reduced no matter how much
you subtract. Remember you are not currency to fall and rise in value.

You do not own yourself to dictate what price you are worthy
of being sold. Stop pricing God's merchandise.

Like a flawless emerald would not require a beautiful setting to dictate its worth, the value of your spirit is intrinsic because it belongs to God. You are not defined by the opinions of men, by mirrors or by compliments.

Although your sins can veil your heart from fully witnessing God, nothing you do can change how God sees you. Your sins and scars can never remove God's presence from your heart, because regardless of who you are or who you have been, God's mercy will always encompass you. Your value is not defined by worldly labels, because although God created this world for you, He says, "I created you for Myself" (20:41).

Our work on Earth is not to become something different, but to awaken from the illusion that we are separate from what we seek. We already carry faith within us; our spirits are and always will be in communion with God. The human soul was not created to become perfect, but to be aware of its completion and its connection with a higher power.

"Enlightenment is when a wave realizes it is the ocean."
THICH NHAT HANH, ZEN MASTER

It is not only through our striving that we spiritually progress, but when we surrender everything that prevents us from seeing that beneath the dust of forgetfulness, we already are what we seek to become. We already are loved by God.

"You wander from room to room, hunting for the diamond
necklace, that is already around your neck."
RUMI

It is not a surprise then that in Arabic the word for a human being is *insan*, which many scholars suggest is derived from the root words *nisyan*, which means "forgetfulness," and *unsiyah*, which means "intimacy, to love, to be loved, and to become close to." At the very root of being human we can see that we were not created to find God, but rather to remember and return to the intimate relationship we already have with Him. Our journey on Earth is not just to God, it is from God, with God, and into the love of God. The path to God is less of a spiritual path and more of a spiritual undressing of all that prevents you from seeing that in this very moment God is with you wherever you are (57:4).

The Infinite Faces of God

Everything on Earth points to God. Everything here has a divine fragrance. As the Qur'an says, "We will show them Our signs in the horizons and within themselves until it becomes clear to them that this is the truth" (41:53), confirming the idea that a divine signpost resides at the core of all creations, and an underlying unity exists among all manifested multiplicity. As Allah says, "the heavens and the earth were joined together as one united piece and then we parted them" (21:30). The Qur'an says that you were united with all of humankind within the embrace of a single soul before you were ever given a separate human existence (39:06).

In essence, God is telling us that everything seen and unseen in existence comes from a single origin. Just as the iron in your blood was made from the fusion of stars and your bones carry the dust of galaxies beyond, you were not only made in Heaven, you were made *from the heavens*. You are not merely living in the universe, you are living as a part of this universe.

> *"Just how infinite colors blossom from the light of a single sun, call it an atom or an Adam, everything was once one."*
>
> ARU BARZAK, POET

The human being is the microcosm of the macrocosm, the bridge between Heaven and Earth, both with a mortal body and an everlasting spirit, both inclined to goodness and inclined to evil (91:7-10). It is the dual nature of man that allows for him to be the perfect receptacle of God's qualities, which is why Allah has chosen us to be His representatives of love upon this Earth. Even though the angels are in constant worship and witnessing of God, their perfection and lack of free will prevents them from experiencing the entirety of God's qualities. After all, how can you experience forgiveness if you never make a mistake?

> *"If you did not sin Allah would replace you with people who would sin and they would seek the forgiveness of Allah and He would forgive them."*[1]

PROPHET MUHAMMAD ﷺ

We human beings were given the trust of free will and intellect so that as a result of that freedom of choice we could come to know and experience God's love. Allah says in the Qur'an, "We offered the Trust to the heavens and the earth and the mountains, but they declined to bear it and feared it, and the human being undertook it. Indeed, he was unjust and ignorant" (33:72). Our ignorance of God, coupled with our ego's inclination toward greediness, makes us humans often unjust and unwilling to rightfully bear the holy responsibility of being God's just representatives on Earth. The status God has granted the human being is not something we should feel entitled to, but a gift we should feel grateful for being given the opportunity to manifest.

The Honor of the Human Being

The Qur'an begs us to reflect on how respected we are by God by asking, "Don't you see that Allah has subjected to you everything in the heavens and in the earth and made complete to you His favors [bestowed His grace upon you] outwardly and inwardly?" (31:20) Despite all that we are given by God, there are still days that our freedom leads us to despair, as we attempt to swim against the current of God's will, feeling the friction between what we want and what Allah knows we need. Despite all our achievements and successes, we still ask ourselves, *How come I never feel good enough? How come no matter what I accomplish I am never fully satisfied?*

We often do not feel good enough because we cannot reach true peace, contentment, and satisfaction, separate from God. It's not through our actions, but through returning to God that we become enough. The hole we carry inside, that we so desperately long to fill, comes from the experience of once being unified with all of existence. After all, how can you long for oneness if you have only ever been a separate body? How can you long for perfection if you have never experienced it? How can you long for an all-encompassing love if you have never tasted it?

> *"If a prisoner had not lived outside, he would not detest*
> *the dungeon."*
>
> RUMI

Our longing for something that this world has not been able to fulfill is the greatest evidence for a world beyond this realm. The Qur'an reminds us of a subtle reality where God planted the seeds of faith, love, and unity in the fertile hearts of all humankind, known as the Covenant of Alast. In a pre-eternal realm, before this world as we know it, every soul that would one day manifest into an earthly form was asked by Allah, "Am I not your Lord?" This soup of souls vibrated into a symphony of affirmation as every single being replied, "Yes, yes, we testify" to the singularity of God. As a result of this covenant, it can be said that at the soul level every person, regardless of conscious belief, is fully aligned with the Divine (7:172).

As a result of God's unconditional love, faith is your divinely gifted birthright. Just as we cannot control our heartbeats or when our cells divide, our spirits are planted in the soil of God-consciousness whether or not we choose to water the seeds. Islam sees belief in the singularity of God as an innate part of what it means to be human. This is why the declaration of faith is seen as the beginning of our journey to fulfilling our purpose on Earth.

The *Fitra* and the Innate Goodness of Man

The innate alignment with the Divine that resides at the heart of being human is often called "the primordial essence" or referred to in Arabic as the *fitra*. The word *fitra* comes from a root word meaning "to split or bring forth." This implies that our work on this Earth is to split the shell of our ego and *bring forth* the divine seeds God has already planted in the garden of our spirits through the generosity of His love.

The *fitra* is the innate disposition to believe in God, worship Him, and believe in His oneness. The Prophet Muhammad ﷺ said that all children are born with the inclination to worship God and live a life in surrender to the Divine.[2] If left alone, a child's natural inclination to believe in God will continuously manifest. When someone follows a path rejecting divine love and instigating evil, it is not as a result of his nature but because of the influence of his parents or the environment in which he was raised. Despite the Qur'an consistently telling the believer to respect their parents, God also says that "We have commanded people to honor their parents, but if they urge you to associate with Me what you have no knowledge of, then do not obey them. To Me is your return, and I will inform you about what you used to do" (29:8).

Regardless of what our parents or any other person chooses to believe, the *fitra* or belief in God's oneness (*tawhid*) is part of the hardware of all human beings. While the software of our minds can be encoded in different ways based on life experience and environment, the hardware of the *fitra* cannot be changed. As the Qur'an says, "Stand firm and true in your devotion to the religion. This is the natural disposition (*fitra*) God instilled in humankind" (30:30). In our natural state of being, we recognize God's light, because we carry an imprint of this light within our spirit. In essence, faith is not setting aside rationality, but rather returning to who you truly are and have always been. This is why many mystics have said that our goal on Earth is not to summit a metaphysical mountain of spirituality, but rather to return to our original childlike state of *fitra* and purity.

Rumi describes the importance of blossoming our innate faith and manifesting our purpose on Earth through the following metaphor:

> "One thing must not be forgotten. Forget all else, but remember this, and you'll have no regrets. Remember and be concerned with everything else, but ignore this one

*thing, and you'll have done nothing. It is just as if a king had
sent you to another country to carry out a specified task.
You go and perform a hundred other tasks, but if you have
not performed that particular task, it is as though you have
done nothing at all."*

RUMI

Our task is to become a holy tree of loving kindness and to share the faithful fruits of our *fitra* with the entire world. It is only when we truly believe in God and submit to Him that we are able to manifest our greatest potential as representatives of God's love on Earth.

Adam and Eve and the Devil

The story of Adam and Eve is not an ancient myth; it is our story. We were created from dust and water, and sent to this world not only to love and worship God and return to Heaven, but also to become a manifestation of Heaven on Earth by reflecting God's qualities of love and mercy upon all creation.[3] As the Prophet Muhammad ﷺ said, "Adorn yourself with Divine Qualities."[4]

Both men and women are called to be mirrors of God on Earth and to work together to create harmony and peace for all people. Just as a pomegranate seed cannot grow into a tree without soil, and soil cannot birth from itself pomegranate fruit without a seed, the divine masculine and divine feminine complement one another on the path of blossoming the soul.

Men and women are not physically identical, but they are equal in value in the eyes of God, for the soul has no gender.[5] As the Prophet Muhammad ﷺ says, "Verily, women are the twin halves of men."[6] In fact the word for "Eve" in Arabic is the same as the Hebrew word *Hawwaah*, which comes from a root word that means "source of life."[7] In essence, every time we reference Eve, we are reminded that although the prophets of God that were mentioned in the Qur'an were men, without women there would be no prophets born into this world. This is why women are seen as the bridges of creation between Heaven and Earth.[8]

The Qur'an does not just honor the holiness of both men and women as the chosen representatives of God on Earth, but also teaches how to overcome our greatest enemy, the Devil. The Devil or Satan, in Arabic is called *Shaytan,* and may also be referred to as *Iblis.* The word *Iblis* is considered to be the Devil's actual name and originates from a root word that means "to give up hope, to despair, to be hopeless."[9] In essence, Iblis is the one who incites hopelessness by attempting to deceive us into believing that we are bad and unlovable based on our actions. In traditional Islamic theology, Iblis is not seen as a fallen angel, because angels do not have free will and so they cannot sin or disobey Allah.[10]

The Qur'an describes the Shaytan as a *jinn,* a creation of God made from smokeless fire that is part of the *ghayb* or unseen realm.[11] Although we cannot physically see the *jinn,* similar to human beings, they have been given free will; in other words, there are both good and bad *jinn.* The Shaytan is not the opposite of God, but a creation of God. Whereas some spiritual paths suggest there are separate gods of light and darkness that balance one another, the Qur'an states that Allah is One, has no equal opposites, and possesses infinite qualities of pure goodness that perfectly complement one another.

The Shaytan has no power, except for what Allah allows him to have (38:82-83). Even though the Shaytan is considered a "clear enemy to man" (17:53), his creation still has a holy purpose. Just as finding the hole in a leaking boat is a blessing because it shows us what needs to be patched, the divine mercy behind the existence of the Shaytan is that he shows us where our hearts are not in alignment with God. In fact, the twentieth-century spiritual master Sheikh Sidi Muhammad Al-Jamal refers to the Shaytan as "the fire at the gate of the garden" because his purpose is to confront and purify our base qualities. As the Qur'an says, "Satan threatens you with poverty and orders you to immorality, while Allah promises you forgiveness from Him and bounty. And Allah is All-Embracing and All-Knowing" (2:268). Some mystics call the Shaytan the guide of darkness or the gatekeeper of Heaven, because it is his voice that tempts us toward the lower qualities of the ego such as envy, lust, greed, and jealousy, showing us the places we need to polish and purify. It is in experiencing distance from Allah that we begin to see the priceless blessing of divine proximity. Although the Shaytan has his place in creation, it is important to remember that the Shaytan is an evil liar, so we should not take his existence lightly.

Iblis was not just a typical *jinn*; narrations from spiritual sages throughout Islamic history have declared that Iblis had worshipped God for a thousand years, with such fervor and passion that he was elevated to be among the angels.[12] Despite not actually being an angel, Iblis enjoyed his celestial rank, until one day Allah declared that he had created a new creation by the name of "Adam" to be His representative on Earth. Allah blew His spirit (*ruh*) into Adam and commanded the angels and Iblis to bow before his new creation. Iblis looked at the hollow clay form of Adam and refused the order of God, declaring, "I am better than him. You created me from fire and created him from clay" (7:12). Just as a match must be struck to unveil the fire it carries within, the creation of Adam created enough friction for the fire of arrogance, that was present but not yet manifested within Iblis, to be lit. Whereas the angels inquired about Adam's creation, they still followed God's command and bowed before the breath of God within Adam; but Iblis was unable to see the reflection of the Divine hidden beyond the human being's physical form.

The Devil's assumption that worth comes from physical substance is a mistake we are still making today. In a way, you could say that Satan was the first documented racist. In reality, our worth is not based on wealth, fame, race, or outer beauty, but based on our good actions and the perfect God who intentionally created us and the seeds of goodness we sow in the garden of our life. Our experience of Allah, ourselves, and the world depends on the polished state of our hearts. As the Qur'an says, "And whoever guards himself for Allah, He shall cover over his evil deeds and grant him a vast reward" (65:5). In other words, our worth is innate, but we can only experience our deep worthiness through the door of good action.

The Qur'an says, "The most noble of you in the sight of Allah is the most righteous of you" (49:13). Since we know that God is unaffected by our actions, we can see this verse as implying that when we do good we unveil the nobility and honor that God has already entrusted to every human being.

The Devil did not understand that what Allah gave to Adam could not be ruined through sin, because our innate worthiness is not earned through good action. Adam was honored before he performed a single good deed, because his initial honor as a human being was not based on his actions, but based on the breath of God (*ruh*) blown into him and the innate goodness (*fitra*) that God planted within him. As the story goes, after the angels bowed before Adam, Allah said to him, "Oh Adam! Dwell—you and your wife—in the Garden and eat freely from it—both of you—but do not come near to this tree, lest you become one of the oppressors [of yourselves and others]" (2:35). Adam and Eve were given all of Paradise, but the Devil was determined to prove that the human creation was unworthy of being so highly honored by God, so he whispered to them, "'Your Lord has forbidden this tree to you only to prevent you from becoming angels or immortals.' And he swore to the two of them, 'Truly I am a sincere advisor to you'" (7:20-21).

After Adam and Eve ate from the forbidden tree, Allah said, "Get down [from this state of innocence and be] each of you [Shaytan and human], an enemy to the other, having on Earth your dwelling and pleasure for a while" (7:24). At this point in the revelation, we see that the real difference between the Devil and Adam comes down to accountability. When Adam and Eve disobey God, they do not blame God or the Devil; they blame themselves and seek God's forgiveness through the following prayer:

> *"Our Lord! We have wronged ourselves. If You do not forgive us and have mercy upon us, we will surely be among the losers."*
>
> QUR'AN 7:23

Eating from the forbidden tree was a means for Adam and Eve to receive the teaching of repentance. Unlike the Devil, whose arrogance was met with divine wrath, Adam and Eve's humility was met with divine mercy, forgiveness, and guidance.[13]

When the Devil disobeyed God, He blamed God and responded by seeking revenge on humankind by saying, "Now that *You* have made me go astray, I shall lie in ambush for them along Your straight path. I will come to them from before them and from behind them and on their right and on their left, and You will not find most of them grateful" (7:16-17). Aside from unveiling the Devil's arrogance, what is incredibly profound about this statement is that the Devil is telling us that the root of disbelief and moral depravity is ingratitude. The deeper dimensions of this verse unveil the secret tactics of the Devil and ultimately teach us how to overcome these temptations through gratitude.

Notice how the Shaytan said that he will ambush us on "the straight path." Just as a thief only robs a house with expensive goods, the Shaytan comes strongest after those who are on the spiritual path and have fostered a sense of faith. Another commentary on the verse suggests that when the Shaytan says he will come from "behind" us it means he will delude us regarding our divine origin, suggesting we are nothing but an accidental creation of a Godless universe. This can also suggest that he will pull us away from the present moment, into a past we cannot change, by fanning the flames of regret and inciting us with feelings of despair. When the Shaytan says he will come from "before" us this implies that he will delude us regarding the Day of Judgment, attempting to convince us that there will be no accountability in the future for our actions, both good and bad.[14]

Then it is said that the Shaytan will come from our right and left, trying to lure us into error through our desires and beliefs. Note that the Shaytan did not say he will approach us from *above* as only revelation descends from above. He also cannot approach us from *below* because when we bow our heads down toward the Earth we represent the station of surrender and humility, whereas the Shaytan represents a station of arrogance. This teaches us a deep secret. When we turn to revelation and are in a state of humility, we are protected from the temptations of the Shaytan. After all, the Shaytan himself says to Allah, "By Your might, I will surely mislead them all, *except*, among them, Your chosen servants" (38:82-83). The "chosen ones" are the ones God blesses with the qualities of faith, sincerity, and humble gratitude.

The Power of Gratitude

The English word "gratitude" comes from the Greek word *gratus,* which means "thankful and pleasing," but also is said to be loosely related to the word "grace." In essence, gratefulness is directly related to Allah, because it is through the doorway of gratitude that we experience Allah's grace and generosity. As Allah profoundly states:

"If you are grateful I will surely give you more."

QUR'AN 14:7

True gratitude or *shukr*, is not based on your circumstance but based on the state of your spirit. Our gratitude does not make God more generous; rather, our gratitude makes us more receptive to receiving all that God continuously gives to us. Being in a state of gratitude is remembering that God loved us before we ever loved Him. When we are grateful we are vibrating at a higher frequency, with more clarity and more awareness of our innate alignment with Allah.

Gratitude is not an emotion; it is more a state of the mind and heart. States of mind are different than emotions because they are like channels on a radio that we can consciously choose to dial into. When we are only thankful when we get what we want, then our gratitude is a product of our ego. True gratitude blossoms through the practice of praising the Divine regardless of the outcome we desire. Sincere gratitude is birthed from the womb of humility, because it is only when we truly believe that God is "the best of planners" (8:30) that our gratefulness is no longer dependent on our outer circumstances, which constantly change, but on a God who is unchanging and eternal. After all, if the Prophet Jonah can glorify God even after being swallowed by a whale, then we too can look beyond our current circumstances and show gratitude for the infinite blessings God is continuously bestowing upon us (37:143-144). In fact, the mystics even say, "We must be grateful for being grateful, because it is by the blessing of Allah that we are grateful to Him to begin with."

When we are in a state of *shukr* or gratefulness we are connecting ourselves to the divine name *Ash-Shakur,* which means the "The Most Grateful."[15] When we are grateful we are closer to our Lord. When we are in a state of gratitude it is always of more value than what we are grateful for—because the gift will perish but the Giver of the gift is eternal. This is why when the Prophet's ﷺ wife asked him why he would undergo so much hardship in prayer and repentance if Allah had already forgiven him, the Prophet ﷺ replied by saying *Afala akuna abdan shakura,* which means, "Should I not be a thankful servant?"[16] In other words, the Prophet ﷺ was not grateful to Allah to gain something, but rather he was grateful because he could not imagine responding to Allah's infinite mercy, grace, love, and forgiveness in any other way. As Rumi says, "Thanksgiving is sweeter than bounty itself. One who cherishes gratitude does not cling to the gift! Thanksgiving is the true meat of Allah's bounty; the bounty is its shell. For thanksgiving carries you to the heart of the Beloved."

The essence of gratitude is experienced through the acknowledgment and appreciation of the gifts Allah has given us. When we appreciate and use His resources and gifts in ways that please Him we are given a greater means of experiencing Him and His divine names. We manifest true gratitude when we use our eyes to see God's signs, when we use our ears to hear God's words, when we use our tongue to remember our Lord, when we use our hands to give charity, when we use our feet to walk the path of truthfulness, love, kindness, justice, and mercy. As Imam Ali says, "When some blessings come to you do not drive them away through thanklessness." Gratitude is the opposite of entitlement and self-management. True gratitude blossoms from the soil of complete trust and surrender to God's perfect will.

Alhamdullilah or "All praise and glory belongs to Allah" is the first thing that Adam expressed when he spoke,[17] and *Alhamdullilah* is among the first words the people of Paradise will say (7:43). If gratitude toward God is the pathway to righteousness and eternal salvation, then we could argue that ingratitude is one of the greatest enemies of faith.[18] This is why one of the ways you can gauge your station of spiritual excellence in Islam is to examine your level of gratefulness.

One of the ways the Qur'an shows us the importance of gratitude is by showing us the detrimental effects of ingratitude. In fact, one of the lessons that the story of the Shaytan shows us is that if you outwardly worship God but inwardly have an ungrateful heart that carries pride, you can fall from the highest heavens to the lowest hell. The arrogance and greed of the Shaytan shifted his focus from the Eternal Gift-Giver to the perishable gift, making his obedience dependent on getting what he thought he deserved. Iblis was already in the Garden, already close to Allah, and yet his ingratitude to God and envy of Adam resulted in him being cast out of Paradise.

"Whoever has an atom's weight of pride in his heart will not enter Paradise."[19]

PROPHET MUHAMMAD ﷺ

Since Allah is the king of oneness and pride and arrogance are states of forgetfulness of Allah, which create separation, the prideful by definition cannot exist before God's singular presence.

Sin and Forgetfulness

Since God declares in the Qur'an, "remembrance of Allah is the greatest" (29:45), being forgetful of the Divine is considered a significant spiritual misstep. As Imam Ali says, "Your sickness is from you, but you do not perceive it and your remedy is within you, but you do not sense it. You presume you are a small entity, but within you is enfolded the entire universe...What you seek is within you, if only you reflect." Here Imam Ali is reminding us that the root problem of humanity is forgetfulness of our innate goodness (*fitra*) and pre-eternal connection to the divine love of God.[20]

In the Bible, the Greek word used for "sin" is *hamartia*, which comes from the sport of archery, translating to "missing the mark." This word beautifully depicts how, when we sin, in addition to turning away from God we are also missing the whole point of what it means to be human. In other words, sin can be seen as a symptom of the human being losing sight of their primordial goodness (*fitra*). Since the goodness of man is a reflection of God's eternal and perfect goodness, our *fitra* cannot be changed through human sin.

> *Just as clouds cannot affect the presence and power of the sun's light, but can alter our experience of the intensity of the light, sin can veil our perception of our inner goodness, but it cannot change it.*

God gave every human being spiritual eyes, to be able to experience and see His signs. Since it is God's generosity and not our obedience to God's laws and rules that gave us spiritual vision, our sins do not have the power to take away what our good deeds never earned us in the first place. However, it is important to remember that our actions have the power to veil us from the gifts that God has given us. Our sins can become a blindfold over our spiritual eyes. Repeatedly sinning without polishing our hearts through the practice of repentance (*tawba*) can prevent us from seeing God's beauty (18:101).[21]

Our sins can turn us away from the light of God's eternal love, making us live in a darkness we subject ourselves to through our own doing. Similar to how when you turn away from the sun you experience darkness, when you turn away from God's love, through sinful actions and forgetfulness, you experience a darkness that feels like wrath. This is precisely why the Qur'an repeatedly illustrates that it is not God who oppresses us but rather we who oppress ourselves.

This distinction is very important. God is not a human being with changing emotions, so all variability we experience in relationship with God comes not from Him but from *our* experience of His love. Although obedience to God's commands and performing good deeds are two ways we *experience* the love of God, our deeds on their own do not make us *worthy* of God, because nothing can be worthy of the One who has given us everything and needs nothing. In truth, we are only worthy of God's love because of God's own generosity. Our worthiness comes from God alone, but our choices and actions are the medium by which we actualize God's gifts. As the Qur'an clearly states, "Man can have nothing but what he strives for" (53:39).

Our experience of the Hereafter is in part determined by our actions, because our actions help to polish the mirror of our hearts, which either reject or receive all that God has given us. As the Qur'an says, "Compete with each other in performing good deeds" (2:148), because "those who believe and do good work, they are the people of Paradise, in it they abide eternally" (2:82).

While good deeds and sincerely serving others helps to align our spirits with God, without purification of the heart there is a veil that prevents us from experiencing the harvest of good action. As the Prophet Muhammad ﷺ said, "Allah does not look at your appearance or wealth, but rather he looks at your hearts and actions."[22] The Qur'an does not just call us to outwardly follow rules, but also calls us to integrate God-consciousness on the deepest levels of our hearts. The Qur'an says, that only he or she will prosper "that brings to Allah a sound heart" (26:89). It is only when outer obedience unites with sincere inner submission that the eyes of the heart awaken to witness and receive the love of God.

> *"On those who believe and perform righteous deeds the Lord*
> *of Mercy will bestow love for them."*
>
> QUR'AN 19:96

It is in turning toward the Divine, being of service to others, and removing the veils of the ego that we begin to feel the love that God has always been pouring upon us.

EGO: "Edging God Out"

Since sin or turning away from God is an act of the ego, it is important to better understand what the ego actually means. It is believed that the ego (*nafs*) or the illusionary sense of self is created when the breath of God (*ruh*) is joined with our mortal body. It is metaphorically said that if the spirit is symbolized by the sun and the body by wet clay, the ego is the translucent steam created when the light of the spirit touches the clay.[23] In other words, like a fog that distorts our vision, the ego is a veil between our consciousness and our spirit. The purification and detachment of the ego is so vital within Islam because the more we purify the illusions of the self, the more we are able to witness the light of Allah.

Just as the dark night is needed to be able to see the stars, the lower ego creates the contrast necessary to experience the spirit. The poet Samani speaks to the balancing effect of opposites when he says, "There must be a garbage pit next to a lofty palace so that all the refuse and filth that gather in the palace can be thrown there. In the same way, whenever God formed a heart by means of the light of purity, He placed the lower self [ego] next to it as a dustbin. This black spot of 'ignorance' flies on the same wings as the jewel of purity...A straight arrow needs a crooked bow. Oh heart, you be like the straight arrow! Oh ego, you take the shape of a crooked bow!"

God breaks us down to break us through because the shell of sin has to be broken before the spirit can flower. God does not test us because He hates us, but because He loves us and sees in us a potential that can only be manifested and unveiled through the fires of purification. Just as muscle must tear to grow, the friction between sin and our inner holiness creates the conditions for spiritual growth. Although in the moment this can be hard to see, it is important to remember that just as the veil of night is needed to see the stars, it is through contrast of pain and pleasure that we come to experience this world.

Even the existence of the human being is like a coin that comes fashioned with two sides: on the one hand, the Qur'an says that you are made in the best of molds (95:4), fashioned with the breath of God's spirit (38:72) and chosen to be His representative of mercy upon the Earth (2:30). On the other hand, the Qur'an describes humankind as fragile creatures made of dust from the same earth they walk upon (23:12); anxious, forgetful, ungrateful, vulnerable to the bite of a fly (22:73), a nothingness in the face of God's eternal reality; a mortal that is passing away a breath at a time, inching toward a death that will arrive without warning (31:34).

Although the word *ego* can be seen as an acronym for "Edging God Out," and acts as a veil that separates us from the oneness of God, it is also the reason that unity carries meaning.[24] Some scholars suggest when Adam and Eve were in the garden they had no real experience of separation from God, and so the holy sacredness of their proximity to the Divine was not fully actualized until they experienced the contrast of distance from God. Some scholars have also stated that Adam and Eve were not sent to Earth as a punishment, but partly because perceived separation may be necessary for the human being to have an experience. Therefore, without the presence of veils the observer and the observed would be one in our worldly physical realm. The veils between us and God are perhaps a product of divine mercy because they allow us to have an experience of God within the multiplicity of His creation.[25]

In order to better understand this, consider the following example: The glass on the helmets of astronauts is created in a shape that deflects the intensity of the sun's light, and protects the astronauts' sensitive eyes from the full luminosity of the sun, assuring they do not go blind. The astronauts' helmets may veil their eyes from the true brightness of the sun, but this veil is a mercy because it allows the astronauts' eyes to have an experience of the light. In this same way, despite the ego being a veil before God, when transformed and purified it allows us to have a true experience of God.

When our ego's inclination to be forgetful of the Divine is met with remembrance of God, our entire perception of reality can transform in an instant. The following story about the thirteenth-century spiritual master and satirist Mullah Nasruddin beautifully illustrates this point:

> A man once came to Mullah Nasruddin, and said, "I am rich but depressed. I have taken all the money I own and have gone in search of happiness, but I have yet to find it." As the man was staring toward the sky in reflection, the Mullah grabbed his bag of money out of his hands and ran away.
>
> The man ran after the Mullah, screaming, "You thief! You thief!" The Mullah ran around a sharp corner and left the bag in the street, where

the man would find it, and then hid behind a pillar. When the man saw his bag on the ground his facial expression changed from despair to joy as he hugged his bag in pure bliss and happiness. After a few moments, the Mullah came out of hiding and said, "Sometimes you have to lose what you have and find it again for you to know the value of the blessing that you have always owned."

Just as Adam and Eve had to leave the Garden to actualize its worth, we were not sent to this Earth as a punishment, but rather as a test and as a means of learning to be grateful for all that God has already given us.[26] We can either be lured by the mortal pleasures of this world into forgetfulness of who and Whose we really are, or we can strive against our ego's desires by being in remembrance (*dhikr*) of God's incomprehensible mercy toward us.

There Is No Compulsion in Religion

In order to understand why God created us with a spirit that longs for unity and an ego that is constantly drawn to individuate, we must first understand that all things begin and end with love. Acquiring intimate knowledge (*ma'rifa*) of God's love is the beginning of our journey. Since we worship The Origin of Love (*Al-Wadud*), loving and being loved by God is what we were created to experience. Even if we have lived a life with more rainy days than blue skies, behind every cloud, the sun of Allah's unconditional love is always present.

It is the love of Allah that takes a mortal moment in time and makes it everlasting. It is through love that we taste infinity. It is through love that we undergo a spiritual alchemy in which our stony hearts are transformed to gold. It is love that pulls a rose out of a sea of thorns, gives wings to a caterpillar, makes granite into rubies, and reminds us we are far more infinite than our weight in dirt. It is through love that the heart can reach God. It is the longing of love that pushes our seedling hearts to reach through an earth of darkness for a light it feels but cannot see.

"How did the rose ever open its heart and give to this world all its beauty? It felt the encouragement of light against its being, otherwise we all remain too frightened."

HAFIZ, 14TH-CENTURY PERSIAN POET

We must not forget that love is the reason there is something instead of nothing because we are created by and for the sake of actualizing God's love. God speaks of this love when He says, "I have not created the invisible beings and humankind except to worship Me" (51:56). At its essence, divine worship is the highest station of love, because you cannot worship something until you love it. But in order for love to exist, so must free will, because love cannot be coerced, it cannot be created by force.

"There is no compulsion in religion"

QUR'AN 2:256

Allah gave us free will, not so we would choose to create evil, but so that we could choose to experience divine love and in turn love God. Had Allah not given us the freedom to choose, without offering the possibility to turn away from Him, then we could never manifest our freedom— there would only be one choice, and as a result, no freedom in denying that choice. Allah allowed for the possibility of our turning away from Him in order for us to manifest our free will and create the possibility for love to exist.

Unwrapping the Gift of Divine Love

Our journey on Earth is about unwrapping the gift of divine love that we were given by God. It is not about achieving, earning, or deserving divine love—the shoreless ocean of Allah's love is already within us.

The endless river of Allah's blessings is already flowing through all of existence, good action is just one of the most important ways we can turn the faucet on and experience Allah's boundless love. The gift of free will creates the contrast necessary to know God, to experience His love, and from a place of passionate gratitude to worship Him.

It is through the human being that the universe comes to know itself, because it is we who have been given the gift of attributing meaning to the forms of creation. When Allah created Adam, the angels asked God why He would create a creation that would bring so much destruction and bloodshed on the Earth. God replied by saying, "I know what you do not know" (2:30). God then tells the angels to prostrate not to the form of Adam, but to the spirit of God reflected within him. In reference to the creation of Adam, Allah says the following:

"I have fashioned him and breathed into him of My Spirit."

QUR'AN 38:72

The Qur'an then mentions another mysterious and distinguishing factor between the angels and Adam, when it says in reference to God, "He taught Adam all the names" (2:31). Some say this refers to giving Adam and all the children of Adam the ability to categorize and make connections between the creations. Others say this refers to the ability to perceive the essence beneath the physical forms. Then there are those that say that what Adam was taught were the names of Allah that are manifested and reflected in all forms of creation, for as Allah says, "Adam was created in My image."[27] This is why many spiritual masters throughout time have said, "He who knows himself knows his Lord."[28]

Although we can reflect God's qualities, we are not God. It is not in knowing ourselves that we know God because God is like us, rather when we come to intimately know our humanity, our limitedness and fallibility, we come to taste something of God's infinite and perfect nature. Just as when you read a beautiful and thoughtful book you are naturally inclined to ponder the brilliance of the author, when we reflect on the intricacy of our creation, it naturally points us to the unfathomable perfection of the Author who wrote us into existence.

To know our Lord, we must learn to embrace our life instead of always trying to escape it. God speaks to us both through our blessings and our trials. When God blesses us with wealth and abundance He is calling us toward His names, The Most Generous (*Al-Karim*) and The Most Grateful

(*Ash-Shakur*). When we stay faithful and hopeful in times of difficulty, we are getting to know God through His quality, The Most Patient (*As-Sabur*). As the Prophet Muhammad ﷺ says, "Amazing is the affair of the believer, verily all of his affair is good and this is not true for anyone except the believer. If something good befalls him he is grateful and that is good for him. If something of harm befalls him he is patient and that is good for him."[29] Both within ourselves and in the greater cosmos, God is opening the door for us to get to know Him through the manifestation of His names.

> *"How we see God is a direct reflection of how we see ourselves. If God brings to mind mostly fear and blame, it means there is too much fear and blame welled inside us. If we see God as full of love and compassion, so are we."*
>
> SHAMS TABRIZI, RUMI'S SPIRITUAL GUIDE

We know God based on the divine names and qualities that are most vibrantly fostered and reflected within us. Knowing ourselves is vital to loving God, for divine love awakens in our spirits when we begin to really taste how needy and desperate we are for God. God planted the quality of His love within us before we even knew who He was, so our longing to love God is a manifestation of Him having loved us first.

Love is not something we create or find in the world; it is a part of who we are. Since we tend to have an affinity toward the goodness of those we resemble, the more we mirror God, the more our love of God blossoms. The more we accompany those who love God and reflect God's qualities of kindness, compassion, mercy, and peace, the more we are drawn into the oneness of His love. We are like the moon: the more we turn away from the darkness of the ignorant ego and toward the eternal light of God's love, the fuller our spirits become.

Worship is the highest station of love. When we experientially learn more about God and how His love both embraces and overlooks our greatest mistakes, we cannot help but worship Him. Sincere worship is not born from the soil of obligation, but from gratitude for all that God has freely given to us before He gave us the mouths to even thank Him.

A simple yet profound way of fanning the flames of gratitude within us is by reflecting on how perfectly God made us. When we reflect on the intricate perfection of our creation we are naturally inclined toward being grateful toward Allah. As we observe the lack of conscious thought that goes into our breaths and into our heart beating, we naturally begin to enter into a state of awe and bewilderment. When we bring awareness to the fact that every time we breathe Allah has intentionally chosen for us to take that breath, we begin to experience that Allah's loving eyes are always upon us. When we turn our worries into worship, through prayer, repentance, and remembrance of Allah's names, our awareness shifts from how big our problems are to how big our Lord is, and we feel peace.

Life Is a Test

The Qur'an describes life as a test, because God sent us to Earth to challenge our own perceived limitations and to help us unveil our vast array of capabilities. Life is not just about Heaven and Hell, it is also about un-veiling who God created you to be, so that you can come to know who God is. The path to God begins with witnessing and experiencing your human qualities, because you cannot actualize what you have not acknowledged. When we shift our perspective from what God is doing *to* us, to what God is doing *for* us, we are able to see that although God may not always give us what we want, He will always give us exactly what we need.

> *"It may be that you hate something and it is good for you and it may be that you love something and it is bad for you."*
>
> QUR'AN 2:216

God knows what soil your seedling soul needs to blossom. He gives you people to love you, to leave you, to inspire you, to doubt you, and to believe in you. Out of His love, God lets the world hurt you and break you, not because He wants to destroy you, but because He wants to show you your hidden strengths that can only be manifested in the cocoon of trials. This is one of the reasons the Prophet ﷺ says, "If Allah wants to do good to somebody He afflicts him with trials."[30] God takes us into the cave of difficulty and pain when there are gems for us to find there. God pushes us to the edge of the cliff when He wants us to learn how to fly. The difficulties we face can act as catalysts for self-discovery and growth.

The core Islamic teaching that "verily with difficulty comes ease" (94:5) is beautifully shown through the popular teaching story of a boy and a butterfly.

> A young boy spent hours watching a butterfly struggle to get out of a hole in its cocoon. Seeking to be of help, the boy grabbed a pair of scissors and carefully slit the cocoon open to help the butterfly out. To the boy's surprise, the butterfly came out with shriveled wings and spent the rest of its life bound to the ground.

The boy did not know that the butterfly's struggle of digging its way out of its cocoon is nature's way of strengthening its wings enough for it to be able to fly. The butterfly does not fly despite its struggle out of the cocoon, but rather because of it. In the same way, our spirit's struggle against the unconscious ego is ultimately what strengthens its muscles. As Rumi says, "If you are irritated by every rub, how will your mirror be polished?"

When we face trials, we are being prepared to manifest our greatest potential, which is hidden beneath the shell of our comfort and conditioning.

We are like photographs; our faith is developed in the darkroom of the trials we face.

In Arabic, the word *fitna*, meaning "hardship," stems from the word *fatanah*, which means "to test gold, burn with fire." Just as gold is heated to extract valuable elements from the useless surrounding material, it is through the fire of our trials that our golden essence is unearthed.

When *fitna* first arrives, it makes little sense; it feels unjust and unfair. For the one who doesn't understand the stages of growth, a seed becoming a tree looks like destruction. When the soil squeezes the shell until it shatters, it looks like punishment, like undeserved pain. But the seed does not curse the sun and rain for breaking it open, because it knows that its potential is far greater than the limit of its shell.

A loving and merciful God recreates you by breaking you out of the cocoons and cages of the past. It is only with patience and prayer that we come to see that heat and pressure help to create the conditions necessary to transform dark coal into a luminous diamond.

> *"God will find a way out for those who are mindful of Him, And He will provide him from (sources) he never could imagine. And whosoever puts his trust in Allah, then He will suffice him. God will accomplish His purpose. God has appointed a measure for everything."*
>
> QUR'AN 65:2-3

Everything on this Earth was created for you to lovingly worship God while experiencing the holiness that resides at the core of all existence. When you are truly aligned with the purpose of being human, the trial and blessing become one. Every experience, every feeling, and every thought is a way that Allah speaks to you and calls to you to return back to His loving embrace. As the Qur'an says, "We tested them with good times and bad, that perhaps they would return" (7:168). It is a blessing to know that both in our moments of ease and in our moments of difficulty, God is equally present and constantly calling us back to Him.

Jihad for Peace

Our spirits striving against the lower qualities of our ego is the great *jihad* of our life. The word *jihad* originates from the root word *jahada*, which means "to strive or struggle."[31] Based on narrations from the Prophet ﷺ, Muslim scholars have broken down the concept of *jihad* into two parts: the lesser jihad and the greater jihad.

The lesser or combative *jihad* is the act of fighting in defense for the freedom of religion, homeland, and basic human rights, while the greater or spiritual *jihad* is striving against one's ego and lower desires. As the Qur'an says, "And why should you not fight in the cause of Allah and for those weak, ill-treated and oppressed among men, women, and children, whose cry is: 'Our Lord! Rescue us from this town, whose people are oppressors; and raise for us from You one who will protect; and raise for us from You one who will help!'" (4:75).

Here the Qur'an is very clearly outlining that Muslims have an obligation to help people who are oppressed, no matter who or where they are in the world. However, the lesser *jihad* is always fought in defense and cannot be declared by civilians, but has to be established by the proper authority figures, acting in accordance with the example of the Prophet ﷺ and the Qur'an (4:59). As the Qur'an says, "Fight in God's cause against those who fight you, but do not overstep the limits: God does not love those who overstep the limits" (2:190).

> *Jihad is not a destination, but the process of striving towards establishing peace where there is injustice and the suppression of freedom.*

Unlike the Romans, who would say, *Silent enim legis enter arma,* which means "Laws are silent during wars," Divine Law stipulates very specific laws during war, to protect against acts of unjust killing and oppression.[32] As a result of the divinely declared holiness of human life (5:32), the rules of defensive warfare in Islam are stricter than those of many modern countries. For example, in combative *jihad* in defense of the freedom of religion, combatants cannot kill women, worshippers, the sick, the elderly, children, non-combatants, or civilians. They also cannot destroy towns, cut down trees, or use fire to destroy the land. Essentially, no bombs may be used, the Earth must be protected, and the innocent cannot be collateral damage.

The combative *jihad* has very specific rules and ends the moment peace is re-established. As the Qur'an very clearly states, "If they propose peace, accept it and trust in God" (8:61). We are called "to deal kindly and justly with anyone" who respects our right to practice our religion freely, who does not drive us unjustly out of our homes, and who does not oppress us (60:8). The Prophet Muhammad ﷺ very clearly and seriously states, "Beware! Whoever is cruel and hard on a non-Muslim minority, curtails their rights, burdens them with more than they can bear, or takes anything from them against their free will, I will complain against the person on the Day of Judgment."[33]

While the lesser *jihad* requires very specific conditions and is fought in a particular context and time frame, the greater spiritual *jihad* is never-ending and applies to all Muslims in all lands and circumstances. While the lesser *jihad* is against a visible tyrant or oppressive enemy, the greater *jihad* is against the invisible enemy of the ego's desires of greed, lust, arrogance, ignorance, pride, envy, anger, and other vices.

The Prophet Muhammad ﷺ reminded us of the importance of the greater *jihad* when he said, "Have I not informed you? The believer is the one who is trusted with the lives and wealth of people. The Muslim is the one from whose tongue and hand people are safe. The one striving in *jihad* in the way of Allah is the one who wages *jihad* against himself in obedience to Allah. The emigrant is one who emigrates away from sins and evil deeds."[34]

We are called to *strive* to reflect the holy qualities of God upon all people, no matter how hard it becomes. When we strive to wake up for dawn prayers, that is a *jihad*. When we protect the secrets of others even when they expose our secrets, that is a *jihad*. When we attempt to bring light and love where we are met with darkness and hatred, that is a *jihad*. *Jihad* can be any act of striving to manifest goodness and beauty for the sake of God.

The idea that the concept of *jihad* is limited to military defense is clearly disproven through the following narration: "A man came to the Prophet ﷺ asking permission to strive in *jihad*. The Prophet ﷺ said, 'Are your parents alive?' He said yes. The Prophet ﷺ said, 'Then strive in their service.'"[35]

Jihad is the act of striving to put everything in its rightful place. Jihad is not only about overcoming our inner struggles with our ego, but also about being a representative of God's justice by protecting the divinely given rights of all people.

It is important that we strive for peace not from a place of hatred, but from a place of love. We must first polish the mirror of our own hearts before we can ever reflect the light of God's justice, mercy, and unity upon the rest of creation.

Polishing the Mirror of the Heart

Similar to a mirror that rusts when it is not polished, the heart can become "rusty" when we are consumed by thoughts of self-management and fail to polish it with the remembrance of God. However, dropping our attention from our mind into our heart and surrendering to God is not easy. In fact, it has been said that the distance between our head and our heart is approximately 18 inches, but it is arguably the longest journey we will spiritually ever take.[36] The spiritual path does not deny the importance of the mind, but if the mind alone reigns over the body, the heart and soul will become enslaved to the ego and its desires. However, when the divinely aligned heart is the king of the body and the mind is its servant, we live in peace and harmony.

It is not a coincidence that the word for "intellect" in Arabic is *aql*, which comes from a root word that can also mean "to restrain," like a rope tethering an animal with a leash to prevent it from escaping.[37] In other words, the value of the intellect is determined by its ability to tether back the animalistic desires within us, so that we have the space to be able to witness and recognize the signs of God.

However, to become a caretaker of the Earth, or mirror of God on Earth, is not only about behavior modification, but about ego and heart transformation. In Islamic theology, the heart is generally considered the "organ of perception," because the world is experienced through the filter of the heart, not the eyes.

"It is not the eyes that are blind, but the hearts."

QUR'AN 22:46

We do not see the world as it truly is, but through the state that our heart is in. When the spiritual heart is veiled with the lower qualities of the ego, such as pride, lust, greed, and envy, we see a distorted perception of reality. As the Qur'an says, "On people's hearts is the stain of that which they do" (83:14). Just as, in the darkness, a pebble and gold look and feel the same, when our hearts are impure and covered by the clouds of sin, the light of distinction fails to penetrate our consciousness, leaving us blind to the truth.

"In everybody there is a piece of flesh, if it is healthy, the whole body is healthy, and if it is sick, the whole body is sick. Beware! It is the heart!"[38]

PROPHET MUHAMMAD ﷺ

Our heart may be the size of our fist, and weigh less than a pound, but in a single hour it can pump 40 gallons of blood through our body. By the power of God, this tiny muscle beats 40 million times a year and 3 billion times during the average human life span.[39] In fact, some scholars have said that if you listen to the heart beating with a stethoscope you can hear the name, "Al-lah, Al-lah, Al-lah."[40] The contraction and expansion the tongue experiences in saying "Allah" is also experienced by the heart, in pumping blood in a very specific oscillatory pattern. Even on the physical level, the heart intimately knows who its Lord is; it is the ego (*nafs*) that forgets the lordship of Allah due to being veiled by its amusement and obsession with the world.

In the Covenant of Alast, in the pre-eternal realm of souls, we all witnessed God outwardly manifested and affirmed that He alone was our Lord. In this world, the heart is called to witness God again, but this time inwardly and indirectly through the way God projects His qualities upon the mirror of creation. The heart that is truly polished does not see the creation, but sees only a reflection of Allah's infinite qualities. This is why when Imam Ali was asked "What is creation?" he profoundly said, "It is like the dust in the air, it only becomes visible when the light of Allah strikes it."

It is only when the heart is purified and realigned with Allah that we see reality as it is, instead of through the veils of who we want to be or think we are, based on the conditioning of our culture and society. The mind does not rule the heart, because the heart has its own spiritual intellect. This is why when the Prophet ﷺ was asked what righteousness is he said, "Consult your heart!"[41]

In fact, scientific studies from the Heartmath Institute have shown that the electromagnetic field of the heart can be measured several feet outside the body—and is 60 times stronger than our brain waves. Plus, the heart of a fetus begins beating before the brain or central nervous system are even developed. In fact, recent studies have shown that the heart has its own set of neurons, with both short-term and long-term memory that can interact with the brain, affecting our emotions.[42]

The heart is also affected by our actions. The Prophet ﷺ teaches us that piety and righteousness are actualized when the soul and heart feel tranquility, and sin is that which creates restlessness and uncertainty in the chest.[43] Knowing that the state of the heart can affect the well-being of the entire physical and spiritual body begs us to ask: how do we transform and awaken our hearts?

The transformation of the heart and purification of the ego is one of the fundamental purposes of divine revelation. Every pillar and practice in Islam serves to purify the ego by turning the heart from the desires of the fleeting world toward the everlasting love of God. The two most powerful ways the Qur'an speaks of how to refine the ego and transform the heart is through the practices of repentance (*tawba*) and remembrance (*dhikr*).

Returning to God Through Repentance

Tawba, or repentance returns us, with love and mercy, to the spiritually aligned parts of ourselves that we tend to lose sight of in the face of our mistakes or sins. We were sent to this Earth as the most beautiful, complete masterpieces of God, but our forgetfulness of our divine origin covers the canvas of our existence with a film that veils us from the divine origin of our spirits. When the Qur'an says, "Allah has not created two hearts in any one man" (33:04), it means that we can either turn our heart to the creation or to Allah, but not both. In fact, a word often used for heart in Arabic is *qalb,* which comes from a root word that also means "to turn, change directions, and return."[44]

It is human to sin or turn away from God, for it is the nature of the heart to be in a constant state of turning between expansion and contraction, between creation and the Creator, and between the mortal ego and our everlasting spirit. The Devil cannot tempt the *qalb* directly because the inner heart is pure and belongs only to Allah. The Devil can only whisper to the chest, known as *sadr* in Arabic, which is sort of like the outer fortress that protects the heart. The stronger the heart becomes through repentance, remembrance, and surrender, the lower the decibels of the Devil's voice become in comparison. This is why the Prophet ﷺ says to Allah, "Oh Turner of the hearts, affirm my heart upon Your religion!"[45]

When we repent, we are purifying the film of the ego to unveil who we are and have always been. We do not become God's representatives on Earth through worldly achievement or knowledge, but by the acknowledgment of how unworthy and incapable we would be of the task without God's grace. This is why those with wisdom pray, "Our Lord, let not our hearts deviate after You have guided us and grant us from Yourself mercy. Indeed, You are the Bestower" (3:8).

It is through boasting in our weakness, that we become receptive to being made strong through the power and mercy of God. Repentance is the act of creating space for God's will to seamlessly move through us without resistance.

It is only when we first surrender our nothingness to God that we become receptive to receiving the fullness of His presence. The following story beautifully depicts the importance of coming to God empty of what we think we know.

A spiritual seeker went to the mountains of Iran to learn from a mystic by the name of Essijan. When the master heard that the seeker wanted to learn about the Divine, she said, "First we must drink tea." When the water had boiled, Essijan poured tea in the seeker's cup until it became full and then began to overflow on the table. Essijan wouldn't stop pouring tea in the full cup until the confused seeker said, "Master, there is no more room in this cup, it is already filled."

The teacher then smiled and said, "Just like you. How can I teach you about the ways of the spirit when you are so filled? You have to first empty your cup of your judgments, past mistakes, opinions, and everything you think you know, if you want to be filled with the awareness of God."

Repentance, in its essence, is the "emptying of your cup" so that you can be filled with the pure light of divine remembrance. One of the best ways to do this is through the recitation of the phrase *Astaghfirullah,* which means, "I seek forgiveness from Allah."[46] Divine remembrance (*dhikr*) is not only about you remembering God through chanting His names, but it is also about being reminded that we are never forgotten by God.

> *Life is not only about reaching Heaven after you die; it is about dwelling in the palace of God's eternal presence while you are living.*

It is through turning our awareness to an unconditionally loving God that our hearts find rest (13:28), and our egos are transformed from what the Qur'an calls the ruling and destructive self (*nafs al-amara*) to the contented and peaceful self (*nafs al-mutmainah*). As the Prophet ﷺ famously said, "There is a polish for everything that takes away rust, and the polish for the heart is the remembrance of God."[47]

However, just as thinking of the ocean will not get you wet, chanting God's names without loving intention is fruitless. As the fifteenth-century Indian poet Kabir profoundly said, "If saying God gave liberation, saying candy made your mouth sweet, saying fire burned your feet, saying water quenched your thirst, saying food banished hunger, the whole world would be free." Remembering God is more than just words on a tongue, it is about actively tuning our consciousness toward the Divine, with intentional words that are followed by actions that actualize our intention.

Returning to God Through Divine Remembrance

In many spiritual paths, repetitive heartfelt chants are used in meditation and prayer practices, as a means of experiencing and communing with the Divine. Hindu and Buddhist traditions use mantras, a holy formula of sound vibration that when repeated over time are believed to help awaken the spirit by inspiring a sense of spiritual transcendence. Linguistically, the Sanskrit word *mantra* is made up of the combination of *man-*, which means "to think," and *-tra*, which means "tool, instrument."[48] In other words, a mantra literally is a "tool for thought or mindfulness."

Fascinatingly enough, the Arabic word *dhikr* is often translated as "remembrance," but is also a tool for mindfulness. The word *dhikr* comes from the tri-literal root *dhal-kaf-ra*, which means "to magnify, praise, to bear in mind, and be mindful." However, in Islamic spirituality, the practice of remembrance or chanting in the form of *dhikr* is not about affirming the self or experiencing spiritual ecstasy, but rather it is a tool to affirm and consistently "bring to mind and heart" the singularity and majesty of Allah.

The power of intentional remembrance is that it brings your awareness to the present moment, which is where God is most intimately experienced. Remembrance is not just a return to God, it is a return to the essence of who you are. Just as darkness vanishes the moment light arrives, since the rust on the heart is a product of forgetfulness, through the very act of remembrance the heart begins being polished.

Like an optometrist adjusting your prescription to correct your vision, remembrance and praise of God realigns, supplements, and heals the eyes of your heart, allowing you to see the truth as it has always been.

Remembrance of God (*dhikr*) is one of the most powerful practices in Islam, because it is one of the greatest ways to open our hearts to receive the unconditional love of God that has always been shining upon us. A powerful practice of remembrance is to chant *Ya Allah* or "Oh Allah" in combination with any of the other 99 divine names of Allah.[49] There are different prescriptions of how many times it is best to chant these names, but the power of remembrance does not come only from the number of times you repeat a particular divine name. The true power of remembrance is derived from the intention and heart you bring to your chanting. It is important to allow permission for yourself to be vulnerable and honest as you invite Allah's divine light into the places where you feel pain, anger, sadness, self-hatred, and doubt.

If we want to experience God more deeply, we must be with God more intimately, through the practices of remembrance, prayer, and repentance. Do not be ashamed of coming to God with your sins, desires, and broken places. It is our hunger, our thirst, and our emptiness that creates the longing for soul food. If we were full, we would never seek for anything. God calls us to Him by inspiring neediness and poverty within us. The names of Allah are like medicine for the needy and wounded parts of our hearts and souls. When we sincerely chant the name of "Allah" or any of the divine names of God, the vibrational sound of the sacred Arabic opens our hearts to being receptive to the divine light of God that encompasses all of creation.

We do not pray to God for His love, we pray to God from having experienced His love. How can we earn God's love when everything we can offer God already belongs to Him? Rumi poetically illustrates this by saying to God, "You have no idea how hard I've looked for a gift to bring You. Nothing seemed right. What's the point of bringing gold to the gold mine, or water to the ocean. Everything I came up with was like taking spices to the Orient. It's not good enough giving my heart and my soul because you already have these. So I've brought you a mirror. Look at Yourself and remember me."

The human journey is not about becoming worthy of having a relationship with God, because as Rumi reminds us, nothing is worthy of God except Himself. After all, how can we "deserve" an infinite God's love through our finite actions? Can we ever pray enough, give enough, love enough to be worthy of being created? Good deeds, being humble, kind, pure, and God-conscious are necessary vehicles that allow us to experience God's love, but our actions alone do not make God love us, because His love is unconditional. We are on this Earth not to find faith or love, but to water the blessings of what God already planted within us.

> *"It is God who has made you deputies on the Earth, raising you in ranks, some above others, in order to test you in the gifts He has given you."*
>
> QUR'AN 6:165

God will ask to what extent we manifested and actualized the gifts He gave us. He will ask if we used our intellect for the benefit of society or to its detriment, if we used our hands to bring peace or to instigate war. He will ask if we wasted our blessings in focusing on materialism or if we used what we were divinely given as a means of supporting those who are less fortunate.

God gave every single one of us unique abilities and talents, and based on what He gave to us, He will evaluate us. God does not grade us on a curve, He compares us to ourselves. Our work on Earth is to receive and cultivate the gifts given to us by God for the benefit of the entire creation.

> *"The meaning of life is to find your gift. The purpose of life is to give it away."*
>
> PABLO PICASSO, ARTIST

God Can Use You Exactly as You Are

We polish our hearts to unveil the interconnectedness of creation, to embrace the places within us where love lives and compassion flourishes, and to see that beneath all outward differences we all originate from a single seed of divine origin. When we fully face God, we become like a holy mirror that contains the entire world within our love. After all, our journey here is not to just connect with the Divine in worship, but once we do this, to return to the creation, as a conduit and reflection of God's unending love on Earth. You are not just pottery fashioned from dust and water, you were sent to be God's eyes on Earth. You were sent as a reflection of love and compassion for all those with hurting hearts. You were sent to reflect God's mercy upon the entire universe.

As the ninth-century Persian mystic Imam Junaid said, "A Muslim is like the earth; even if impurities are thrown on it, it will blossom into a green pasture." We are called to be like a date tree, so rooted in the love of God that when people throw stones at you, you reply with fruits that taste sweet. Do not live your life in reaction to what people have done *to* you, but live your life in gratitude for all that God has done *for* you.

> "The servants of The Most Merciful are they who walk modestly upon the earth, and if the ignorant address them, they say, 'Peace.'"
>
> QUR'AN 25:63

We are called by God not to react to the ignorance of men, but rather to live a life that reflects the love and wisdom of God. To serve Allah means to serve His creations, because how can you truly love the Creator if you do not deeply revere and love what He creates? We are called to be mothers of creation, called by God to take all the creatures of the Earth under our wings of compassion and care for them as if they are our own children. As the twentieth-century scholar Seyyed Hossein Nasr says, "Man is the bridge between heaven and earth. On the one hand, he is to leave earth for heaven; on the other, he is to bring back heaven on earth. He is to serve as a conduit, a channel, for Divine Grace."[50]

There is no prerequisite to beginning the journey of reflecting God's love upon the universe. God can use you exactly as you are. If shepherds, orphans, prisoners, and refugees were called to be prophets, then you better believe that God can use you in this very moment as a catalyst of change.

> God's mercy accepts us as we are, but He loves us too much to let us stay the same.

Just as a seed sprouts when it is kissed by the light of the sun, when we are open to receiving the light of God's love, we too transform. It is when we align with our divinely inspired spirit that we awaken within us a sacred longing for justice, a passion to bring mercy and kindness to hurting hearts, and a burning desire to see the world in alignment with the laws of divine love. When we surrender before God, allowing Him to act through us, we not only transform, but our divine alignment creates a magnetic force that pulls others toward the pole of divine compassion, mercy, and love for all creatures without discrimination. It is not through our ability that great things happen, but through God's grace.

Noah's ark was built by an old prophet in the desert, and it survived the flood that drowned his world—while the world's greatest engineers built the *Titanic,* declaring, "Not even God Himself could sink this ship," and yet it sunk on its first voyage.[51] When our effort and striving is rooted in faith, our actions lead to lasting results beyond our wildest imagination. Our work is not to change the world. Our mission is to serve and love the world, believing that when we serve God and His creations from a place of love, by the virtue of God's mercy the world begins to heal.

We live in a *uni-verse,* meaning there is only one. There is no third world, there is only one world. The Qur'an intimately speaks to our interconnected nature by reminding us that we all come from a single soul. Islam's call for actualizing our oneness can be understood through the South African phrase *ubuntu,* which roughly translates to "I am what I am because of what we all are."[52]

In order to better understand the powerful wisdom of the word *ubuntu* and how it fosters the Islamic ideal of community, consider the following story.

> An anthropologist once told a group of African children that he had put a basket of fruit beneath a tree in the distance, and whoever got there first could eat all the fruit. The children smiled at the man and then grabbed each other's hands and ran to the tree together. As they all sat down joyfully eating the fruit together, the anthropologist asked why they ran as a group, knowing their reward would be less when shared. The children smiled again and replied, "*Ubuntu,* I am because we are."[53]

In the context of faith, someone who follows the philosophy of *ubuntu* is someone who knows how God manifests His love most completely when we are aware of our interconnectedness. Just as a single drop of water is seemingly powerless, but many drops together can create a current strong enough to carve stone into shapes as magnificent as the Grand Canyon, *ubuntu* reminds us that our true power as human beings is unleashed when we unite and work together. As a mystic once said, "We are each angels with one wing, we can only fly by embracing each other." When we see the fulfillment of another's needs as being as important as our own, we are actualizing what it means to have faith.

> *"None of you has faith until he loves for his brother what he loves for himself."*[54]
>
> PROPHET MUHAMMAD ﷺ

Just as when the sun shines, it shines on everyone, and when the rain falls, it pours on everyone—we were created as divine representatives to manifest God's glory upon all of His creations. As the Prophet Muhammad ﷺ says, "All humankind is from Adam and Eve. An Arab has no superiority over a non-Arab, nor a non-Arab has any superiority over an Arab. Also, a white has no superiority over black, nor a black has any superiority over white except by God-consciousness and good action."[55] To be a true Muslim means to look at every creature of God and say the following:

> *I honor the sacredness of your life, regardless what you believe; if the Creator of the universe has decided to create you from the spirit of His love, then by virtue of your very existence, you are more than enough for me.*

God did not create us, against all odds, so that we could spend the precious gift of our life judging others, or deciding who deserves mercy and forgiveness. We are called to compassionately advise others from a place of genuine love, but in the end God is the only one who can judge. Part of our purpose on Earth is to love all creatures, without borders and boundaries. As Rumi says, "Inside the great mystery that is, we don't really own anything. What is this competition we feel then, before we go, one at a time, through the same gate?"

We all came from the same origin and we will all return to the same God who created us. Since we all come from one soul, what happens to each person on some level either positively or negatively effects each and every one of us. The divine calling of humankind to be the caretaker or representative of God on Earth is beautifully expressed in Judaism with the teaching of *Tikkun Olam* or "To repair the world." The idea behind *Tikkun Olam* is that if we can see what needs to be repaired and healed in the world, we have found what God has called us to fulfill in His name. However, if we find ourselves only seeing what is broken and wrong with the world, then it is we ourselves that need to be healed. We are a part of this world, so when we change ourselves the world changes too. After all, we can only give to others what we ourselves contain.

This is perfectly articulated in the following story of the Prophet Jesus from the teachings of the twelfth-century Persian poet Attar.

> Jesus and his faithful disciples entered a town where the villagers started to scream at Jesus with profanities and false accusations that were not befitting of his holy stature, kind demeanor, and gentle heart. Jesus turned his face toward them, returning every harsh remark with a merciful prayer to God for their happiness and success in life. One of his disciples turned to Jesus and said, "Oh master, why are you praying for these terrible people? How are you not filled with righteous anger toward their hateful remarks?" Jesus kindly looked at his disciple and replied, "My dear brother, I can only spend from what I have in my purse."

Just as whether you squeeze an orange harshly or softly, it will only produce orange juice, Jesus carried no hate within him, so when harsh words squeezed him, only love poured out. How we reply to the world has nothing to do with the world and everything to do with what we carry in our own souls. No one has the power to make us feel angry. The world can only unveil the anger we already carry within us. It is only when we become a garden blossoming with the qualities of God that we can offer the divine fruits of peace, love, compassion, and mercy to others too. The human journey is insightfully illustrated in another ancient story that has been orally passed down throughout the years.

> A traveler was wandering through a town, searching for hope, when he came across a crippled beggar, then an old woman getting beaten, and then the funeral of a baby. He fell into a spell of pain, distraught from the despair, famine, and destruction he witnessed. He ran out of the town into the vast silence of the desert at night and screamed to God, "Oh why God! Why is there so much pain? Why is there so much oppression, so much injustice? Why don't You do something?"

> The man was crying as he was punching the desert floor with his fists, crying over and over again, "Why don't You do something, Lord? Why is there so much war, and cancer, and hatred? Why must so many people starve themselves to sleep? Why must children be homeless? Oh God why don't You do something? Why don't You quench the flames of our sadness? Why don't you bring joy where hope is lost? Why don't You do something? Why don't You just do something?!"

> The poor man dug his knuckles into the hot sand and screamed until he fell into an ecstatic state, and heard the Divine reply, "I did do something. I created you."

Unveiling Your Divine Purpose

We have each been created with different thumbprints by God, as a reminder that every one of our imprints on this world is unique. As the Qur'an says, "God has made the Earth a wide expanse for you so that you may walk thereon spacious paths" (71:19-20). We share the call to worship God, but how we serve God within what He has prescribed can still be as diverse as there are creatures in the universe.

"There are a thousand ways to kneel and kiss the earth."

RUMI

Don't compare yourself to others, for every person carries a unique divine song in their soul, a melody of love, kindness, mercy, justice, freedom, and oneness that is longing to play in the concert hall of creation. Everything in existence is in a symphony of praise for the Divine. Knowing this encourages us to surrender to the unique song that God composed and wrote in the pages of our heart before we were ever sent to Earth. We can begin the process of unearthing this divine purpose by asking ourselves the following simple, yet powerful question:

What breaks my heart the most?

What moves you and inspires you with the most passion is the seed that carries your purpose. As Rumi says, "Feel yourself being quietly drawn by the deeper pull of what you truly love." Your heart is the compass that will lead you to the sacred work you have been called by God to do. Your *fitra,* that primordial alignment with the Divine, is your soul's compass. When you tune into this inner guidance you will always find the path that awakens your spirit and excites your senses.

Your blessings, your trials and triumphs, your journey of falling and rising, your gifts and talents—they are all connected. Your true calling is held in the arms of your deepest wounds. God only breaks you to remake you, because breakdowns come before breakthroughs. Everything that God has written into your path was meant to prepare you for this exact moment. God wants you to come as you are, not as you think you should be.

"This place where you are right now, God circled on a map
for you."

HAFIZ, 14TH-CENTURY PERSIAN POET

As long as your heart is beating, you have a purpose. God is intentional, so He does not keep anyone on Earth that doesn't have to be here;

if we are blessed with more life, it is because someone in the world needs us. If we are alive, it means that what we were sent to this earth to create has not yet been accomplished. As Rabbi Nachman of Breslov said, "The day you were born is the day God decided that the world could not exist without you."

This world needs you. You matter beyond what words can capture, because the God who created all of existence chose to create you. In the Qur'an Allah says, "We did not create the heavens and the earth, and everything between them except for a specific purpose" (46:03). We may all be vastly different from one another when we are separate, but like puzzle pieces we each have a unique space to fill in order to complete the picture of oneness on Earth.

> *"Make room for one another in your collective life. Make room and in return God will make room for you."*
>
> QUR'AN 58:11

When Allah created the creation, He said, "Be! And it is" (36:82). Allah already gave us everything we need; our work is to follow the path He paved, heed the guidance He gave, and let His perfect will unfold within us like the petals of a rose, surrendering to the divine light of His love. As we walk the spiritual path, our will begins to align with God's will.

> *"When the forgetful man gets up in the morning, he reflects on what he is going to do, whereas the intelligent man sees what God is doing with him."*
>
> IBN ATA ALLAH AL-ISKANDARI, 13TH-CENTURY MYSTIC

It is only when we define ourselves as *faqir*, or as the Buddhists say, accept our state of "holy poverty" that we will see that only when we are completely empty of the world are we able to be entirely filled with the eternal presence of God. It is only when we choose to give up everything that we become truly free. It is only when we own nothing that we have nothing to lose and thus become shareholders of everything. Like the clouds floating freely across the skies without the need to grasp the air as their own, or the birds who call the entire Earth their homes, when we let go of grasping and holding on, we become receptive to receiving all that God has written for us to enjoy.

> *"Listen carefully: Unless a grain of wheat is buried in the ground, dead to the world, it is never any more than a grain of wheat. But if it is buried, it sprouts and reproduces itself many times over. In the same way, anyone who holds on to life just as it is destroys that life. But if you let it go, reckless in your love, you'll have it forever, real and eternal."*[56]
>
> **THE BIBLE (JOHN 12:24-25)**

Echoing the beauty of this Bible verse, the Muslim mystics describe the transforming power of a humbly surrendered heart before God through the following story:

> As a raindrop fell from a pregnant cloud, it looked at the ocean and said, "Who am I compared to this infinite sea?" The raindrop's humility inspired the heart of an oyster to open its shell and let the raindrop inside, transforming it into a beautiful pearl.[57]

It is through our acceptance of our finiteness and fallibility before God that we are primed to be transformed through His infinite love. One of the words for "love" in Arabic is *muhabbah,* which comes from a root word that means "to erase." This implies that knowledge of *Al-Wadud,* The Most Loving, begins with erasing all attachment to the self. As Rumi says, "Be melting snow. Wash yourself of yourself."

When we enfold our will into the will of God, we erase the seeking of the self, in exchange for what the Divine seeks to create through us. To know a singular God, all separation must vanish, for it is only when the lines between lover and the Beloved dissolve that we begin to see the world as it is rather than as we project it to be. We don't fall *in* love with God, we fall *into* the love of God. It is always God who is the doer, it is always God who is loving us. As Rumi says, "Knock, and He'll open the door. Vanish, and He'll make you shine like the sun. Fall, and He'll raise you to the heavens. Become nothing, and He'll turn you into everything." Just as a reed plant has to empty itself to become a flute, we must be empty of the ego for God's breath to flow through us, making us a unique instrument of His will in the symphony of His all-encompassing love and mercy.

> *My Lord, help me faithfully walk the straight path of return into Your embrace of love. "My Lord! Open for me my heart. And make easy for me my mission" (20:25-26). As my beloved Prophet ﷺ says, "Oh Allah! Inspire my heart to guidance and save me from the evil of my soul."*[58] *Lord, inspire my heart to turn to You in fear and in hope, in failure and in success, in happiness and in sorrow, and for me to seek for You and reach for You in all the moments of my life. "Our Lord! Perfect our light, and forgive us. Surely You have full power over everything!" (66:8). In Your illuminating names I pray, Ameen.*

Reflection: Healing Your Heart with the 99 Divine Names

We can never know God's essence, but we can experience the healing power of His divine names. The following practice is a powerful way to strengthen our relationship with Allah, even through the trials He has written for us to face.

- Next time you find yourself in a conflict, ask yourself, "What was I needing that I didn't receive?" If you are struggling to identify what you are needing, it will help to journal about the conflict you are facing. One way to do this is through *free-form writing*. Set a timer for 5–7 minutes and write without stopping until the buzzer goes off. If you feel stuck, write about not knowing what to say. Just keep writing without stopping and with no filter.
- Once you have written about how the conflict made you feel, go back and circle or put a star next to any key words/sections that

feel important. Take a moment to feel what emotional, spiritual, or physical needs of yours were unfulfilled. Notice places where you were needing love, compassion, kindness, someone to trust, safety, protection, forgiveness, patience, mercy, strength, to be heard, to be held, or to be comforted.

- Once you identify your need or needs, go to the appendix to the "The 99 Divine Names of Allah" section and pick out a name of Allah that most closely relates to what you are needing.

  - For example, if you identify your deeper need is to be heard or seen, try the names *As-Sami'* (The All-Hearing) or *Al-Basir* (The All-Seeing). If you were needing respect, try the name *Al-Muiz* (The Honorer). If you discover your deeper need was for compassion or mercy, try the name *Ar-Rahman* (The Most Merciful). If you were needing love or forgiveness, try the names *Al-Wadud* (The Most Loving) or *Al-Ghaffur* (The Great Forgiver).

  - The first several times you do this practice, it may be challenging to identify your deeper need. If you still feel uncertain about which name to use, you can try this practice with the all-encompassing name—*Allah.*

- Once you identify what divine name most closely fits your need, ask yourself where in your body you are feeling this unmet need. Do you feel discomfort in your stomach? Anxiety or tightness in your chest? Constriction in your throat? A helpful way of identifying where you physically hold your emotions is by scanning your body through your imagination. Start with the top of your head, notice if you have any tension in your head or neck. Slowly work your way down your arms, chest, stomach, legs, all the way to your toes, allowing your body to show you where you are holding any tension or unmet needs. Put your hand over where you feel constriction, or if no particular place in your body stands out, just place your hand on your heart and bring your awareness to the space under your palm.

- Find a comfortable place to sit, with your back straight and your body grounded.
- Recite the divine name you have chosen 100 times, as you slowly pull the vibration of each letter into your heart or wherever you feel constriction.
- Notice how you feel afterward.
- Repeat this process for every unmet need you are feeling.
- How is it different, turning to Allah to fulfill your needs instead of turning to yourself or to other people?

Reflection: Gratitude Journal

Generosity blossoms in the soil of gratitude. The more aware and grateful we are for our blessings, the more open-hearted and generous our hearts become. As mentioned before, the Qur'an shows us that we experience God's generosity through our gratitude: "If you are grateful I will surely give you more" (14:7). Since what you focus on or magnify becomes bigger, when you focus on your blessings, you find more for which to be grateful.

One of the most powerful ways to water the seeds of gratitude and generosity is with a gratitude journal. The key to making this practice effective are the three E's: emote, extend, and exercise. First, you want to engage and connect with your *emotions* when you are writing about the things for which you are grateful. The second is to *extend* your gratitude beyond just your own circle, by contemplating the things you are grateful for within the greater community (the farmers that grew your food, the builders that built your house, the sun rising every morning, the clouds that bring rain, etc.). Lastly, you want to make sure you set the intention of *exercising* this practice daily, because the more you take time to express gratitude the more you will notice the abundant blessings God has given to you.

- Buy a journal or make your own.
- Devote a few moments, every morning when you wake up or

at night before you go to sleep, to writing down 3–5 things for which you are grateful.

- If you have trouble coming up with things to be grateful for, consider the following that may apply: you can read, you can write, you are healthy, you can walk, you have the ability to think, you have a warm bed and a place to sleep, you have something to eat, you are safe, you have the means to go to school, you are loved, you have faith, you can see this page or hear these words.

- Make sure to engage your emotions and really *feel* gratitude for the things you have written down. If you are struggling to connect emotionally with what you are feeling grateful for, sometimes it is helpful to consider what it would be like if you did not have that blessing in your life. For example, if you are grateful for your eyesight, sit with what it would be like to not be able to see.

- At the end of the week, read out loud the things you are grateful for, being conscious of how gratitude may have affected your relationships with yourself and Allah.

- How does it feel to focus on your blessings on a daily basis?

"Alif. Lam. Ra. A Book has been revealed to you, so that, by the permission of their Lord, you would be able to bring forth humankind from the darkness into the light—to the path of The Mighty, The Praiseworthy."

QUR'AN 14:1

"Let the Qur'an be the springtime of my heart, the light of my chest, the remover of my sadness, and the reliever of my distress."[1]

PROPHET MUHAMMAD ﷺ

3

THE MYSTERIOUS WORLD OF THE QUR'AN

The Qur'an is a divine letter of love sent from Allah. It shows us all the ways He has loved us before we were ever given the chance to love and to know Him. Every word of this revelation is infused with divine mercy, perfumed with a love that's unconditional and a grace that's completely independent of human action. The Qur'an is not a destination or wall—it is a window. It does not call us *to* it, but rather calls us to look *through* it and toward the mysterious essence of God that animates everything in existence. It reminds us that, since everything in creation is a manifestation of God's love, by virtue of our very existence we can never be outside the boundless ocean of divine love and mercy.

The Qur'an is unique in that it exemplifies a book in which the author is in love with the reader and the reader seeks to know this love. Since the beginning of time, humanity has been sent revelations from God as a means of guiding the human being toward the divine path of peace. More than just a book of laws, the Qur'an is known as the *Al-Furqan* or "The Criterion." This is because it is a light of discernment that allows us to distinguish between the path of return to The Origin of Love (*Al-Wadud*) and the paths that lead us astray from actualizing the essence of who we are and Whose we are.

The Mysterious Power of Recitation

The Qur'an is an oral reminder of God's omnipresence that serves to unite and gather all souls within the oneness of God. In fact, the word *Qur'an* originates from the triliteral root *qaf-ra-hamza,* which means "to recite, read, gather, collect, and join." Holistically, it can be said that the entire message of the Qur'an is focused on the concept of *tawhid,* which literally means "to make something one." Reciting God's word acts like a reset code. It interrupts the negative patterns of our worldly conditioning by shedding light on the places where we resist divine union with God.

By divine design, the Qur'an will confront your ego, challenge your subjective truths, rub against your resistance to surrender, and shatter your limiting pictures about both who you are and who God is. By its very nature, parts of the Qur'an will trigger you, because this revelation is like a pure mirror. You see in it what you bring to it. If you come with hatred and separation, you will see the hatred of your own heart reflected back to you. If you come reflecting divine qualities of love, mercy, kindness, and majesty, you will experience a taste of God's beauty.

> *"A drop of rain can fall into the mouth of a seashell or a snake, but in a seashell, it turns into a pearl and in a snake, it turns into poison."*
>
> IMAM ALI

Whatever you see in this book points to your own state of consciousness. Every word of the Qur'an is a lantern that illuminates the darkness of our fears, penetrating the caves of our subconscious, shedding light on the parts of ourselves we do everything in our power to hide.

The Book of Allah begins the process of healing our hearts through bringing deeper awareness to the places where we have turned away from God. As the famous psychologist Carl Jung says, "One does not become enlightened by imagining figures of light, but by making the darkness conscious." The purpose of the different principles of faith revealed within the Qur'an is to unveil your hidden darkness and sins, as a means of offering you healing and divine forgiveness. The declaration of faith (*shahadah*) shows you your places of lordship, prayer (*salat*) brings to light your false idols, fasting in the month of *Ramadan* strengthens your will power and makes you more God-conscious, paying the alms tax (*zakat*) unveils your inner greed, and the pilgrimage (*Hajj*) allows you to see your attachments to this world. Islam holistically confronts all the facets of your ego, because it is only through the light of awareness that the seeds of change begin to blossom. As the beloved daughter of the Prophet ﷺ Fatima Zahra teaches us, "The wisdom in the Qur'an will take you from the darkness of ignorance to the light of knowledge."

The Qur'an Is Not Actually a Book

When Allah refers in the Qur'an to the "Mother of the Book" (43:4), He is actually referring to the Preserved Tablet (*Al-Lawh Al-Mahfooz*). This is a "book" that is said to be in the highest levels of Heaven and carries the decrees of God, the words of the Qur'an, and all other revelations within its mysterious pages. Although we refer to the Qur'an as a "book," it is actually not the written words of revelation, but the *recitation* of those words.

> *The Qur'an is a reflection of God's speech manifested on the human being's tongue.*

Whereas words on paper are limited to one focal point, when words are spoken aloud they emanate in waves of vibration in every direction. Whereas words on paper can be very much separate from the reader, since the Qur'an is the recital of God's words, to experience the Qur'an you must interact with it—you must bring the words of Allah inside of your mind and heart and then outwardly recite them. There is a scientific significance to this practice as well. Studies have shown that the combined action of speaking and hearing ourselves out loud significantly increases the likelihood that what we are reading will be stored in our long-term memory.[2]

The words of the Qur'an were put into writing and bound in a book, known as the *Mus'haf,* as a means of preserving and spreading the holy message of God. Since the beginning of revelation, the Prophet's ﷺ followers were both memorizing and writing down verses of the Qur'an on parchment, stone, animal bones, pieces of leather, and cloth. Within 20 years of the Prophet's ﷺ death a complete written version of the Qur'an was compiled together, copied and sent all over the Muslim world. However, it is important to point out that the chapters of the Qur'an are not compiled in the order in which they were revealed. Narrations suggest that the Prophet Muhammad ﷺ would review all revealed scriptures with the Angel Gabriel during the month of Ramadan, at which point Gabriel would dictate where each verse belonged. Some scholars have suggested that the Qur'an was divinely commanded to not be in chronological order, so that it is not read like a storybook. In a deeper sense, the order of the Qur'an serves as a reminder that our relationship with God is not linear or one-dimensional, because God is beyond both time and space.

While the written Qur'an is highly respected and honored, nothing that is done to the written words of the Qur'an have any effect on its holiness. Just as a thousand oceans cannot turn off the light of the moon, because it is not the source of its own light, you cannot diminish the light of the Qur'an, because it is a reflection of God's eternal speech, reflected in the mirror of this worldly realm.[3] Thinking you can erase, defile, or burn the reflection of the Qur'an on Earth is like punching the mirror and thinking the person reflected in it will be harmed. After all, the *Mus'haf* is a three-dimensional manifestation of God's words, which are held in heavenly realms, beyond anything we could comprehend (*Al-Lawh Al-Mahfooz*). The Qur'an reiterates the bewildering nature of God's words when it says, "If the sea were ink for writing the words of my Lord, it would run dry before those words were exhausted—even if We were to add another sea to it" (18:109).

The First Word of Revelation: *Iqra'!*

The Qur'an descended directly from the majestic throne of the Divine, from the highest heavens through the celestial bridge of the Angel Gabriel, streaming into the heart of the Prophet Muhammed ﷺ. It was 610 AD when Muhammad ﷺ at the age of 40 received the first words of the Qur'an.

He was meditating in a cave on the Mountain of Light (*Jabal an-Nur*) when the Angel Gabriel embraced him with the light of revelation.[4] "*Iqra'!*" Muhammad ﷺ was commanded: "Read!" The Angel called to Muhammad ﷺ again and said, "Read!" and then again, and said, "Read in the name of your Lord Who created [all things]. He created the human being from a clot. Read, for your Lord is the Most Generous, [it is He] Who taught by the pen, He taught man what he did not know" (96:1-5).

The vibration of divine majesty poured in as the eyes of the Prophet's ﷺ heart opened to the reality that the Qur'an was not made of letters, but that it was a divine frequency of light imprinted within his very spirit. Just as the human body carries an intangible soul, the letters of the Qur'an carry the sacred sound code of divine light. The Qur'an is a living text that was sent to "bring forth humankind from the darkness into the light" (14:1). By the power of divine love, the message of the Qur'an has a way of nourishing the seeds of our innate goodness. In fact, some scholars have suggested that when rain is mentioned in the Qur'an it is a metaphor for the merciful word of God, and that the dry earth is a metaphor for the human heart. Just as rain falls from the clouds in the sky, bringing the dead earth to life, the Qur'an descended from the heavens, bringing to life the dead hearts of humankind.

> "Can't you see the earth dry and lifeless—and suddenly when
> We send down waters upon it, it stirs and swells and puts
> forth every kind of lovely plant!"

QUR'AN 22:5

The Message of the Qur'an

The core message of the Qur'an is strict monotheism. The oneness of God is the foundation in the garden of revelation; everything sprouts from it. While the prophets of God were sent throughout history to both share God's words and to manifest the divine message into action for their people in their time, the message has always been timelessly the same:

God is one, and only He is worthy of being worshipped.

Although everything within the Qur'an points to the ultimate supremacy and singularity of God, some additional major themes of the Qur'an include: who God is, the creation story of humankind, the role of the Devil, the unseen world and the angels, the afterlife, Heaven and Hell, the stories of the major prophets sent by God, the deeper dimension of divine revelation, the core pillars of faith, natural phenomena, how to worship God, how to purify the ego, how to polish the heart and awaken the soul, how to live a moral life, how to honor your family, how to conduct business ethically, the importance of having a faith-based community, and how to become a representative of God's love on Earth.

Beyond themes and concepts, the Qur'an contains real-life stories of loss and gain, brokenness and healing, sin and redemption, oppression and justice, darkness and light; and consistently points to the perishability of this world and the eternal nature of the life to come. The Qur'an constantly gives glad tidings to those who inspire goodness and have faith and warns against those who create corruption on Earth and reject the truth (4:165). The Qur'an shows us that it is through worshipping God that we manifest our full potential and unveil our true purpose on Earth.

The revelation teaches us not just how to experience God, but how to interact with Him. It speaks extensively on the mercy and forgiveness of God, while also speaking to the justice of God, which will hold us accountable for the hearts we break and the truths we knowingly reject.

The Qur'an also illustrates stories of incredible human beings throughout time, overcoming enormous difficulties and struggles through trust and reliance on God. These stories are recounted by God as a reminder that regardless of what difficulties we are facing, when God is our guide we can summit whatever mountain we have been written to traverse. The Qur'an shows us that things don't always go according to our plans, but God's plan for us will always be the best possible outcome.

Take the example of the Prophet Joseph, who was thrown into a well by his jealous brothers, sold into slavery, wrongly accused, and thrown into jail, only to rise to be one of the most powerful advisors to the King of Egypt. Joseph could not have predicted that it was through prison that he would reach the palace; but God had a far better plan for him that he could ever imagine (12:1-111). Or what about the Prophet Abraham, who was unjustly catapulted into a deadly fire, only to find that God cooled the flames and transformed it into a garden for him (21:69). Or take the example of Moses, who was stuck between the Red Sea and the strongest army known to man; but since his eyes were on God and not on the barriers he faced, God parted the Red Sea and saved the faithful Moses from the unjust Pharaoh (26:60-68). The Qur'an also speaks about the Virgin Mary, whose being pregnant with Jesus jeopardized her pristine reputation and life. Despite what seemed like a dire situation, Mary trusted God and followed His order to fast from speaking for three days. When Jesus was born, it was he who miraculously spoke in the cradle, in his mother's defense (19:26-33).

The Qur'an reminds every person that is struggling, every heart that is broken, and every soul that is hurting that even if it feels like you are facing a hopeless situation know that there is refuge and healing with God.

> *"If God supports you, none can overcome you. Yet if He forsakes you, who is there then that can help you? Let the believers put their trust in God."*
>
> QUR'AN 3:160

X = God Is Unconditionally Merciful

The Qur'an makes more sense if we approach it as an algebraic equation with a given x, before we jump to interpreting or solving for *y.* The Qur'an begins all of its chapters, aside from one, with the given *x* = *Bismillahi Ar-Rahman Ar-Rahim,* which translates to "In the name of God, the Lord of Mercy, the Bestower of Mercy."[5] Only once the Qur'an declares *x = God Is Unconditionally Merciful* does it then tell us, with that in mind, to go and solve for all our *y*'s—or, better said, *whys.*

Every question we ask, every doubt we carry, and every difficulty we face can only be understood once we accept the given *x,* in this case the absolute belief that Allah is merciful and loving, without conditions. With that being said, all interpretations of the Qur'an that do not come from a place of mercy and love go against the soul of the revelation, and must be rejected and exchanged for a perspective that honors the heart of people, while speaking the truth of the message as it has been revealed.[6]

Islam is a religion of surrendering in peace to *Ar-Rahman,* The Most Merciful. Therefore, if an interpretation of the Qur'an does not carry mercy alongside justice, it is not from Islam, but from the ego of man. If, in reading the Qur'an, we do not become more merciful both toward ourselves and others, we may claim to have read the Qur'an's words, but we certainly did not experience the reality of its truth. As Allah asks, "Will they not meditate on the Qur'an or are there locks on their hearts?" (47:24) The Qur'an is open; it is our hearts that can become closed, preventing us from experiencing the revelations' holy wisdom.

Why the Qur'an Was Revealed in Stages

Like a seed carries the potential of the entire tree within it, many scholars believe the seed of the entire revelation of the Qur'an descended on the Night of Power (*Laylatul Qadr*), from the highest heavens to the first heaven (97:1). Just as it takes a seed time to become a tree, the Qur'an's 114 chapters and more than 6,200 verses took 23 years to descend from the lowest heaven to our world. However, it is not just the Qur'an that was revealed gradually—everything Allah has brought into existence in this world progresses in stages. The Qur'an beautifully alludes to this notion in the following verse:

"So I call to witness the rosy glow of sunset, the night and its
progression, the moon as it grows into fullness; surely you
shall travel from stage to stage."

QUR'AN 84:16-19

In the practical sense, since much of the Qur'an was revealed in response to questions people asked and circumstances the Prophet ﷺ was facing, it only made sense that the revelation would be revealed after, rather than before, the question was asked or conflict was faced. When the Prophet ﷺ was asked why the Qur'an did not unveil itself all at once, the Qur'an replies by saying, so that "We may strengthen your heart" (25:32).

Just as climbers must take time to acclimate to the increasing
altitude of higher peaks, or scuba divers must equalize to the
increasing water pressure as they descend deeper into the
ocean's depth, the human heart requires time to integrate
revelation before delving deeper into the message.

It can be said, then, that the silence or space between revelations was part of the revelation, because without that silence we would not be able to integrate the message fully. Just as the space between words gives a sentence meaning, or the silence between notes creates rhythm, God is telling us that even in the silence, His mercy is present.

The Secrets of *Alif, Lam, Mim*

Every word and vibration in the Qur'an is intentional, whether or not we comprehend it. In fact, some of the chapters of the Qur'an begin mysteriously with different combinations of Arabic letters such as *Alif, Lam, Mim* and have baffled scholars for hundreds of years. Some scholars have suggested these mysterious letters are symbols that hold numerical values that hint at mystical secrets. Other scholars have said the letters are hidden abbreviations or codes that point to other words—*Alif* being a reference to Allah, *Mim* referring to Muhammad ﷺ, *Nun* referring to *Nur* or "The Divine Light," and so on.

Although the majority opinion is that since the meaning behind these letters is only known by Allah, they serve to remind us of our ignorance in the face of Allah's all-encompassing knowledge.[7] In essence, Allah is reminding us from the very beginning of the revelation that to be guided we have to humbly acknowledge our intellectual poverty and neediness. It is not a surprise, then, that when Allah uses these letters in the Qur'an He follows it up with a verse about the wisdom, power, or mysterious nature of divine revelation. As the Qur'an says, "*Alif. Lam. Mim.* That is the Book about which there is no doubt, a guidance for those conscious of Allah" (2:1-2).

Linguistically, these letters also have a powerful outward impact. To understand this effect, we have to understand that starting a chapter with "*Alif. Lam. Mim.*" is akin to starting a sentence in English with "A, B, C." Some scholars suggest that Allah uses these simple letters as a way of confronting human beings and inspiring them to contemplate how with the same simple letters they use to speak, Allah has manifested a masterpiece of language beyond their understanding.

Interestingly enough, these letters occur 29 times in the Qur'an, which mirrors the 29 letters of the Arabic language, with the inclusion of the *hamza,* or glottal stop. To better understand this, consider the following metaphor:

> *Just as all the elements within a human being are present in the earth, but if we collect the exact recipe of physical ingredients and mix it with water we cannot create life, we have access to all the letters of the Arabic language that are used in the Qur'an, but we cannot create anything like it because, like the creation of life, the Qur'an carries a divine secret beyond human comprehension.*[8]

Despite the linguistic perfection of the Qur'an, Allah does not ask us to passively believe its divine origin. Instead, Allah directly confronts the listener, who doubts the divinity of the Qur'an by falsely declaring that the Prophet Muhammad ﷺ is its author by saying, "And if you are in doubt about what We have sent down upon Our servant [Muhammad], then produce a chapter like it and call upon your witnesses other than Allah, if you should be truthful" (2:23). Since this challenge was first made more than 1,400 years ago, no writer has managed to mirror the Qur'an in Arabic in a thoughtful and intellectual way. The Qur'an's linguistic arrangement is so unique in the Arabic language, that for those who are experts of classical Arabic, the recitation of the book itself can be powerful enough to prove its divine origin.

This is why Allah says that if words recited by human beings were allowed to "cause the mountains to move, or the earth to be torn apart, or the dead to speak" (13:31), the Qur'an would have been the first recital to be able to do so. The power of this holy text is alluded to again in God's saying, "Had We sent down this Qur'an upon a mountain, you would have certainly seen it humbled and torn apart in awe of Allah. We set forth examples for people in order that they may reflect" (59:21). It is amazing to think that a majestic and powerful mountain would crumble beneath the word of God, but the garden of the human heart has been honored and created specifically by God to be able to receive the rains of revelation.

How to Read the Qur'an from the Heart

When we approach the Qur'an, we are interacting with the holy words of the Creator of existence. The Prophet ﷺ reminds us of the divine mercy that accompanies the Qur'an when he says, "Whoever recites a letter from the Book of Allah, he will be credited with a good deed, and a good deed gets a ten-fold reward. I do not say that *Alif-Lam-Mim* is one letter, but *Alif* is a letter, *Lam* is a letter and *Mim* is a letter."[9] The Qur'an is so powerful that when it would be revealed to the Prophet ﷺ it would cause him to sweat profusely; if the Prophet ﷺ was traveling when the revelation came down, the weight of God's word would make the animal he was riding buckle to the floor.[10]

We must not forget that the Qur'an is a profoundly powerful reve-lation that was sent from Heaven as a mercy to this Earth. This book is a manifestation of the speech of God; it is a picture of eternity that is mysteriously being reflected into our mortal realm. It is only through the grace and mercy of God that our hearts can be opened to a revelation that transcends the human mind. The soul of the Qur'an cannot be read, it can only be transmitted.

The Qur'an says, "There has come to you from Allah a light and a clear Book" (5:15). The Qur'an descended with a light, because you cannot read the Qur'an in the darkness. Just as physical light is a necessity for the eyes to be able to see, spiritual light is a necessity in experiencing God's word. The Prophet Muhammad ﷺ is the light that illuminates the Qur'an and allows humankind to access this divine revelation. In addition to his sayings and the way he lived his life, the Prophet Muhammad ﷺ said he left behind "The Book of Allah and my household."[11] However you define the word "household" or *ahlul bayt,* this small group of faithful believers are a doorway to understanding the deeper dimensions of the Book of Allah, the Qur'an.[12] This is why, after praying for God to open our hearts to His message, the first step to receiving revelation is to connect to the heart of the Prophet Muhammad ﷺ and his family (*ahlul bayt*). We can also connect to the deeper teachings of the Qur'an through the examples of the most righteous amongst the Prophet's ﷺ followers (*sahabah*), or by sitting in the company of the living friends of God (*awliya*).

It is important that we have an experienced guide walk us through the landscape of revelation and help us understand the hidden secrets of the scripture. Any literate person can read the Qur'an's words, but not everyone can digest its deepest truths. The Qur'an is the living word of God, so the same verse is never experienced the same way twice. It is an interactive and highly intelligent book.

> We don't just read the Qur'an; the Qur'an reads us. It looks
> into our hearts and, based on the purity of our intentions
> and the capacity of our spirits, it unveils or covers the soul
> of its secrets.

As Rumi says, "The Qur'an is like a shy bride"—you have to approach it with respect and reverence for it to unveil itself. This is precisely why the door to revelation is opened through *adab* or "courtesy and politeness."

It is important to remember that most of the followers of the Prophet ﷺ were not literate or educated. Understanding the deep essence of the Qur'an is not a matter of how much worldly knowledge you have acquired as much as it's a matter of the level of sincerity and humility in your heart. This is why the mystics call us to move from "the knowledge of the tongue to the knowledge of the heart," because the light of God cannot be understood by the mind, it can only be experienced through a heart that is open and witnesses God's greatness. Perhaps this is why Allah describes the Qur'an as "a reminder for him who is in awe of God" (20:3).

To read the Qur'an from the heart, we have to be conscious about the level of respect and intention we bring to the book. If we approach the Qur'an with an agenda of debating others, we run the risk of projecting on the book what we want to see rather than what has been revealed. When we read only the parts of the Qur'an that resonate with us and ignore the parts we don't agree with, we run the risk of shaping the scripture around our likes and dislikes, instead of allowing the book to shape us.

It is not self-righteousness or ego-based consciousness that is the precursor to receiving revelation, but an awakened and humble heart. Our loving Lord tells us that the Qur'an will not be understood by just anyone, because "this is a message for everyone whose heart is wide-awake or who listens while he is present" (50:37). Reading the Qur'an from the heart begins with repentance, because until we let go of our subjective opinions and biases, we will end up seeing the Qur'an not as it is, but through the filters of our misperceptions and projections.

It is the mind that overthinks and challenges revelation. Allah says, "This Book has no doubt in it—guidance for the God-conscious" (2:2). The Qur'an is void of errors; it is the interpretations of man that are flawed. This is why, before we even open the book, the Qur'an calls us to not only be ritualistically and outwardly pure, through ablution (*wudu'*), but also to inwardly purify our hearts, through repentance of everything that prevents us from fully witnessing God. The Qur'an says, "Most surely it is an honored Qur'an, in a Book that is hidden; None shall touch it save the purified ones" (56:77-79).

To approach the soul of the divine revelation you have to come purified, humble, and empty of your attachment to the self, because a singular God cannot be experienced where there is multiplicity. Allah calls you to drop all other distractions and "Recite the Qur'an calmly and distinctly [with your mind attuned to its meaning]" (73:4). Allah then tells us that if we want to benefit from the recitation of His words, we must be in a state of God-consciousness: "When the Qur'an is recited, then listen to it and pay attention that you may receive mercy" (7:204).

Just as minerals and vitamins change the composition of the body, if we allow our souls to consume the words of the Qur'an, its medicinal vibration can transform and heal our spiritual bodies. Although the accurate recitation of the Qur'an in Arabic has many benefits and blessings, God is merciful and encouraging toward those who struggle with the pronunciation.

> "Verily the one who recites the Qur'an beautifully, smoothly, and precisely, he will be in the company of the noble and obedient angels. And as for the one who recites with difficulty, stammering or stumbling through its verses, then he will have twice that reward."[13]
>
> PROPHET MUHAMMAD ﷺ

It is important to remember that our spirits are already acquainted with divine revelation, because our essence and the Qur'an come from the same source—Allah. This is why it is in the praise of God that our wandering and nomadic souls find a place of rest and home. When we surrender to the recitation of the Qur'an in Arabic, the same holy light that created us envelops our entire essence, whether or not we understand the words being recited.

The heart is always in communion with God. It is the noise of the mind that prevents us from being aware of that innate connection. Just as a seed has to break to take the raindrop in, we have to come humble with the shell of our ego broken for the message of the Qur'an to truly penetrate our deepest hearts.

The Transforming Power of Scripture

In relationship to us, the Qur'an has a beginning and an end, because we are subject to time. But Allah says that, "We sent the Qur'an down" (97:1), implying that since the Qur'an is an unveiling of the divine attribute of His speech, the essence of the message has no beginning or end in relationship to God. It begs us to ask, how could a finite human mind comprehend the speech of an infinite God? What could a limited being say about a limitless revelation? What could our subjective perceptions unveil about an Absolute Truth (*Haqq*)? To better understand the significance of the Qur'an, we must go back in time to the story of a man who was given the answer to these questions not through words, but through an incredible example:

> A man once asked a spiritual master, "What is there to gain from reading the Qur'an if we will never fully understand it? What's the point of reading the same book over and over again?" The old sage responded by taking the young man to a well, where he emptied a big bag of black coal, and handed the dirty bag to the man. The sage told the man to fill the bag with water. The man said, "But master, this is a cloth bag, the water will seep through the fabric." The old man said, "If you trust me, then do as I say," and then he left.
>
> For the next few hours, the man kept filling the bag with bucket after bucket, only for the water to keep seeping through the cloth. By the time the sage returned, the man was exhausted and defeated. The sage looked at the empty bag and smiled. The confused young man asked, "Why are you smiling? I have no water in this bag."
>
> The old man replied, "Your bag may not have been able to contain the water, but over time the water you poured within it washed away all

the darkness of the coal that had stained the bag, making the bag as beautiful as the day I bought it. It is similar with the Qur'an. You will not be able to contain the entire revelation, but the more you recite it and allow the vibration to flow through you, the more it will purify you. The revelation of God was not sent to give you something you do not have, but rather to remove every veil in the way of your seeing that you already are what you seek to become."

We carry the path to Heaven inside of us. Divine revelation is just the light of awareness that allows us to access that inner knowing. The Qur'an has been the same for more than 1,400 years, and yet those same words interact differently with us depending on where we are in our lives. To better understand this, consider the following example: Fire can both make a hot air balloon fly thousands of feet above the ground, and burn an entire forest down. It can burn incense into ashes, make gold into liquid, and transform liquid water into vapor. Just as the essence of fire is constant, but what it reacts with results in different outcomes, the Qur'an is one revelation, but its manifestations are infinite, due the innumerable shades of the human experience.

We are called to read the Qur'an again and again not because the message of the revelation changes, but because we change. Therefore, the same message interacts differently with our spirits, hearts, and egos depending on where we are on the path of God. As they say, "The beauty of the Qur'an is that you cannot change its message, but its message can completely change you."[14]

Revelation Meets You Where You Are

The Qur'an does not just speak to people of a particular time, it speaks to the timeless soul of the human being. It does not only refer to stories of the past, it also speaks to the urgency of the present, while calling us to be conscious of the implications of our actions in the future. Every struggle between good and evil, between prophet and imposter, between peacemakers and tyrant rulers exemplifies archetypes that exist in our lives.

The Qur'an is timeless. Through the language of metaphor and allegory, every story, battle, and victory cited in the Qur'an speaks to you directly. Do not just read the Qur'an—put yourself in the shoes of every character. Do not just try to understand the Qur'an, strive to experience it with all of your senses. This is how the living Qur'an becomes awakened and integrated into your field of vision. This is how reading the Qur'an goes from being passive to being active. You have to enter the ecosystem of revelation and plunge into the depth of its ocean.

Do not read the Qur'an judging those that came before you; instead, ask yourself why you are being told these stories. If we read the Qur'an without categorizing ourselves as either Muslim or non-Muslim, we have a much better chance of objectively learning from the text. When we leave behind our labels, we are able to objectively look at the characteristics and behavior traits spoken about and see which category we actually fall into, based on our actions. This can be a very humbling experience, because where it may be easy to verbally affirm our faith, it is an entirely different thing to put that faith into practice.

When reading the Qur'an, it is important to know that every verse is speaking directly to you. Listen carefully. This book is your story. What is it confronting? What it is calling you to do? What is it reminding you of that you once knew but may have forgotten?

The Qur'an speaks both to the scientist and the shepherd, to the artist and the businessman, to the poet and the politician. Its words meet each seeker exactly where they are in their spiritual journey. There are scholars and mystics alike that have said that every verse of the Qur'an has seven depths of meaning, the last of which only God knows, which the Qur'an confirms by saying, "no one knows its hidden meaning except Allah" (3:7).

Some mystics have described the Qur'an as a river that, from the outside, looks like just one current, but once you step into the revelation you will experience the richness and mystery of the different currents of meaning hidden within its unified outer flow. The more faith we cultivate, the deeper we can dive beneath the surface of literalism and find the hidden pearls of divine wisdom.[15]

The Power of Metaphors and Symbolism

The verses of the Qur'an are not always straightforward and clear (*muhkamat*); the revelation also includes verses that are allegorical, symbolic, and metaphorical (*mutashabihat*) (3:7). The vague language or imagery used at times in the Qur'an is part of what makes the text timeless, because it speaks to readers of all times, of vastly different intellectual capabilities, through the language of symbolism.

> *"If religion had not, on the one hand, expressed its ideas in common, familiar language, it would have been incomprehensible to the people of that age; but if it had expressed its ideas in common language, religion would have had no meaning in later times. It was therefore necessary that religion should speak in images and symbols that would become comprehensible with the development of human thought and science."[16]*
>
> **ALI SHARI'ATI, 20TH-CENTURY SCHOLAR**

Regardless of the Qur'an's beautiful symbolism, powerful prose, and many scientific discoveries, the Qur'an is not a book of *science*, it is a book of *signs*. The Qur'an points us to the beauty and bewildering majesty of creation as a means of returning us to the Creator.[17]

While earthly books are written through the subjective eyes of a human author's perception of reality, the Qur'an introduces itself as the pure word of God and so it is an unfiltered, perfect reflection of love and truth.

> *"The superiority of the speech of God over other speeches is like the superiority of God over His creatures."[18]*
>
> **PROPHET MUHAMMAD** ﷺ

The words of the Qur'an are not the interpretations of human beings, but the pure unadulterated speech of God manifested into a language that is understood by man. Every verse of the Qur'an is referred to as an *ayah*, meaning "sign," because every word of revelation is a signpost that is pointing toward God. Although we cannot witness God directly, we can experience Him through the reflection of His names throughout the entire cosmos. If we see creation as a manuscript of God, then the Qur'an can be seen as the spiritual Rosetta Stone that helps us translate this subtle language into divine guidance. This is why we are not called to just read the Qur'an; we are called to "ponder on its signs" (38:29), as only the souls that are willing to take it to heart can actualize the essence of its deeper meaning.

Individual verses of the Qur'an can only be understood in relationship with the entirety of the book's message of mercy and love. Just as studying the heart outside of the human body would give you an incomplete picture as to the purpose of the organ, a verse of the Qur'an, cherry-picked and studied separately from the historical context and overall message of the revelation, would give you an incomplete interpretation.

The Healing Vibration of Revelation

Within the Qur'an resides all the answers to the soul's questions of how to approach and experience God. The Qur'an is not just a collection of rules and regulations, but is, as Imam Ali describes, "An ocean whose depth shall not be fathomed; A spring that shall not be exhausted by those who draw from it; peace for whoever dwells on it; a guidance for whoever follows it; a cure after which there is no malady; a shelter for whoever seeks healing; a light which does not alternate with darkness."

The Qur'an is a lullaby for the spirit and an alarm for the ego.

While its words are calming to the spirit, bringing it into a restful state of peace and contentment, it is a wake-up call for the ego, confronting it with the light of awareness. It acts like a spiritual flashlight that extinguishes the darkness of moral and spiritual evils. Just as a seed cannot become a tree until it breaks its shell and lets the light in, we cannot fully be transformed by the Qur'an's healing power unless we remove the veils that separate our hearts from God.

The Qur'an teaches us that surrender in Islam is to give up our perceptions of how things *should* be, in exchange for being receptive to God's love to manifest through us. The Qur'an is a bridge from this world to the highest heavenly realms; it is an open invitation from God to come sit in His presence. The words of the revelation are not just letters that capture meaning, but rather placeholders for the sacred vibration of Allah's words, whose divine composition mysteriously transforms and unveils the human spirit of all that prevents it from uniting with The Origin of Love (*Al-Wadud*).

> "*The Holy Qur'an, we must always remember, does not contain the human speech and thought of the Prophet Muhammad, but is the Divine Song of power and love sung directly by Allah, the ultimate Source of the universe, through the personal, cultural, and spiritual being of His Prophet. The Holy Qur'an, in its depth, is direct revelation, regardless of whatever historical studies are made of its surface. No meditation upon the Qur'an, no matter how strong the inspiration or how broad the scholarship, could begin to equal the Arabic original, simply because the Arabic Qur'an remains in the realm of revelation. This is a living revelation, occurring afresh each time the Holy Qur'an is sung or chanted, for these Arabic words are the actual resonance of Allah Most High, and thus they transmit healing, protecting, transforming, and illuminating power directly from the Source.*"[19]

LEX HIXON, "THE HEART OF THE QUR'AN"

The notion that the words of the Qur'an can have a profound effect on the human being is wonderfully illustrated through the following story:

A wealthy merchant invited a famous doctor and a sheikh to dinner to ask them to help his sick daughter. The merchant asked the sheikh to pray for his daughter and the sheikh said, "I will read verses of the Qur'an for your daughter and ask my beloved Lord to heal her, leaving no trace of illness." The famous doctor interrupted the sheikh by saying, "Are you crazy? What is this nonsense? Science has advanced enough for us to know words don't heal people, medicine heals people." In response the sheikh screamed, "You stupid man! What do you know about the healing power of God's word?" The surprised doctor's face lit up in anger as he screamed with a vengeance, "How dare you call me stupid!"

The clever sheikh then said, "Oh, please forgive me for calling you stupid. But did you notice how simple words made you insanely angry? If words from a stranger can make your eyes red, your heart beat faster in rage, your adrenaline spike, and your blood vessels constrict, making your blood pressure rise, then surely God's perfect words have the power to heal."

Since the Qur'an is from Allah its words are more mysterious and powerful than we can ever imagine. After all, it was God's speech that created us and everything else in existence so it's reasonable to assume God's words can have a tangible effect on us.

"Be! And It Is."

The power of revelation is illustrated in the Qur'an when Allah says everything was created through His saying *kun faya kun* or "Be! And it is" (36:82). From a single word *kun* or "Be," all of existence was set into motion.[20] *Kun*. We are here. *Kun*. We are gone. *Kun* is being said again and again, as everything is constantly both sprouting from and withering into the embrace of God. This is the hidden power of revelation.

The words of the Qur'an are like rays from the sun—whatever it shines upon, it transforms.

Although it is beneficial and necessary to have the Qur'an available in many languages, it is important to remember that the rhyme, rhythm, cadence, and overall linguistic beauty of the Qur'an is significantly minimized when it's translated from its original Arabic. This is important to understand because the words of the Qur'an are not just letters—they are seen as a sacred sound code of divinely arranged Arabic letters, which serve as a healing balm for the wounds of the soul. The words of revelation carry spiritual power beyond the human understanding of the language of Arabic; the Qur'an has a unique way of bewildering the mind and awakening the heart.

While the Qur'an was often revealed through the Angel Gabriel coming to the Prophet ﷺ in the shape of a man, it also at times was revealed through a spiritual medium that the Prophet ﷺ described as "a voice which resembles the sound of a ringing bell."[21] It is hard to ignore the vibratory nature of a bell's resonance and how that reiterates the notion that revelation is more than just words that carry meaning.

> *"We send down of the Qur'an that which is healing and mercy for the believers; as for those who are unjust, it only increases their loss."*
>
> QUR'AN 17:82

Scientists today have also discovered the incredible power of speech in the form of vibration and energy. The famous physicist Albert Einstein unveiled the power of vibration through the equation $E=MC^2$, which showed how energy and matter are interchangeable; as a result of the implications of this theory, some have suggested that the vibrational, energetic quality of words can theoretically affect matter.[22] Revolutionary scientific studies performed at the University of Helsinki in Finland have also shown that DNA can be repaired through frequency and vibration.[23]

When we open our consciousness to the melodic recitation of the Holy Qur'an, fireworks go off in our brain and our hearts find rest as new connections are made in the pathways of our faith. As Imam Ali said, "The words of Allah are the medicine of the heart."

> *Our hearts are like solar panels, our spiritual light is generated from consistently turning to and drinking in the light of God's word.*

The words of the Qur'an help to transcribe the spiritual code hidden beneath our physical forms. The more we saturate ourselves in the ocean of revelation, the more we will be filled with the presence and truth of God.

Everything Is a Manifestation of God's Speech

Old manuscripts of the Qur'an were often embellished with borders that incorporated arrows that pointed outward, away from the text. These arrows were symbols that led the reader off the page and into the world; these arrows reminded the reader that God is not confined to the pages of scripture. After all, God said "Be!" and spoke us into existence, so everything we see and experience is a manifestation of divine speech (36:82).

> *"We will show them Our signs in the horizons and within themselves until it becomes clear to them that this is the truth. Is it not enough that your Lord witnesses everything?"*
>
> QUR'AN 41:53

We are called to read beyond just the reflection of the Qur'an that is contained in a book.[24] We are called to read the revelation that graces the pages of the outer world and the holy words of God that are hidden in the folds of our inner realm.[25] Imagine if you saw every ocean wave as a sign of God, every breeze as an *ayah,* every person as a *surah,* and every moment as an opportunity to know God through the creation He spoke into existence.[26] Imagine how your life would change if you approached a blade of grass, a ladybug, or another human being with the same reverence you approach revelation. After all isn't everything in existence a manifestation of God's speech?

Memorizing the Qur'an

Since the oneness of Allah is encoded in the hearts of humankind, hearing the words of the Qur'an will feel familiar to the soul in a way that cannot be fathomed by the mind.[27] The Qur'an itself says, "We have certainly made the Qur'an easy for remembrance, so is there anyone who will remember?" (54:17)

Even if we look at it literally, the Qur'an's unique rhyming patterns, rhythm, cadence, repetition, and usage of literary devices such as palindromes and ring compositions make the revelation not just extraordinary but easier to memorize. Scientists have shown that rhyming patterns assist in acoustically encoding memories. Since rhyming words carry similar sound codes they tend to be more easily linked together in the brain.[28] Since the Qur'an is recited out loud and often heard repeatedly during prayers and at mosques, it becomes easier to memorize.[29] This is perhaps why the Qur'an is considered by many to be the most memorized book in the world, with an estimated several million people today having memorized the text cover to cover.[30]

Although Allah says, "We have sent down the Qur'an, and We will be its Guardian" (15:9), the mass memorizations of the Qur'an since the time of the Prophet ﷺ have inevitably made it virtually impossible for anyone to alter this text. All Muslims have access to the Qur'an exactly as it was revealed to the Prophet Muhammad ﷺ more than 1,400 years ago. Part of the beauty of Islam is that its revelation is not only for holy men and religious scholars, but for every single person, from every class and culture. As the Prophet Muhammad ﷺ beautifully said, in the eyes of God, "All people are equal as the teeth of a comb."[31] Our closeness to God and our connection with the Qur'an are not determined by our wealth, beauty, or knowledge but by the intentions behind our actions, the state of our hearts, and the sincerity of our love for Allah and His messengers.

A Linguistic Miracle and Divine Reminder of Oneness

The fact that the Qur'an was not written down by the Prophet ﷺ himself, as it was revealed makes the symmetry and precision of the revelation even more miraculous. Although many sources claim that the Prophet ﷺ had scribes to write down the different verses of the Qur'an as he recited them, the majority of scholars believe he himself could not read. The Qur'an confirms this claim through the following saying, "So believe in Allah and His Messenger, the unlettered prophet, who believes in Allah and His words, and follow him that you may be guided" (7:158).

To be unlettered today would be a disadvantage, but the illiteracy of the Prophet ﷺ further illustrated his utter dependence on revelation. His inability to read, made him incapable to look to himself or the outside world for knowledge. In *Ideals and Realities of Islam*, scholar Seyyed Hossein Nasr profoundly describes the importance of the Prophet ﷺ being unlettered: "The Word of God in Islam is the Qur'an; in Christianity it is Christ. The vehicle of the Divine Message in Christianity is the Virgin Mary; in Islam it is the soul of the Prophet. The Prophet must be unlettered for the same reason that the Virgin Mary must be virgin. The human vehicle of a Divine Message must be pure and untainted. The Divine Word can only be written on the pure 'untouched' tablet of human receptivity. If this Word is in the form of flesh the purity is symbolized by the virginity of the mother who gives birth to the Word, and if it is in the form of a book this purity is symbolized by the unlettered nature of the person who is chosen to announce the Word among men...The unlettered nature of the Prophet demonstrates how the human recipient is completely passive before the Divine. Were this purity and virginity of the soul not to exist, the Divine Word would in a sense become tainted with purely human knowledge and not be presented to mankind in its pristine purity."[32] The Prophet ﷺ was not swayed by human interpretations because he drank directly from the spring of divine wisdom.

If the Qur'an was written by a human writer, we would have naturally seen over a 23-year period a maturing happen, but the voice of the Qur'an stays timelessly consistent in a language that is both majestic and profound. In the time of the Prophet ﷺ, there were no online databases, no search engines, and yet the Qur'an is filled with dozens of examples of correlated words being used exactly the same amount of times. For example, the word for "this life" and "the next life" are each used 115 times, while the words for "angels" and "devils" are each used 88 times. The Qur'an is so specific that the phrase "they said" is used 332 times, while the word "say" is also used exactly 332 times.[33] There are dozens of more numerical correlations all throughout the revelation, which brilliantly illustrate the thoughtfulness and perfection of Allah's words.

Keeping in mind that many scholars suggest the Qur'an was not written down and compiled in its entirety during the 23 years that it was being revealed to the Prophet Muhammad ﷺ, would it be humanly possible to create a revelation that is this balanced and precise? It would arguably be impossible without divine guidance and inspiration.

As miraculous as this revelation is, the Qur'an is not seen as a new message to humankind. Rather, the Qur'an is seen as a light that illuminates all that we already have been given by God, "confirming what came before it, as He [Allah] revealed the Torah and the Gospel" (3:3). Just as the Prophet Muhammad ﷺ was sent "to be a mercy to *all* worlds" (21:107), the Qur'an was not just sent for Muslims, but is also "a reminder for *all* the worlds" (38:87).

The Qur'an was not meant to replace the Bible, Torah, or other holy scriptures; it was meant as a capstone and confirmation of the truth revealed to all divinely chosen prophets sent to this world.

The prophets are like different rivers throughout time that all pointed to the same ocean of unity.

The Qur'an itself says, "Say: We believe in God and what He has revealed to us and to Abraham, Ishmael, Isaac, and their descendants, and what was revealed to Moses, Jesus, and the prophets from their Lord. We make no distinction among them and to God we have submitted ourselves" (2:136). The major differences between the truth sent down to all divinely chosen prophets is not in the heart of the message, but in man's preservation and interpretation of that scripture over time.[34] The Qur'an never describes itself as a replacement of the original message of Abraham, Moses, or Jesus, but rather as a reminder of God's oneness in the Arabic language.[35]

Due to the Qur'an's unparalleled linguistic perfection in the Arabic language, numerously confirmed scientific proofs, profoundly accurate historical predictions, and ability to speak to the human soul it is considered to be a divine miracle. It's important to understand that God does not randomly send miracles with His prophets, but in His divine perfection, tailors them specifically to the audience and context of their time.

Take Moses, for example. The time of the Pharaoh was one of extravagance, arrogance, and magicians, so the divine signs that were sent with Moses dwarfed the magic of the era with plagues, staffs turning into snakes, and the parting of the Red Sea. Whereas the miracles sent through Jesus were in the realm of healing, raising the dead, purifying the lepers, and giving the blind back their sight—because the people of his era were skilled in medicine and prided themselves on the advancement of human knowledge.

During the time of the Prophet Muhammad ﷺ, the expertise of the Arabs was neither in magic nor medicine but rather in language. Allah sent the Prophet Muhammad ﷺ a miracle in the form of a book unparalleled in its linguistic beauty, fitting neither the conditions of poetry nor of prose—or any other style that had ever been heard by the Arabs. Where poets wrote from a place of fleeting passion, the Qur'an originated from the womb of Absolute Truth (*Haqq*). While Arab writers strived to arrange letters in ways that pointed to a realm beyond the sum of the words themselves, the Qur'an's structure itself was beyond form, for it pointed to a divine reality beyond time and space. Whereas we can only read about the divine miracles that were manifested during the time of the other prophets, the beauty of the miracle of the Qur'an is that we can directly experience it with our own senses in this present moment.

The Qur'an Was a Game-Changer

In the 23 years it took for the Qur'an to unveil itself on Earth, its words did not just change the hearts of people spiritually—the Qur'an confronted every aspect of how people lived their lives. What was remarkable about this revolution of change was that it affected not just social or religious spheres, but also the political and governmental norms of Arab culture.

The Qur'an changed the way people dressed, spoke, ate, prayed, conducted business, treated women, and interacted with their parents. Through the revelation of the Qur'an, the Prophet Muhammad ﷺ established equal rights among people of all colors, eradicated the class system and tribalism, abolished alcoholism, and established a justice system that was both revolutionary and inclusive of people of all socioeconomic statures.

One of the most revolutionary ideas was the rights of women. Through the Qur'an, Allah confronted the sexist culture of seventh-century Arabia by declaring that men and women were of equal worth in the eyes of God. In a culture of misogyny where men would bury their infant girls alive, the Qur'an gave women the right to vote, inherit money, and own property. Additionally, the Prophet ﷺ made education compulsory for every Muslim girl.[36] The Qur'an serves to remind us that there is more to being a representative of God on Earth than praying privately in our homes. We need to stand up for the rights of others, demand equality, and respect people of all cultures and races. The Qur'an doesn't just teach us to let go of our biases, it shows us how to transform our judgments into opportunities for greater understanding and connection.

The Qur'an does not just lead us, it liberates us from the grips of the ego. It does not just guide us; it helps us grow past the shells of our limiting beliefs. It does not just confront us; it consoles us with God's infinite mercy. It reminds us of our holy purpose, of how incredibly valuable we are in the eyes of God, and inspires us to live a life not simply based on our present limited capacity, but to trust that when we depend on God all things are possible by virtue of His infinite and all-encompassing power. The Qur'an is not meant to only be recited, it is meant to be taken in like the fragrance of a rose, deep within our essence, allowing it to permeate in the deepest recesses of our being. The Qur'an was sent as a pathway of return to God.

> *"This Qur'an is the rope of Allah, and it is the clear Light and Healing. It is a protection for the one who clings to it and a rescue for the one who follows it. It is not crooked and so it puts things straight."*[37]
>
> **PROPHET MUHAMMAD ﷺ**

In a sense, the Qur'an is a divine GPS. This acronym is not for Global Positioning System, but rather for God Positioning System. In other words, the Qur'an warns us when we are going in the wrong direction, by reminding us that our ultimate goal is not to chase after this world but to return to the straight path of knowing, loving, and worshipping God.

The Qur'an not only reminds us of the human being's divinely inspired potential, but helps us to course-correct toward actualizing that potential. Just as the thick atmosphere of the Earth protects it from asteroids and harmful radiation, the light of the Qur'an and the remembrance of God come together to create a spiritual atmosphere around our souls, protecting us from constant attacks of sin and forgetfulness.[38]

> *On the darkest nights of our souls, the Qur'an is a faithful companion with embracing arms. For every feeling we are experiencing, the Qur'an has a soothing verse, and for every pain we carry it has a timeless remedy.*

The Qur'an is like a spiritual iron that straightens the creases of our spirit through its powerful transmission. The revelation has a mysterious way of decoding and recoding our spiritual mainframe from the emotional traumas and patterns of the past. God's words are a source of medicine for the broken heart seeking to be whole again, truth for the confused heart seeking clarity and certainty, and guidance for the lost and straying heart seeking to be found.

We are called not to just read the Qur'an—but to become a manifestation of its message. We are called to be a mercy to all the creations of God, by bringing light where there is darkness, feeding the hungry, forgiving those who wrong us, taking care of the orphans, being generous to the needy, being kind to our parents, and through sincere worship becoming a vessel of God's unconditional love for the entire world. It is not how much of the Qur'an we read or memorize, but how much of it we internalize that makes a difference. After all, the Qur'an was not sent to passively inform our minds; rather, it was sent to actively transform our hearts.

Oh Allah! Open for me the flood gates of the Qur'an. Let
its words wash me of all illusion, let its light swallow all the
darkness that surrounds me, and allow its healing power to
mend the broken places within me. Oh Allah! Make the Qur'an
my faithful companion on the straight path to You. "My Lord!
Cause me to enter whatever I may do sincerely and cause me
to leave it sincerely and grant me supporting authority from
Your presence" (17:80). In Your powerful names I pray, Ameen.

Reflection: "Contemplate the Qur'an with Love"

When we reflect on verses of the Qur'an with love and awareness, we open ourselves up to experiencing the revelation in a different way. Anytime you come across a verse of the Qur'an that is difficult to comprehend, or one you would like a deeper understanding of, consider doing the following practice.

- Begin by choosing a verse of the Qur'an you want to further contemplate. If one does not come to mind you can begin by choosing one of the beautiful Qur'an verses from the list below:
  - "We are closer to him than the jugular vein" (50:16).
  - "Wherever you turn, there is the face of Allah" (2:115).
  - "To God we belong and to Him we shall return" (2:156).
  - "Indeed, Allah will not change the condition of people until they change themselves" (13:11).
  - "It may be that you hate something and it is good for you and it may be that you love something and it is bad for you" (2:216).
  - "Oh My servants who have transgressed against their souls! Do not despair of the mercy of Allah. Indeed, Allah forgives all sins. Indeed, it is He who is The Forgiving, The Merciful" (39:53).
- On a piece of paper, write the verse you chose, in both English and Arabic. If you cannot read Arabic, write down the transliteration

of the Arabic in English so you can experience the original recitation of the verse.

- Every morning when you wake up, make the following prayer before you recite the verse you have chosen: *"Oh Allah, through Your generosity please open the doors of my heart and help me understand the wisdom of the Qur'an. Oh Allah, allow me to only receive from this verse the knowledge that would benefit me and bring me closer to You."*

- Once you make a heartfelt prayer to Allah, read the English translation of the verse, followed by reciting it 3 times silently and 3 times out loud, in Arabic. Your pronunciation does not have to be perfect, just do your best.

- Take a moment to reconnect with your breath and contemplate the meaning of the verse.

- Spend 3–5 minutes silently repeating the verse in Arabic as you observe your natural breathing pattern.

- Write down any insights that come up.

- Repeat this process with the same verse every day for a week.

- At the end of the week, read over your daily insights and observe how your reflections may have deepened or transformed as the week progressed.

- How do you feel about this verse now?

Reflection: "Healing with Divine Sound"

The recitation of the Qur'an in Arabic has a resonance with the power to awaken and inspire the hearts of those who intentionally listen. In order to make a deep connection with the Qur'an, it can be helpful to follow these steps:

- Begin by taking a few moments of silence while reconnecting with your breath.

- Now take 5 deep breaths, slowly breathing in through your nose and out through your mouth.

- Bring your awareness to the area of your spinal column in the space behind your heart. Notice how the sensations of this area change as you breathe in deeper.
- Pick a chapter (*surah*) from the Qur'an that you feel drawn to and play an audio recording of it.[39]
- As you listen to the *surah* you chose, bring your attention to the sounds of the words, the vibration, the pauses, and the emphasis made on certain letters.
- Use your breath to consciously breathe in the vibration of each letter you hear into your heart.
- Notice and observe any insights or sensations that come up during or after your experience.

"Islam can be summarized in three sentences: Be with the Creator, without creation. Be with creation, without ego. Wish for others what you wish for yourself."

SHAYKH ZAKARIYA
AL-SIDIQQUI

4

THE SPIRITUAL DIMENSIONS OF ISLAM

Islam is not only a religion, it's a way of life that can physically, mentally, and spiritually transform a believer. God did not send the Prophet Muhammad ﷺ to begin a new religion; rather, He sent him to reignite our relationship with the Divine. However, the Qur'an does not just speak to our relationship with God; it also guides and counsels us in our relationship with all that God created. The Qur'an beseeches us to treat ourselves with more mercy, to be kinder to others, to be more compassionate toward all of Allah's creatures, and to be conscious and intentional in our use of earthly resources.

"Do what is good as God has done what is good to you."
QUR'AN 28:77

Islam is a journey of lovingly serving God for the blessing of the life we were given, but could do nothing to ever earn. Our life is a loan from

God, which is why the word *din,* which is often translated as "religion," is originally born of a root word meaning "debt." Thus, in essence, by walking the path of Islam we are also seeking to pay our debt to God, who has given us life.[1] However, God doesn't ask us to pray to Him because He is lacking something; rather He is asking us to plug into God-consciousness as a way of recharging the battery of our own souls.

Many people make the mistake of thinking that religion is the means by which human beings seek God. The truth is, Islam is a journey of unveiling the secret that God is and has always been with us. We may not be able to perceive God directly, but He is reflected in everything.

Islam is not a path about obtaining God's love; it is a path that teaches you to strive, persevere, and unveil what you have already been given. Islam is not just a series of practices and actions; it is a light that helps grow the seeds of our most authentic selves. Islam is not merely outward obedience to Divine Law; it is a cultivation of inner faith. It is not only about celebrating what is right and standing up against what is wrong; it is about bringing mercy, beauty, and excellence to our words, thoughts, actions, and deeds. Islam is the path of showing you how to become who you already are.

We are all born with spiritual wings, Islam simply reminds
us how to fly.

You Are Inherently Good

Islam is not limited to solely the outward worship of God, it provides a means of unveiling all the ways you are a reflection of God's beauty and majesty. The Qur'an says that God has planted within all humankind a seed of innate goodness, known in Arabic as the *fitra.*[2] This primordial nature of goodness, placed in our hearts, inclines us toward actions that are righteous, beautiful, and in perfect alignment with the Divine. On the soul level, all of humankind is in a perfect relationship with God, regardless of what they choose to outwardly believe. This primordial goodness that exists at the soul of every single person longs to manifest itself the way a seed longs to unfold the hundreds of blossoms hidden in its unseen potential. The path of Islam teaches the seeker how to water the spiritual garden of the soul, which has already been tilled and sowed by God's abundantly overflowing love.

One of the main purposes of Islam is to unveil this innate goodness. All the prophets were sent by God to remind us that in this very moment we are already everything we seek to become. On the path to God, every step is the destination. The divinely inspired version of ourselves is not found out in the world, but exists beneath the misperceptions of who we think we are. This is precisely why the Qur'an says, "Religion in the sight of God is surrender" (3:19), because it is only when we surrender our subjective perception of reality that we become receptive to what God is choosing to manifest through us in the present moment.

There is a well-known story in the Qur'an, in which God tells the Prophet Moses that he must first surrender his attachments in order to receive divine revelation. Allah says, "Oh Moses, Indeed, I am your Lord, so remove your sandals. Indeed, you are in the sacred valley of Tuwa. And I have chosen you, so listen to what is revealed [to you]" (20:11-13). The spiritual sages say that when Moses is being asked to take off his sandals, it is symbolic not only of removing his attachment to this world—but Allah is also asking him to surrender his attachment to the spiritual path itself.[3] After all, we are not called to be "Islam worshippers," we are called to be worshippers of Allah alone. Our religion is not our destination, but the practices, principles, and teachings of Islam are necessary provisions on the path to Allah.

Islam: To Surrender in Peace

In Islam, the path of self-surrender has three stations: *islam, iman,* and *ihsan.* The first station, *islam,* is primarily focused on the actions of the limbs being in alignment with Divine Law (*sharia*). Since *islam* is based on the *sharia,* it is important to understand that the word *sharia* is often used to mean "Divine Law." However, *sharia* more literally translates to mean, "a path to the watering hole." This implies that the purpose of divine guidance is to guide human beings through the desert of ignorance to the oasis of faith.

The *sharia* can essentially be broken into two categories: laws concerning how to practice the pillars of Islam, and laws concerning all other matters in a Muslim's life. Although there are countless different perspectives when it comes to Divine Law (*sharia*), some of the core principles of *sharia* are the following: preservation of religion, protection of the holiness of life, fostering and honoring of the intellect, preservation of the sanctity of the family, and protection of property.

It is important to point out that the *sharia* is based on the Qur'an or sayings of the Prophet ﷺ, but it also contains the interpretation of scholars over time, who naturally differed from one another; as a result, there can be vast differences in how people experience specific issues and nuances. Nonetheless, the one main objective that connects the different interpretation of scholars is the call to "enjoin what is good in all of our affairs, while warding off and protecting against all that is evil." The *sharia* is like a flashlight—meant to guide us through the darkness of confusion and uncertainty unto the straight path. However, just as we follow maps but do not worship them, we are not meant to worship revelation or the *sharia*, but to surrender to the guidance of God and follow the path He paves for us.

Islam begins as an external surrendering of the body to the clearly stated prohibitions and commands of God.

> *"Islam is to testify that there is nothing worthy of worship*
> *except God and that Muhammad is the messenger of God,*
> *to perform the ritual prayers, to pay the purifying alms, to*
> *fast in Ramadan, and to make the pilgrimage to the Sacred*
> *House if you are able to do so."[4]*
>
> **PROPHET MUHAMMAD** ﷺ

The word *islam* means "to surrender, to submit" and comes from the triliteral root *sin-lam-mim,* which also can mean "well-being, completion, freedom, and peace." Linguistically, then, the word *islam* can be said to mean "to surrender in peace," for it is only when we submit as a servant to God that we are liberated from the enslavement of our ego. Similar to how the gravitation of our orbiting moon helps stabilize the Earth as it rotates around its axis, the practices of Islam help to ground us, preventing us from wobbling into temptations that would prevent us from actualizing our true potential.[5]

To surrender is not to give up, give in, or to lose; rather it means *being with* what Allah has written for you by embracing, in faith, gratitude, and with complete trust, that "Allah is the best of planners" (3:54). Submission to Allah begins with acknowledgement that every moment we have been given is a gift from Allah that we can neither ignore nor change.

> "What is meant for you, will reach you even if it is beneath two mountains. And what is not meant for you will not reach you even if it's between your two lips."
>
> IMAM AL-GHAZALI, 11TH-CENTURY MYSTIC

Surrendering to Allah and believing the supremeness of His decree does not mean we stop striving to better ourselves. The Prophet ﷺ said, "Trust in Allah, but tie your camel,"[6] which means we are called to always trust in God, but we must still use our common sense; we must still struggle with our entire souls for the sake of establishing peace on Earth. The Prophet Muhammad ﷺ clearly states the importance of standing up and physically doing our part against oppression when he says, "Whosoever of you sees an evil, let him change it with his hand; and if he is not able to do so, then [let him change it] with his tongue; and if he is not able to do so, then with his heart, and that is the weakest level of faith."[7]

Trusting God's will does not mean we stop actively enjoining goodness and standing up against injustice. Surrendering to Allah does not mean we stop trying; it means we stop thinking we can control the outcome of the choices that we make. By surrendering, we let go of how we think things should be, and become flexible, to move with the breeze of Allah's decree.

As the mystics say, "Blessed are the flexible, for they shall not
be bent out of shape."[8]

When we surrender to God we change the flow of intention and energy behind our actions. We do not act from fear of loss or poverty, but from a place of trust in God. The concept of surrender is beautifully described in Taoism as *Wei Wu Wei,* meaning to "Do without doing."[9] When we surrender to God, we are like a grain of sand surrendering to become the mountain, or like a drop of rain surrendering to become the entire ocean. If we feel resistance in surrendering to God and trusting Him, it is important to not judge ourselves. In fact, the awareness that we feel resistance to surrendering is a blessing, because it brings our attention to the places within us where we struggle to rely on God. This awareness opens the door to repentance and remembrance of God, offering us the opportunity to turn from self-reliance to God-reliance.

The observance of outer laws establishes a uniform moral structure, molding and furnishing a container to foster faithfulness. Just as everything in existence has a form (body) and an essence (spirit), and the purpose of that form is to carry the essence, the purpose of our obedience to the Divine Law, through *islam,* is to create the soil necessary for the seed of faith, or *iman,* to be cultivated.

Iman: Walking in Faith

While *islam* refers to the realm of activity, *iman* refers to the intellectual understanding of faith and relates to our perception of God, the unseen, and the Hereafter. While the station of *islam* is apparent, outward, and can be seen, *iman* is hidden, inward, and related to the unseen reality of the heart and soul. *Iman* is when we delve past the surface and into the spirit of revelation. *Iman* is the inner reality of worship. It is the cultivation of divine presence and knowledge within the human heart, which brings value and meaning to our outer actions. *Iman* is the state of allowing God's love to open our hearts to the light that streams between every word of scripture, the way the petals of a spring flower open to the warm sun.

"Iman is to believe in Allah, His angels, His books, His messengers, the Last Day, and to believe in destiny both its good and its bad."[10]

PROPHET MUHAMMAD ﷺ

Iman is having faith in the unseen and trusting that God always has our best interests at heart. Faith is about *tawakul,* or sincere trust that whatever Allah chooses for us to experience, be it a blessing or a trial, is ultimately in service of our deeper witnessing of Him. Since faith blossoms in direct relationship with our trust in God, we can water the seeds of our faith through chanting and meditation. For example, we may chant or repeat the Qur'anic verse, *Hasbuna Allah wa ni'ma al Wakil,* which means, "Allah is sufficient for us and He is the best Protector" (3:173). When we practice this powerful chant of remembrance or *dhikr* while experiencing fear or doubt, it increases our receptivity to the love and light of God, which further nourishes the seeds of faith within us.

At its core, surrendering in faith is the acknowledgment that although we may not have power over the outcomes of our life, we always have the freedom to choose the state of our spirit, in meeting the trials and blessings that are written for us. Some make the mistake of thinking faith is a feeling, when in fact in many ways it is a choice to be open to what Allah has already given us. At its essence, faith is having the trust and patience to hold on to your relationship with God through the changing winds of your feelings and circumstances.

Islamic sages have said, "Faith is comprised of two things: one half is patience and the other half is gratitude."[11] Patience is a necessary element of fostering faith, because sometimes it takes time to unveil the divine purpose behind God's will. Patience and true reliance on Allah lead to gratefulness, because when we understand that God always wants better for us than we could ever imagine for ourselves we are naturally inclined toward being grateful. To have *iman* is to believe that although the future is unknown, our God is known and forever faithful. To have faith is to proclaim that although we don't know what tomorrow will hold, we know that God is already there, embracing and protecting our souls.

*"If you were to rely on Allah as He should be relied on,
He would provide for you as He provides for the birds.
They go out early in the morning hungry and return in the
evening full."*[12]

PROPHET MUHAMMAD ﷺ

In the Qur'an, Allah says that He "guides to Himself whoever turns to Him" (42:13). The cultivation of faith begins with praying to God to open our hearts to experience His love. By His wisdom, God guides whom He wills and those who desire to be guided. It is not God but our egos that are the barriers to faith. We find it difficult to trust in God because we are relying on ourselves instead of on God.

To foster faith in God, it helps to reflect on the fact that all of the decisions we make are based on a biased perception of the past, an incomplete view of the present, and an unknown future. Whereas the Qur'an says to us, "You have been given very little knowledge" (17:85), God sees the past, present, and future completely, as His wisdom is perfect across time and space. When we realize how limited our knowledge is, we are naturally more inclined to trust God's perfect wisdom over our incomplete vision. Faith automatically blossoms when we remove the walls of the ego, because faith is not something we find, but something that blossoms from the inside.

Our *iman* often grows when we acknowledge all the good that God has already done for us. The faithful fully submit to God's will, saying, "God is enough for me. There is no god but He. In Him I have put my trust. He is the Lord of the Mighty Throne" (9:129).

Iman fosters within us as we begin to trust God with the depths of our hearts. In the Qur'an Allah calls out a group of Bedouins who tried to claim they had *iman* by saying, "The Bedouins say, 'We have believed.' Say, 'You have not [yet] believed; but say [instead], 'We have submitted,' for faith [*iman*] has not yet entered your hearts" (49:14). This verse points out that *iman* is not acquired through robotic submission, but rather it is fostered when we sincerely believe and obey God from the depths of our hearts.[13] Obeying God's command without sincerity or love leads to emptiness, while saying you love God but refuse to follow what He asks of you is a sign of inner conflict and hypocrisy.

Our outer actions are a good litmus test for the reality of our internal state, and vice versa. It is important to understand that our spiritual journey will have ups and downs; just as your breath goes in and out, and ocean waves rise and fall, our faith goes through cycles. Every mountain has both a base camp and a summit, and as long as you are alive your faith will have peaks and valleys. If your faith were never-changing and constant, then you would have no reason to call upon God. In the Qur'an, Allah very clearly states that our faith will be tested.

> *"Do the people think that they will be left to say, 'We believe'*
> *and they will not be tried?"*
>
> QUR'AN 29:2

The first step of being Muslim is to profess your faith, but until you put your beliefs into action you don't actually possess faith.[14] Faith is not something we can put in a bank and lock up. It is not stagnant; it is something that is alive and constantly flowing like a river. Since God is infinite, the journey of faith is endless.

> *The mystics say that there are only two rules on the path to*
> *God: begin and continue.*

So long as we are on Earth, there is no finish line that we can reach where we can stop trying or striving toward growth. In the same way that if a bodybuilder stops working out, he begins to lose the muscle that he has gained over time, when we stop doing our practices, our faith weakens. It is important to understand that just as there's no magic pill to obtaining the physical body we seek to have, there is no shortcut to becoming spiritually strong.

The secret to walking the path of Islam is not in pretending to be perfect, but in proclaiming your weaknesses before God. When you understand that it is your deficiency that creates the space to experience God's generosity, you come to see that God calls you to Him through your humanity and fallibility. Sometimes we have to fall on our backs before we face the heavens. Sometimes we have to be broken before we seek God to mend our hearts. Sometimes we have to become sick before we call upon the Healer. God is not forsaking you, God has not forgotten you—rather, your Lord is calling you, through your pain and struggle, to rely on Him in a deeper way.

> *"Faith is the bird that feels the light and sings, while the dawn is still dark."*
> RABINDRANATH TAGORE, 20TH-CENTURY INDIAN POET

Linguistically, the word *iman* is often translated as "faith," but it comes from the root word *amana*, which means "to make one safe and secure," implying that faith anchors one in the safety and protection of God.

Imam Ali says, "Iman is confession with the tongue, verification with the heart, and action of the body." It is not a passive declaration of belief, but rather faith put in action. The sign of true *iman* is that it affects how you interact with the entirety of creation, not just the Creator.

> *The best of people are those that bring the most benefit to the rest of humankind."*[15]
> PROPHET MUHAMMAD ﷺ

The more committed we are to abiding by God's laws and becoming a reflection of divine love on Earth, the greater our container for *iman* becomes. Without *islam, iman* cannot be contained, and without *iman, islam* is like a body without a soul; it is lifeless and inflexible. Outer obedience and active inner faith strengthen one another like threads joining to create a braid.

Ihsan: Seeing God Everywhere

When we combine outer practice (*islam*) and inner faith (*iman*) with the awareness of God's omnipresence, we enter into the mysterious realm of *ihsan*. The station of *ihsan*—or, as it is sometimes called, "spiritual excellence"—is achieved when we transcend the duality of the outer and the inner, and enter into the singular presence of God.

It is only when the sun of the ego sets that the true everlasting light of the soul and the innate beauty within the human being can rise. This refining of the soul to be in pure alignment with God is the essence of the station of *ihsan*. In defining *ihsan*, the Prophet ﷺ famously said:

> "It is to worship God as though you are seeing Him, for even
> if you cannot see Him, you know that He sees you."[16]
>
> PROPHET MUHAMMAD ﷺ

Even at the higher levels of spiritual awareness, our sight will falter, but our refuge from our fallibility and faltering is to trust that God will never falter in His witnessing of us. *Ihsan* is when you are in a constant state of awareness of Allah's all-encompassing love for you. When we understand that God sees us even when we don't see Him, we are reminded that His mercy and love are not dependent on our fragile vision of Him, but on His All-Encompassing Sight (*Al-Basir*).

Seekers in the state of *ihsan* are like servants before a loving king, conscious of every step they take and every word they say, beautifying their actions out of gratitude for being welcomed into the king's palace of kindness. Linguistically, *ihsan* is "to make something beautiful," for when we are truly aware of God's all-encompassing goodness we cannot help but reflect the beauty of His presence. In this transcendent state of being we manifest "spiritual excellence"—not from the ego or in order to be praised, but out of being in love with God.

Ihsan is a state of goodness which is independent from the creation and seeks no reciprocity or applause. When someone is living in a state of *ihsan* they see the creation as nothing but a reflection of the Creator. In a sense, then, *ihsan* has two main dimensions: being consistently present, and being God-conscious in all of our states. A *Muhsin* or one with *ihsan* is constantly striving to be present with whatever face God meets them with moment to moment. A *Muhsin* is not only constantly turning to God for guidance through prayer and remembrance, but also constantly seeking opportunities to serve God's creation. To be in a state of *ihsan* is to know that God is everywhere by His knowledge, that He is reflected in everything by His names, and that His love is the breath behind all that exists.

The eighth-century spiritual master, and descendent of the Prophet ﷺ, Imam Ja'far As-Sadiq, taught his students that people worship God in one of three ways: the worship of the slave, who worships God out of fear of punishment; the worship of the merchant, who worships God seeking a reward; and the worship of the free, who worship God out of love and gratitude, which is the best form of worship.[17] It is only when we worship the Divine out of love that our worship transforms our entire being. This is the station of *ihsan*.

When all of existence becomes a mirror for God, every place becomes sacred, every voice becomes revelation, every face becomes a reflection of God—making every moment a chance to witness the Divine and to be witnessed by the Divine. Whereas *islam* focuses on outer actions, and *iman* focuses on inner certainty, *ihsan* is the world of intention, where all that we do is for the sake of God alone. As the Prophet ﷺ said, "Actions are rewarded in accordance with their intentions,"[18] meaning that the more sincere our intentions, the more valuable our actions of submission to the will of God become.

The Qur'an says, "Whoever turns his face to Allah and is a *Muhsin* [one who has *ihsan*] for him is a reward from His Lord and there is no fear for him, nor shall he grieve" (2:112). Much of our grief and fear in this life comes from our desire to change the past or to control the future. Since in the station of *ihsan* the seeker has surrendered their will before the will of God and fully trusted Him, when they meet God in the next life they will experience no fear or grief.

In *ihsan,* our attachment to the separate self dies, as we awaken in the reality of God's singularity.[19] Whereas *islam* refers to the physical, and *iman* relates to the intellectual, *ihsan* is about the spiritual dimension. In a deeper sense, *islam* is the actions that can be seen with the eyes, *iman* is the beliefs that cannot be seen but are held in the heart, while *ihsan* journeys beyond the duality of inner and outer to be in the presence of God alone. The expansive and unifying state of *ihsan* is poetically illustrated in the following poem:

> "*Out beyond ideas of wrongdoing and rightdoing, there is a field. I'll meet you there. When the soul lies down in that grass, the world is too full to talk about. Ideas, language, even the phrase 'each other' doesn't make any sense.*"[20]
>
> RUMI

In this profound poem, Rumi is reminding us that within the oneness of God's presence there is no self, there is no other, there is only God and so the multiplicity of words will always fall short of expressing the experience of the *Muhsin* in the mystery of divine unity.

The Stations of Ecstatic Love

The stations of Islam are simply three different depths into the ocean of divine love. The mystics poetically describe the correlation of love and the stations of *islam, iman,* and *ihsan* through the analogy of three butterflies before the flame of a candle.

The first butterfly sees the smoke from a flame rising in the distance and declares, "I know about love." This butterfly is in the station of *islam,* because she uses her rational intellect to outwardly deduce from the smoke that she sees the presence of light. This realm of knowing is known as *ilm al-yaqin,* or the "knowledge of certainty."

The second butterfly actually sees the light and feels the heat from the flame and declares, "I know how love's fire can burn." This butterfly is in a station of *iman,* because she not only intellectually believes in the presence of light but she has directly experienced the flame. This realm of knowing is known as *ayn al-yaqin,* or the "eye of certainty."

The third butterfly flies directly into the flame, dissolving itself within the light. This butterfly is consumed by love and so she has no words to offer. It is in the station of *ihsan*, because she has disappeared and become entirely embraced by the light of what she loved. This realm of knowing is known as *haqq al-yaqin*, or the "truth of certainty."

The places inside us where we are terrified by the flames of the truth are the places where our ego refuses to relinquish control and rely on God. We only know the truth to the extent that we surrender our separations and limits to become consumed by the truth of God. After all, one of the core missions of the Islamic path is to guide the seeker beyond just knowledge *about* God, to the experience and knowledge *of* God.[21]

It is only when we marry the outer with the inner that the door to having an intimate relationship with God is opened. If we neglect to integrate the outer actions of religion with the inner purification of the heart in a harmonious way, we will find our faith feels chaotic and imbalanced. If we ignore the outer rules and moral laws of the religion, we will be ungrounded, like a feather ruled by the passing winds of our fleeting desires. If we neglect the spiritual side of the path, our worship will lack passion and love, making us inevitably rigid and even fanatical in our approach to God.

It is only when we surrender our body, mind, and soul to God that we will be able to manifest the true message of peace that exists at the heart of the path of Islam. We are not called to follow Islam, we are called to *become* it. We are called to surrender, like grains of salt, into the infinite ocean of God's grace and abundance. When we surrender our will, mind, heart, and soul in this way, we don't lose ourselves, but instead become receptive to all that God seeks to create through us. This is the purpose of our creation: to let go of all that is bound to pass and become one with God's everlasting love.

> *Oh Allah, I do not seek to worship You from fear of pain or for longing for pleasure, but I seek to worship You for Your sake alone. My Lord, help me surrender my will within Your will. Help me move without resistance on the rivers of Your decree. Oh Allah, help me surrender to You like the seas, the moon, the stars, the mountains, and galaxies. Please help me to surrender to You like the leaves in the breeze. Allow me to*

give You all of myself by removing the veils of doubt and fear. Allah, guide me on the path of truth and help me dedicate my life to You alone. I pray that You make my heart grounded in the fertile soil of faith. Allah, please always remind me that only in You will I find peace, ease, and the keys to the innermost secrets You have hidden inside of me. My Lord help me be humble, honest, kind, and faithful as I walk this path You have paved from You to You. In Your supreme names I pray, Ameen.

Reflection: "Making Every Action into Worship"

Since worship is like nourishment for the spirit, the way oxygen is for the body, the more we infuse our day with acts of praise, the more lively our souls will feel. The question inevitably becomes, how can we be in a constant state of prayer when we have worldly obligations? The secret lies in the intention! Anything can be an act of worship if you make the intention of getting closer to Allah through that act. To reach the state of *ihsan*—to be in a perpetual state of awareness, worship, and witnessing of God—we have to begin bringing God-consciousness into everything we do. In order to better explain this, let's run through a list of daily activities, alongside intentional prayers that can be used to heighten our awareness of Allah.

- When you wake up in the morning, take a few deep breaths and bring your awareness to your heart. Before getting out of bed try saying, *"Oh Allah, You are The Awakener, Al-Ba'ith, thank You for giving me another chance to love, worship, and surrender to You more completely. As I get out of this bed this morning, help me step deeper into my faith and to feel the peace that comes from proximity to You."*
- Before brushing your teeth, you can say, *"Oh Allah, You are The Most Generous, Al-Karim. As I brush my teeth, may You allow the words of my mouth to spring from Your source of love, peace, and kindness. Allah, help me purify my tongue*

from the remembrance of anything other than You."

- When taking a shower, try saying, *"Oh Allah, You are The Most Pure, Al-Quddus, as I wash my body may I also wash away the mistakes of the day and my forgetfulness of You. May the blessing of water unveil the purity of my soul, allowing me to receive the light of Your mercy."*

- When putting on your clothes, you can say, *"Oh Allah, You are The Provider, Ar-Razzaq, as I dress my body with clothes that you have provided for me, may You dress my spirit with the cloak of holiness and light."*

- Before eating try saying, *"Oh Allah, You are The Nourisher, Al-Muqeet, thank You for this food before me, may this food serve to strengthen my body and keep me healthy and energetic to make my worship of You passionate and infused with love."*

- Before driving or getting on public transport, you can say, *"Oh Allah, You are The Bestower of Safety, Al-Muhaymin, may I safely travel from where I am to where I seek to be, both in this life and the next."*

- Before working, you can say, *"Oh Allah, You are the Creator, Al-Khaliq, as I begin this project, help me to reflect Your qualities of creativity, strength, and peace into my work. Allah, use me as a vessel to bring others closer in proximity to You."*

- Before seeing friends, try saying, *"Oh Allah, You are The Most Merciful, Ar-Rahman, may I interact with others in a way that reflects Your qualities of kindness, mercy, love, and compassion."*

- Before sleeping, you can say, *"Oh Allah, You are The All-Aware, Al-Khabir, while I sleep tonight, keep my heart awake in remembrance of You."*

- Take a moment and write down 2–3 other activities you do on a daily basis. Make sure to add an intentional prayer alongside each activity.

- Notice how your daily activities feel different when you bring the presence of Allah into them.

"And seek forgiveness of your Lord; then turn to Him wholeheartedly. Verily, my Lord is Merciful, Most Loving."

QUR'AN 11:90

"Oh son of Adam, so long as you call upon Me and ask of Me, I shall forgive you for what you have done, and I shall not mind. Oh son of Adam, were your sins to reach the clouds of the sky and were you then to ask forgiveness of Me, I would forgive you. Oh son of Adam, were you to come to Me with sins nearly as great as the Earth, and were you then to face Me, ascribing no partner to Me, I would bring you forgiveness nearly as great as the Earth."[1]

ALLAH

5

TAWBA: REPENT AND RETURN TO UNITY

No matter how far astray we have gone, no matter how far from God we have wandered, no matter how many sins we have committed, no matter what we have done or said, there is no place too far for God's infinite forgiveness and mercy to reach. One of the greatest gifts God has given us is the practice of *tawba*. One of the most commonly associated words with the Arabic word *tawba* is "repentance," but *tawba* actually more literally means "to return." *Tawba* is a hopeful reminder that our everlasting spirits cannot be irreparably stained by our mortal actions or words.

When we turn to Allah asking for forgiveness, we are in essence returning to who we really are, by removing the veils of sin that have prevented our true vision. As Allah says, "It is not the eyes that are blind, but the hearts" (22:46). *Tawba* purifies our heart so that Allah's light can penetrate our soul, giving us divine insight. In this way, repentance turns our inner gaze from a place of ego-consciousness to God-consciousness, returning our hearts from this mortal world and its fleeting desires to Allah and His eternal peace.

When we engage in sincere *tawba,* we reach out to Allah, praying for Him to cover our sins with the cloak of His mercy. At its essence, *tawba* is about tuning into and connecting with how loved we are by God. We don't have to understand every cause and effect of our mistakes in order to repent, because *tawba* is the act of surrendering the entire matter into the hands of Allah.

God's Guidance Begins and Ends with Forgiveness

The first prayer human beings made was one of forgiveness, when Adam and Eve ate from the forbidden tree and said: "Our Lord! We have wronged ourselves. If You do not forgive us and have mercy upon us, we will surely be among the losers" (7:23). Allah responded to this prayer by forgiving Adam and Eve as the Qur'an says, "Then Adam received from his Lord [some] words, and He accepted his repentance. Indeed, it is He who is the accepting of repentance, The Merciful" (2:37). The very first guidance God gave to us is to seek His forgiveness, and among the final prayers we human beings will make on the Day of Judgment will be a prayer seeking God's forgiveness. It has been said that as we approach the gates of Heaven we will pray that Allah amplifies the light of our heart by praying, "Our Lord, perfect for us our light and forgive us. Indeed, You have power over all things" (66:8). Asking for forgiveness is not something we should be ashamed of doing, but something God expects and wants us to do.

> *"A bad deed which you regret in your heart is a thousand times better than the good deed that makes you feel proud."*
>
> IMAM ALI

The Arabic word for "seeking forgiveness" is *istighfar* and is related to the Arabic word *al-mighfar,* which means "covering the head from something harmful." In other words, *istighfar* not only covers our sins with the mercy of God, but it also protects us from the harm that we inflict on our own souls.[2]

The act of seeking God's forgiveness is itself a protection from the consequences of our own actions. *Istighfar* is not just about seeking forgiveness from our sins, it is also about seeking forgiveness for not doing enough. Since as human beings we will always fall short in worshipping and serving God as He deserves, we seek for forgiveness for even our good actions, relying on God's mercy to fill in the gaps of our deficiencies. Whether we get distracted during prayer, or seek worldly praise for our acts of kindness, we are in desperate need for God to constantly cloak both our sins and our good deeds with the garment of His loving forgiveness.

> "Why do you not seek forgiveness of Allah that you may receive mercy?"
>
> QUR'AN 27:46

When we seek God's forgiveness, God actually elevates our station. As the Prophet Noah says in the Qur'an, "My people, seek forgiveness from your Lord and turn to Him in repentance. He will send you abundant rain from the sky and add strength to your strength. Do not sinfully turn away from Him" (11:52). When we respond to our humanity by seeking forgiveness and returning to God, He responds by raining upon us His blessings of grace. It is not in being perfect that we access God's mercy, but through *tawba* and seeking forgiveness.

Returning to the Oneness

Another word for repentance is "atonement," which can also be read as "at-one-ment," reminding us that when we seek forgiveness we become *at one* with God's mercy and love. Repentance is the act of emptying and breaking all the idols and gods we have placed in the sanctuary of our hearts before the one true God. We seek forgiveness for making gods of our desires, reputation, envy, money, fame, or other people's opinions. In essence, every sin we commit is an act of reaching toward the world for that which only Allah can give to us. Just like a shadow points to the light, sin points to the places within us that depend on the world to fulfill our needs instead of Allah.

When Allah makes us aware of a sin we committed, He is not punishing us, but rather inviting us toward His presence. In this way, the moment we are drawn to sincere repentance, we are in effect unveiling the forgiveness that Allah has already written for us to experience. Someone asked the great eighth-century mystic Rabia Al-Adawiyya, "I have sinned much; if I repent, will Allah forgive me?" She profoundly replied, "It is the opposite; if Allah forgives you, you are capable of repentance."

As the Qur'an says, Allah "calls you that He may forgive your faults" (14:10). It is not our repentance that leads to forgiveness, but Allah's infinite mercy and forgiving nature that acts as a divine force of gravity, returning us to who we have always been beneath the dust of forgetfulness and sin.[3] The fact that *tawba* means "return" implies that in every moment we have everything we need to walk toward Allah. In essence, *tawba* makes room for the blessings that Allah has already written for us to experience.

Begin Right Now

Our path of return to God begins exactly where we are. We are not meant to be worthy of God before we turn to faith, but rather it is through God's all-encompassing mercy (*Ar-Rahman*) that we are made worthy. In other words, there is no such thing as being too bad, too lost, or too broken for a God who created everything in existence to fix and repair. Rumi says, "Water says to the dirty, 'Come here.' The dirty one says, 'I am ashamed.' Water says, 'How will your shame be washed away without me?'" Even if we keep making the same mistake or falling for the same temptation, God calls us to keep seeking the cleansing waters of His mercy.

Do not listen to the voices that say you are too imperfect for a perfect God, that you are too filthy to be cleaned, or too horrible to be redeemed—no matter the life you have led, your mistakes or sins can never be greater than God's mercy.

> *"Oh My servants who have transgressed against their souls! Do not despair of the mercy of Allah. Indeed, Allah forgives all sins. Indeed, it is He who is the Forgiving, the Merciful."*
>
> QUR'AN 39:53

The Prophet Muhammad ﷺ said, "Satan said: 'By Your might, Oh Lord, I will continue to mislead the children of Adam, as long as their souls are in their bodies.' The Lord said: 'By My might and majesty, I will continue to forgive them, as long as they seek my forgiveness.'"[4] Ultimately, our greatest loss is living a life without asking God for forgiveness. Allah is *Al-Afuw* or "The Pardoner," whose forgiveness is like a divine presidential pardon: He completely eradicates the record of our sin and removes all the negative consequences of our choices. The mercy of God is why the Qur'an beseeches us to seek for forgiveness.

> *"Glorify the praises of your Lord and ask for His forgiveness. Verily, He is ever accepting of repentance."*
>
> QUR'AN 110:03

Do not be discouraged if you find yourself facing a problem or temptation that you thought you had already conquered. Spiritual progress follows the shape of a spiral: even when it seems like you are going back to where you started, you can actually be ascending in a deeper way. The practice of *tawba* is a means of spiritual course correction, in which we realign our hearts and intention toward Allah.

A modern-day example of the importance of checks and balances is airplanes. An airplane spends 90–95 percent of its time off course, due to weather and human error; the only way it reaches its desired destination is through constant course correction.[5] No matter how much we stumble off the straight path, we can still reach the destination of divine eternal love, so long as we keep striving to return.

Transforming Your Temptations into Prayers

Becoming more spiritual and God-conscious does not mean we're no longer tested with the voices and thoughts of temptation conjured by our ego, but rather that we have more awareness around the voices that call us toward darkness, shame, and separation. Just as the stars are always in the sky, but we only can see them in the darkness of the night, the voices of the ego and Devil may remain present. The difference between someone close to God and someone turned away from God is not in whether or not they are tempted, but rather in where they are focusing their attention.

The more we turn to God's light, the brighter the skies of our mind become and the dimmer the stars of the ego and Devil appear in comparison. Instead of looking to self-reliance to overcome temptation, we are called to lean into God. The Devil is an expert at using our imperfections to make us feel unworthy of having a relationship with God. If we try to fight the Devil we will always lose, so the only way to overcome the Devil is through the help of God.

> *"Those who are aware of God when a passing impulse from*
> *the Devil touches them, they bring God to remembrance and*
> *at once they see things clearly."*
>
> QUR'AN 7:201

No matter what the Devil tempts you with, instead of fighting the temptation or trying to figure out a way around it, go to Allah first. A powerful way to do this in practice is to respond to every temptation with a prayer. Take a moment and be conscious of the distractions or temptations you're experiencing. Whenever you are being drawn away from your heart and toward something that is against one of the commands of God and feels like it will not serve the holiness of your heart, you are being tempted by the Devil.

The voices of the Devil might sound like, *You are not good enough, you will always fall short...you will never overcome this addiction, you are too sinful for God...this is not that big of deal, just one more time and then you can give this up, God doesn't really care...God will not accept someone as bad as you anyway, so you might as well do what feels good.* You may even notice how the Devil thrives on hopelessness and despair. The Devil will use your shortcomings to instill fear and shame within you, trying to make you feel you are not worthy of having a relationship with God.

Once you are conscious of the voice of the Devil, don't fight his voice or be drawn into it; rather, turn it over to God in the form of a prayer. For example, if the Devil tempts you with lust, ask Allah for help in turning your desires toward Him. If the Devil tries to get you to stop praying, ask Allah for help in being more attentive in prayer. If the Devil attempts to shame you through shortcomings in your faith, ask Allah to help purify your intentions. When you become aware that the Devil attacks the places in your faith that are the weakest, his whispers of temptation actually become doorways into how to strengthen your faith and become closer to God.

When we turn away from Allah's light, like the Earth when it turns away from the sun, we fall into a state of spiritual darkness, not because Allah punished us but because out of our free will we chose to turn our awareness away from the light of truth. However, the darkness of separation is an illusion; Allah is closer to us than the very breath in our lungs. Repentance is returning our awareness to the divine connection we are already plugged into, by awakening us from the illusion of separation from God. When we return to face Allah through repentance, Allah not only forgives our sins, but the sins themselves become reminders of Allah's mercy and forgiveness. In this way, our sins become symbols of Allah's love and thus serve to return our gaze to the face of the Divine.

As the Qur'an says, "Except those who repent and believe, and do righteous deeds, for those, Allah will change their sins into good deeds, and Allah is All-Forgiving, Most Merciful" (25:70). Allah blesses us beyond what we deserve and gives to us without accounting from the storehouses of His grace. God is consistently seeking to forgive us; repentance is just one of the ways we can access His eternal and overflowing mercy.

> *"Our Lord descends to the lowest heaven in the last third of every night, and He says: 'Who is calling upon Me that I may answer him? Who is asking from Me that I may give to him? Who is seeking My forgiveness that I may forgive him?'"*[6]

PROPHET MUHAMMAD ﷺ

Turning Toward God

When we repent, we are simultaneously turning away from sinful actions and turning toward God for realignment on the straight path of truth. It is important to always ask God for help, but we must also strive to live by the principles that Allah has called us to foster within ourselves.

> *"Allah will not change the condition of a people until they change themselves."*

QUR'AN 13:11

When we turn from our sins, and actively and intentionally turn towards God's light, everything changes. Albert Einstein famously said, "No problem can be solved from the same level of consciousness that created it." In other words, repentance helps us change our state of mind and heart, shifting our frequency from ego-consciousness to God-consciousness—allowing us to tune into the channel of divine love that is continuously being broadcasted in every single moment. The Qur'an says, "Allah loves those who repent and those who purify themselves" (2:222), because repentance allows us to experience God's love by removing the veils of illusion and sin.

God's love for us does not change with the tides, it does not strengthen and weaken like the waxing and waning moon; it is consistent and unconditional for "God is independent of all creatures" (3:97). It is not Allah's love for us that changes, rather it is our awareness of His love that can become veiled. This is why how we act can have a profound effect on what kind of reality we experience. As the Qur'an says, "Then as for him whose measure of good deeds is heavy, He will live a pleasant life" (101:6-7). Through repentance and good deeds, God gives us the ability to open the blinds created by sin, allowing the light of God's love to come inside our hearts, bringing with it endless waves of peace and contentment.

When we realize that repentance is not something *we have to do,* but rather something *we get to do,* our whole life begins to change. We begin to see that when Allah gives us the awareness that we have sinned, He is not shaming us, but actually calling us back into the arms of His love. As Rumi says, "The wound is where the light enters," because it is in our weaknesses that we taste God's strength, it is in our shortcomings that we experience God's perfection, and it is in our brokenness that we feel God's mercy.

A perfect metaphor for this is found in an ancient practice in Japanese art called *Kintosukuroi,* meaning "golden repair." In *Kintosukuroi,* pottery that is broken is repaired with gold or silver lacquer, as a way of embracing and celebrating the beauty that comes with being broken.[7] The beauty in our imperfections is that, through repentance, our scars transform from moments of regret to reminders of God's mercy and compassion. It feels freeing to know that the ways in which we fall short are doorways back into the divine presence of perfection. As one mystic profoundly put it, "Oh my Lord! I am my weakness, but You are my strength."

The Infinite Power of God's Forgiveness

The Prophet ﷺ expressed God's incomprehensible mercy through a profound story he once told his companions about a man who had unjustly killed many people.

> There once was a man who, after killing 99 people, suddenly felt a sense of remorse and wanted to know if there was any chance that

God would forgive him. He found a holy monk and asked him if he would be forgiven by God if he repented. The monk made the mistake of saying that he would not be forgiven, so the man became angry and killed the monk.

Then the man sought out a famous scholar and told him that he had killed 100 people and wanted to know if there was any chance he would be forgiven. The scholar knew that in order for the man to change, his environment would have to change, so he replied, "Who stands between you and repentance? Go to such and such land; there [you will find] people devoted to prayer and worship of God, join them in worship, and do not come back to your land because it is an evil place."

The man made sincere repentance and set out on a journey toward a holy land of faithful believers. However, before he reached his destination, the man died. Upon his death, the angels of mercy and the angels of torment began to argue over who would take his soul. The angels of mercy said, "This man has come with a repenting heart to Allah." The angels of punishment said, "He never did a virtuous deed in his life."

God then sent a third angel, in the shape of a human being, to mediate between the two sides. The mediator said, "Measure the distance between the two lands. He will be considered to belong to the land to which he is nearer." The angels measured the land and found the man was closer to the land of piety, so the angels of mercy were commanded to collect his soul. Some commentators say that the distance that was measured was at first against the man, but Allah, through His mercy, stretched the earth in the man's favor.[8]

It's important to understand that on the Day of Judgement, those who have wronged, hurt, or killed people, will be held accountable for their actions in a perfectly just way. This story is not saying that we can do whatever we want and then passively seek forgiveness, but rather it is reminding us that we are redeemable if we sincerely turn back to God. This story reminds us that the light of divine compassion has a way of transforming even the hardest hearts. Mercy does not create the space for evil, hopelessness or feeling as if we are not redeemable or are inherently bad is what turns us away from God. As an ancient proverb says, "The child who is not embraced by the village will burn it down to feel its warmth." We must be less like the judgmental monk and more like the wise scholar. We cannot change the world through fear or shame. Change happens when we make the path easy for people, when we inspire them toward their greatest potential through hope and love. As the great scholar Imam Al-Ghazali said, "Half of the weight of the spread of disbelief in the world is carried by religious people who made God detestable to His creation through their terrible conduct and terrible speech." Our calling is not to judge people, but through love to inspire them toward their greatest potential.

> "Treat people with ease and do not be hard on them; give
> them glad tidings and do not make them run away."[9]
>
> PROPHET MUHAMMAD ﷺ

Forgive to Free Yourself

Tawba is not only about returning to God—it is also about returning to the creation as a mirror of God's mercy, compassion, and forgiving nature. When you forgive others, it is like pointing a flashlight into the mirror: you get back the grace you gave.

> "Good and evil are not equal. Repel evil with good and you
> will find that your enemy has become your close friend."
>
> QUR'AN 41:34

Forgiveness happens when you choose to see a person for their innate goodness, not their manifested evil—choosing to see someone for who God created them to be, rather than defining them by their worst actions. Responding to someone who wronged you by wronging them would be like trying to put out a wildfire by pouring gasoline on it. As the civil rights activist Martin Luther King, Jr. said, "Darkness cannot drive out darkness; only light can do that. Hate cannot drive out hate; only love can do that."[10] Forgiveness is not just about freeing another soul from the cage of their mistakes, but also about freeing ourselves from the prison of blame and judgment.

When we forgive others, we are releasing ourselves from the burden of someone else's transgressions.

The Prophet Muhammad ﷺ said, "Do not do evil to those who do evil to you, but deal with them with forgiveness and kindness."[11] We are called to forgive even those who are not sorry, even if the apology is insincere, not because someone deserves it, but because our heart deserves peace. When we hold onto anger as a means of punishing others we end up hurting ourselves more than anyone else. As the Buddha said, "Holding onto anger is like drinking poison and expecting the other person to die." Forgiving others frees us from the chains of our own anger. On the spiritual path, being merciful to others is one of the fastest paths of return into the presence of divine mercy.

"Those who are merciful will be shown mercy by The Merciful."[12]

PROPHET MUHAMMAD ﷺ

Opportunities for forgiveness are divine gifts, because they are moments when Allah is calling us closer to Him, through the embodiment of His qualities of forgiveness, patience, compassion and mercy. Not only do we get to know God more through emulating Him, but when we forgive others Allah in turn forgives and purifies us of our past sins. As Allah says in the Qur'an, "Whoever gives up his right as charity, it is an act of atonement for himself" (5:45). When we forgive others for the sake of Allah, He returns the favor by forgiving us for the sins that weigh heavy on our hearts. As the Qur'an says, "Let them pardon and overlook. Would you not love for Allah to forgive you? Allah is Forgiving and Merciful" (24:22).

It is important to point out that Allah has given us the right to seek justice. Nonetheless, whenever we are wronged, it is important to ask:

Is choosing to not forgive this person worth missing out on experiencing God's forgiveness? God calls us to forgive the unforgivable in others, because God continuously forgives the unforgivable in us.

> *As a mystic once said, "Be like the flower that gives its fragrance even to the hand that crushes it."*[13]

Even when we are wronged by others we must not wrong them. As lovers of God we are called to reflect the Divine's loving qualities upon all people without discrimination. Forgiveness does not mean we don't hold people accountable for their actions, but that we do so with compassion and mercy.

Forgiving Ourselves

We tend to compare our inner reality with other people's outward illusion of perfection, making it harder to forgive ourselves than others. God's mercy will always outweigh our sins, but the scales of self-hatred are often heavier than our feelings of self-love. We must learn to forgive ourselves for the things we did not know, before we had the opportunity to learn them. Everybody has perfect vision when they look back in hindsight, but if we want to move forward we must learn from the past, not live in it.

The following story wonderfully depicts how when we refuse to forgive ourselves, we hurt not just ourselves but all those around us.

> Several people were sitting on a small boat in the middle of the ocean when one of the passengers took out an axe and started chopping into the wooden floor beneath his feet. The other passengers cried out in horror, "What are you doing?" The man replied, "None of your business. I am doing this to my own portion of the boat!"

We are all on one boat—what happens to one of us affects the collective consciousness of the entire world. When you do not forgive yourself, and choose to punish or hurt yourself, all of humanity suffers. *Tawba* is not just about asking God for forgiveness, it is also about seeing ourselves as worthy enough to receive His mercy. The first step to self-forgiveness begins by looking at ourselves through the eyes of God, instead of through the eyes of our sins.

When we sin and turn to God in humility, our reliance on God increases. As Rumi says, "Where there is ruin, there is hope for a treasure." The awareness that we've sinned is cause for gratitude, because it creates a path of return to Him. Our inclination to repent is a sign that God is calling us toward Him. The Devil wants us to be occupied with our mistakes, because as long as we are looking at our humanity our eyes are turned away from the divine perfection of God. As long as we are looking at our sins, we are losing the opportunity to witness God's forgiveness.

It is important to be reminded that our fallibility cannot make an unchanging God love us any less. So the next time you make a mistake, don't allow yourself to drown in shame; instead, choose to consciously return your heart to Allah, for it is only in His remembrance that you can truly find peace. The doors of God are always open for those who sincerely seek to be in His presence. Every single day God gives us a new chance to be welcomed into the arms of His grace.

> *"And whoever keeps His duty to God, God will appoint a way out for him."*
>
> **QUR'AN 65:02**

Our God is faithful and His mercy wraps around us more completely than the arms of a loving mother embracing her infant child. The lights of His love, forgiveness, and mercy are always surrounding us; we simply have to open our eyes and receive His divine qualities that are already manifesting both within and around us.

How to Repent: The Path to Loving Forgiveness

A beautiful way to understand the steps of *tawba* is through the ancient Hawaiian practice of *Ho'oponopono*. In the Hawaiian tradition of healing, this powerful chant of repentance and reconciliation means "I'm sorry, please forgive me, thank you, I love you." This phrase is perhaps one of the most concise depictions of the essence of *tawba*. When we commit a sin, first we turn to Allah in regret for our sinful actions (I'm sorry), then we seek forgiveness and purification from the effects of our sin from both Allah and those we may have hurt (please forgive me), we then thank Allah for the invitation to return to His embrace of love and acceptance (thank you), and finally we set the intention of living a life aligned and rooted in the unifying love of Allah so that we don't repeat the same mistake (I love you).

When we are practicing *tawba,* we are not just asking God to forgive us, we are asking God to also return us to Him. The first step of this return begins by acknowledging the places and ways our hearts have turned away. It is important to allow ourselves to feel the guilt and remorse that manifests from having turned away from God. We are not called to punish ourselves, but to access the sincere grief of being disconnected from God.

Once we connect with our regret and guilt, we then want to tune into where we are holding these feelings in our body. When we feel where we are physically carrying resistance, anxiety, guilt, disappointment, or any other feeling that is coming up, we are ready to begin the healing practice of *tawba.*

We begin by placing our hands where we feel we are holding the weight of sin, and we call upon Allah to bring his healing light into this place of pain. Once we have made our intention to Allah, we take a deep breath in and on the exhale we recite *Astaghfirullah,* which means, "I seek forgiveness from Allah." When we repeat this chant consciously, bringing this sacred phrase to the places we feel constriction, we begin to feel a blossoming peace within us.

> *"If anyone constantly seeks forgiveness, Allah will appoint for him a way out of every distress and a relief from every anxiety, and will provide sustenance for him from where he could never imagine."[14]*

PROPHET MUHAMMAD ﷺ

Although *Astaghfirullah* is one of the most common chants of seeking forgiveness, one of the most profound and well-known prayers of repentance in Arabic is *Astaghfirullah al-'Azeem al-lazi la ilaha illa Huwal-Hayyul-Qayyum wa atubu ilaih,* which translates to "I seek forgiveness from Allah, The Mighty, whom there is none worthy of worship except Him, The Living, The Eternal, and I turn to Him in repentance."

The Prophet ﷺ said that if we establish a practice of reciting this prayer of forgiveness, even if our sins were as much as the foam on the vast oceans of the Earth, we would still be forgiven by the infinite grace of God.[15]

Returning to the Path of Love

Repentance is not about punishment, it is about returning to the path of love. We are called to sit in the fire of regret as a way to purify ourselves from the inclination to return to the same sin.

> *"Pure repentance is feeling sorrow in the heart, seeking forgiveness with the tongue, and having the intention to never do it again."*
>
> IMAM ALI

Every moment is an opportunity to turn to God. Regret and remorse are not meant to be utilized as a form of self-punishment, but to minimize our ego's longing for worldly desires through humility and neediness for Allah. Fostering a sense of remorse or guilt is not the same as shame, for sincere guilt is a product of our pure conscience that reminds us who we are by turning us away from sin and returning us to our essential goodness. Where guilt says something we *did* is wrong, shame says that *we* are wrong. If we respond to sin with shame, we run the risk of wallowing in our mistakes, instead of acknowledging our neediness and turning to God for help.

Although sin can veil the innate goodness of our souls, it cannot alter it. If we were truly bad, then there would be no point in repenting, for there would be no authentic good self to return to God. Just as polishing only makes sense if there is a diamond beneath the dirt, repentance only makes sense because we carry an innately good spirit beneath the dust of forgetfulness and sin. As Rumi says, "When they ask, 'How long will you boil in the fire?' Reply by saying, 'Until I am pure.'"

Repentance is the key to unlocking and escaping the prison of our limited perception of ourselves, so that we can see beneath what has happened to us, what the world thinks of us, and beyond our actions and words, there is a pure soul within us that is holy and perfectly beautiful. Perhaps this why the Prophet Muhammad ﷺ said, "By Allah! I ask for forgiveness from Allah and turn to Him in repentance more than seventy times a day."[16]

Repentance and remembrance of God helps to polish the rust on the mirror of our hearts, allowing us to see the beauty of Allah that is constantly being reflected through us. When we remember who God is, when we praise and magnify Him, when we come needy and desperate for His forgiveness, we actualize who we truly are beneath the weight of our sins. Repentance is letting go of our baggage, because we understand that by Allah's mercy we are not defined by our past. As the mystics say, "The ocean refuses no river," so how could an infinitely merciful God refuse any sinner? We are not worthy of God's forgiveness because of our repentance, but because God's mercy embraces all things, including our sin. This is why the mystics cleverly repent to Allah by saying: "Oh Allah, plead on my behalf with Yourself, do what is worthy of You, not worthy of me!"

> *"My Lord! Forgive and have mercy for You are the best of those who show mercy" (23:118). My Lord, return my heart to You when I turn away, remind me of You when I am forgetful, and guide me on Your path of grace with every step I take. Oh Allah, turn my gaze from my mistakes toward Your mercy. My Lord, in my faultiness, help me see an opportunity to return to You, in my*

*brokenness help me see Your healing power. Oh Allah, let
my shamefulness be cleansed with the waters of Your love
and let my sins be covered with the cloak of Your perfection!
In Your forgiving names I pray, Ameen.*

Reflection: "Deeper Dimensions of Tawba"

In every moment of our life, through our actions and intentions, we
are either in alignment or disconnection with our souls. To assure we are
not unconsciously choosing to oppress ourselves, it helps to have a daily
practice of accountability. The following exercise is a simple but powerful way to live by design instead of by default. For the next week, take 5
minutes every night before you sleep to mentally scan your thoughts and
actions of the day.

- Bring awareness to the moments that you witnessed God, honored your heart, and emulated divine qualities of love, kindness,
  forgiveness, peace, and unity.
- Celebrate these moments and express gratitude to Allah for
  bringing you closer to Him through His qualities.
- Once you have fully honored the spiritual successes of the day,
  bring awareness to the moments you felt forgetful of God in
  your actions or thoughts.
- Instead of judging or shaming yourself for these actions, show
  gratitude to Allah for showing you the places you turned away,
  so that you have the opportunity to course-correct.
- Take a moment to experience the feelings of remorse that come
  up and use the fuel of regret as a means of turning to God in
  repentance by saying: *Astaghfirullah al-'Azeem wa atubu ilaih*,
  which means "I seek forgiveness from Allah, The Mighty, and
  turn to Him in repentance."
- Repeat this chant 33–100 times.
- Be conscious of where you may be being hard on yourself.
  Remind yourself that Allah's mercy is and always will be greater

than your worst sins. Place your right hand on the center of your chest and make the intention of opening your heart to Allah's loving and merciful forgiveness.

- Allow yourself to experience a moment of gratitude, by saying, "*Alhamdullilah,* thank you my Lord for calling me back to You, by blessing me with the awareness that I have turned away."
- Make the intention of increasing the activities that brought you closer to God and diminishing the actions that turned your heart away from God.
- This may be difficult at first, so continuously turn to Allah and ask for His help in keeping you aligned with Him.
- Reflect and observe how your state may change over the course of the week. Journal about these changes.

Ash-hadu an la ilaha illa Allah

I TESTIFY THAT THERE IS NO GOD BUT GOD

Wa ash-hadu anna Muhammad-an rasul Allah

AND I TESTIFY THAT MUHAMMAD IS THE PROPHET
OF GOD

6

SHAHADAH:
THE ECSTASY OF
ONENESS

A seeker becomes a Muslim through the proclamation of the Testimony of Faith, known as the *shahadah*. The *shahadah* is our first doorway into the divine ocean of Islam. It creates the framework for deepening the process of surrendering to the Divine, both outwardly and inwardly. The *shahadah* begins with the intention of emptying the heart of all false gods, whether it be our attachments, desires, or beliefs, before affirming the existence of the one true supreme God. The second portion of the *shahadah* is testifying to the prophethood of Muhammad ﷺ; in essence, making the intention to follow in his footsteps. When a person declares from the heart in Arabic, *Ash-hadu an la ilaha illa Allah. Wa ash-hadu anna Muhammad-an rasul Allah*—which means "I testify there is no god but God. And I testify that Muhammad is the Prophet of God"—they are considered to be a Muslim.

It's important to point out that faith is not something we have to obtain or earn, but rather it is the journey of unveiling what we have already been given by God. Whereas disbelief leads to covering the self with illusions and misperceptions based on musings of the ego, faith is the journey of uncovering and discovering the higher self. The word for "disbelief" is often used interchangeably with the Arabic word *kafir,* which literally means "the one who covers the truth." In fact, when a farmer plants a seed in the earth and covers it with soil, in Arabic it would be said that he is performing the act of *kufr.* In a spiritual context, a *kafir* is someone who covers the priceless jewel of faith in their own heart. In the Qur'an, the word *kufr* is used as the opposite of *shukr* or gratitude, because covering up the truth is the greatest act of ingratitude. As the Qur'an says, "We bestowed wisdom on Luqman, saying, 'Be grateful to God: he who is grateful, is grateful only for the good of his own soul. But if anyone is ungrateful (*kafara*), then surely God is Self-Sufficient and Praiseworthy'" (31:12). For the Muslim, a true disbeliever is not one who is genuinely seeking the truth, but rather one who is aware of God's existence, but out of arrogance or ingratitude refuses to obey Him. In other words, being a *kafir* could be understood as a state of resisting the natural state of what it means to be human.

Nonetheless, it is important to point out that you can never force someone to convert or accept the message of Islam. The merit and value of faith comes from a human being's freedom to choose whether or not to accept what God has already given to them. This is why the Qur'an very clearly states, "There is no compulsion in religion" (2:256). Every single person on Earth already carries the seeds of faith within them; how those seeds grow depends on what God has planned for them and to what extent they strive spiritually.

"Whoever believes in Allah—He will guide his heart."

QUR'AN 64:11

If God wills for the human being to remove the weeds of falsehood and the veils of misperception (*la ilaha*), the divinely sown seeds of faith will naturally flower in the omnipresence of His light (*illa Allah*). There is a hilarious and profound story of the comical Mullah Nasruddin that beautifully depicts the notion that we human beings are a treasure chest and the gems of faith reside within us, not outside.

> One night, Nasruddin was crawling on hands and knees under a street lamp outside his house when a few of his neighbors came over and asked him what he was doing. The Mullah replied, "I have lost my keys and I am trying to find them!" His neighbors decided to help the Mullah search for his keys. After about 20 minutes, one of his neighbors asked, "Oh Mullah, do you remember the last time you had your keys?" The Mullah very confidently replied, "Yes! I was in my house." The neighbors all confusingly looked at each other, until one of them asked, "Then why are we looking for them out here on the street?"

> The Mullah casually replied, "Because the light is better here. My house is dark this time of night." The Mullah then stood up, looked each confused neighbor in the face, and then profoundly said, "How often do you search out in the world for the keys you carry inside of you? Don't travel the Earth in search of answers that are already in the treasure chest of your heart. The question and the answer come from the same place. Have the courage to dive inside, there are many keys and pearls awaiting to be discovered."

What we seek is within us; it cannot be found in the outer world. As Rumi says, "Why are you knocking at every other door? Go, knock at the door of your own heart."

Shahadah, Part 1: "I Testify That There Is No God but God"

Our work on Earth is not to find God out in the world, but rather to look inside and remember how close He already is to us. In fact, the word *shahadah* does not just mean "to testify," but also refers to something that is visibly witnessed. The visible witnessing that the *shahadah* represents is the soul's witnessing of the lordship and oneness of Allah during the Covenant of Alast.[1] When we bear witness to God's oneness in the present moment, we are in effect reaffirming our witnessing of God in a subtle world beyond our conception of time and space. When we say *la ilaha illa Allah,* we are not just saying, "There is no god but God," but also that there is nothing real in existence but God, because He is both the origin of all existence and the only destination of return.

Just as any number divided by infinity reaches toward zero—relative to God's infinite eternal nature, every finite form is reaching toward nothingness.

> *"All that is on Earth will perish but forever will abide the face of your Sustainer full of Majesty, Bounty, and Honor."*
>
> QUR'AN 55:26-27

Investing in any goal, outcome, or destination other than God is like investing in ice in the desert; with the passage of time you are bound to lose. If we make our desires our gods, we suspend ourselves in a constant state of anxiety and instability, for our emotions are constantly changing and fluctuating. When we take multiple forms as our god, we experience a constant state of chaos, because where there are multiple wills present there is friction, creating a lack of harmony (21:22). Where there is separation, there exists difference of opinion, which results in conflict and resistance. This is why the Qur'an says, "Allah puts forth a parable of a man belonging to many partners at variance with each other, and a man belonging entirely to one master: Are those two equal in comparison?" (39:29) If you take this world as your god, you become a servant of everything created; but if you take Allah as your one Lord, then everything on this Earth will serve you in the mission of spreading divine love and kindness.

All of the prophets of God were sent with the same message of reminding humankind of God's singularity and supremacy. As the Qur'an says, "We sent a messenger to every community, saying, 'Worship God and shun false gods'" (16:36). It is only when we surrender our will into the will of a singular supreme God, dissolving all separation in the embrace of the Divine, that our heart can finally taste the heavenly peace it so desperately seeks. The Prophet ﷺ confirms this through saying, "He who died knowing that there is no god but God will enter Paradise."[2]

To better understand the power of *la ilaha illa Allah,* it helps to break it into two parts: *la ilaha* or "There is no god" and *illa Allah* or "but God." When we break the phrase apart like this, we can see that God does not want us to come declaring only His existence, but He wants us to begin by declaring the nonexistence of everything else in creation. When we experience periods of loneliness or hopelessness, asking why people always have to leave, why nothing lasts forever, why everything around us feels like an illusion, we are in a state of *la ilaha,* which is a holy part of the process, so long as we keep walking to *illa Allah.* Feeling like this fleeting world will let us down is not void of the truth, but if we stay stuck in this place of negation, we will be veiled from witnessing God's love and care.

> *Do not place a period where God has placed a comma,
> because God's plan stretches beyond your moments of
> doubt and fear.*

If you can see your emotions as train stations you're riding through—instead of as your final destination—your feelings will not go against your faith (*iman*), but actually can serve to help your faith blossom. We must learn to bring all that we are to God, and trust that He can handle it. Our feelings of loneliness, sadness, and isolation are all perfect precursors to faith, so long as we keep steadfastly walking on the path to God.

The worst thing we can do is think that something we're feeling is so wrong and horrible that we isolate ourselves from God, thinking we're not worthy of being in His presence. We must remember that Allah doesn't expect us to be perfect; after all, our sense of self-worth is not dependent on us, but on God. When we bring our poverty, our neediness, and our nothingness to God, He meets us with His generosity (*Al-Karim*), His ability to satisfy all needs (*As-Samad*), and His richness (*Al-Ghaniy*). Just as if you want light in your room you must open the blinds, if you want the shadows and dark places in your being to dissolve, you have to open your heart to the light of Allah. In essence, all of existence is just a reflection of the light of God's grace manifesting into different forms.

> *"There is only One Light and 'you' and 'I' are holes in the lamp shade."*

MAHMAD SHABISTARI, 14TH-CENTURY PERSIAN POET

The separation we feel from God is just an illusion, for He is with us wherever we are. The "distance" between us and God is created from our forgetfulness. This is why when we find ourselves in a situation of uncertainty, doubt, or separation from God, it helps to sit in remembrance and repeat *la ilaha illa Allah*. This practice of remembrance shines the light of God through our veils of forgetfulness reminding us of our proximity to the Divine. It is helpful to remember, as we recite these holy words, that the passion that inspires us to seek God is a flower that blossoms from the seeds of faith God Himself planted within our souls. As Rumi says, "We are all knocking from the inside," longing for that which we already are but have yet to open our eyes to.

La ilaha illa Allah is the act of shedding the veils of creation, only to find that beneath everything created is the fragrance of an uncreated Creator. It is removing what is finite to find what is infinite; removing the multiplicity to find what is singular. The heart that actualizes *la ilaha illa Allah* becomes the metaphorical throne of God, because when we empty our hearts from all that is created, nothing remains but a polished mirror reflecting the eternal Creator. As Rumi says, "You have to open your hand to be held." You must first empty your cup of all illusion, for it to be filled with the light of Allah. You have to let go of what is perishing to be in the presence of the Eternal.

Whatever we carry in our hearts is what we are consciously and subconsciously witnessing. This is why the *shahadah* begins with an emptying of all the false idols we have consciously or subconsciously been holding on to. One way of understanding the value of this emptiness in relationship with *la ilaha illa Allah* is through the letter *Alif*. In Hebrew, *Alif* is often a silent letter that holds the structure of a word together. In Kabbalah or Jewish mysticism, they say the *Alif* is the nothingness that holds together all of existence.

Since it is in the state of emptiness that we create the space for everything, the negation of *la ilaha* must precede the filling of *illa Allah*. When we say, "There is no god but God" the lower case "god" refers directly to false idols such as material wealth, people, our desires, and anything we worship aside from Allah. Just as when you download new software you first have to uninstall the old version, before we declare God's oneness we have to negate all idols we carry within us. The spiritual value of this negation is humorously articulated through the following story.

> A mystic master by the name of Radiyya was once so overcome with divine love that she loudly declared, "Oh Allah, I am nothing, I am a nobody, I am less than morning dew dissolving in the presence of Your light!"
>
> One of Radiyya's students was inspired by his teacher's words and decided to also declare his nothingness before the majesty of Allah. When Radiyya overheard her student's utterances she turned to him and said, "Who do you think you are to declare that you are nothing?"

Radiyya was profoundly reminding us that nothingness or annihilation of the attachment to the ego before Allah is a high station. After all, nothingness or emptiness (*la ilaha*) is the precursor to true embodiment of faith (*illa Allah*).

When we place *la ilaha illa Allah* between us and the world, it creates the space necessary to be able to interact with the world in a healthy way. In psychological terms, to be a *shahid* or a witnesser of the ego is the doorway to mental and emotional freedom, because the first step to change is creating the space to become aware of the need for change. When we are too enmeshed in our feelings or the trials we are facing, it is like we are trying to read a newspaper with our face pressed against the page. Contemplating and meditating on *la ilaha illa Allah* as a means of detaching from the world and our ego creates the space necessary to witness the events of our life, instead of being triggered and ruled by them.

When we have fully self-actualized what it means to say *la ilaha illa Allah*, we become aware that wherever we turn from the east to the west there is only the face of God. Nothing exists without God's mercy and without Him continually sustaining it. This is why everything points back to God, by the very nature of its existence. This is profoundly illustrated through the following story:

> A great mystic once saw a child with a lit candle and was inspired to teach him something of the mystery of life. He pointed to the flame and asked, "Where did this light come from?" The boy bewilderingly looked at the light, then looked at the mystic. The boy then suddenly blew the candle out and said, "But where did it go?" The mystic was speechless. The child had unveiled a profound truth: where the light came from was the same place to which it would eventually return.

This passage exemplifies the Qur'anic verse, *inna lillahi wa inna ilayhi raji'un*, "To God we belong and to Him we shall return" (2:156). In the singularity of Allah, beginning and end, past and present, form and essence are integrated and united in a way that shatters the mind. Truly actualizing *la ilaha illa Allah* is understanding your complete and utter dependence on God. In the face of the Divine, all separation vanishes; there is no man, no woman, no outer or inner, because in the embrace of His all-encompassing love, the rivers of multiplicity unite in the ocean of His singularity.

Shahadah, Part 2: "I Testify That Muhammad Is the Prophet of God"

Once a seeker actualizes the soul's innate knowledge of God's existence and the desperate need for divine care, the question inevitably becomes, what to do with this knowledge. For the Muslim, the Prophet Muhammad ﷺ is the answer to this question. Over the 23-year period the Qur'an was revealed, its words were not written in a format that was accessible by the masses. When the Prophet's ﷺ followers thought of the Qur'an they would most likely think of the Prophet's ﷺ face and his voice reciting the words of revelation. In a sense, the message sent by God and the messenger were inseparable. The Prophet Muhammad ﷺ is fundamental to the Islamic declaration of faith because he represents what belief in God's singularity looks like in action. He is described as a "mercy to all worlds" and an "illuminating lamp" of guidance and discernment on the path of return to God (21:107, 33:46).

He is not just a messenger, but an embodiment of the message—a "walking Qur'an," a full moon reflecting the sun of divine oneness.[3] He is the epitome of what it means to actualize the human destiny of being simultaneously the humble servant of God and His chosen divine representative on Earth. It is through following his example that we can distinguish truth from illusion.

The importance of following in the footsteps of the Prophet Muhammad ﷺ can be beautifully exemplified by a phenomenon in the sport of cycling known as drafting. When cyclists ride in a group, the leader of the pack breaks the wind, creating a draft, through which those who are following him can peddle significantly faster, with less effort than cycling on their own. In essence, Muslims are all riding in the draft of the Prophet ﷺ on the path to God. He breaks through the winds of doubt, hopelessness, and fear through his leadership, allowing us to ride on the straight path of love with the least resistance.

The Qur'an may describe the Prophet Muhammad ﷺ as the "seal of the prophets," (33:40) but he is not solely the last chapter of prophethood, he is the bind of the book of prophecy. The message that he was sent with encompasses the essence of all divinely sent revelations that came before him. Like a fractal that carries the same image in the part as it does in the whole, the true revelation that was sent to all the prophets of God was the same message of God's oneness that was sent with the Prophet

Muhammad ﷺ. The Qur'an calls Muslims to say, "We make no distinction between any of His messengers" (2:285). If every prophet of God represents a puzzle piece in the picture of revelation, Muhammad ﷺ is seen as the final piece, which led to the completion of the divine message. He is seen neither as the Divine nor as angelic, but regarded as a mere mortal who was immersed in the sacred presence of God (18:110). It is said that when he prayed he became so empty of himself that only the remembrance of God remained. He fasted not just from food and water, but from everything between his spirit and his Lord. He not only gave his money and time to those in need, but he offered his entire being in charity before Allah.

The Prophet ﷺ actualized the true meaning of *la ilaha illa Allah* by his will being fully dissolved into the will of God. Therefore, the Prophet's ﷺ actions were a reflection of God's qualities manifested on Earth. Allah speaks to the station of this reality when He says the following:

> *"I am his hearing with which he hears, his seeing with which he sees, his hand with which he grasps, and his leg with which he walks. Were he to ask of Me, I would surely give it to him; and were he to ask Me for refuge, I would surely grant it to him."*[4]
>
> ALLAH

The Prophet Muhammad ﷺ is not only the vehicle of revealing the map of guidance, but he himself is a manifestation of that map. This is why in the Qur'an Allah says, "Whoever obeys the Messenger has obeyed Allah" (4:80). The Prophet ﷺ is a pure mirror of the Divine, a perfect instrument of God's will in service of all humankind.[5] Allah sent the Prophet Muhammad ﷺ as He sent prophets before him as a "bringer of glad-tidings" of God's mercy and forgiveness, a "warner" of God's justice, and a reminder that our actions have consequences (2:119).

The Prophet ﷺ was not sent as a king to rule the world, but rather sent to be like the humble Earth—a safe place for those who were afraid, a guide for those who were lost, in service of those who were poor, and an inspiration for those who were hopeless. He was not sent to make bad people good; rather, he was sent, like spring, to bring the dead seeds of faith back to life through divine mercy and light.

Who Was the Prophet ﷺ?

The Prophet Muhammad ﷺ traces his lineage to the Prophet Abraham, who is considered the father of monotheism by many Jews, Christians, and Muslims.[6] The Prophet Muhammad ﷺ was born in 570 AD in Mecca and died in the year 632, at the age of 62, in Medina. However, it wasn't until the Prophet ﷺ reached the age of 40, that the Angel Gabriel was sent to reveal the first words of the Qur'an to him.

After spending some time privately preaching to those he knew, God eventually commanded the Prophet Muhammad ﷺ to publicly call the polytheistic Arabs toward monotheism. Before the Prophet ﷺ announced to the tribe of Quraysh of Mecca that he was chosen by God as a prophet sent to reveal the Qur'an, he said, "Oh Quraysh! If I say that an army is advancing on you from behind the mountains, will you believe me?" The crowd responded, "Yes; because we have never heard you telling a lie."[7]

The people of Mecca trusted Muhammad ﷺ so much that they would call him *Al-Sadiq*, the truthful one, and *Al-Amin*, the trustworthy one. Despite his impeccable reputation for honesty, the overwhelming majority of Meccans rejected him as a prophet of God. Nonetheless, Prophet Muhammad ﷺ kept preaching the message of Islam, despite facing strong resistance both from many members of his extended family and from the most powerful tribal leaders of Mecca.

After withstanding several years of constant emotional and physical abuse from the Meccans, the Prophet ﷺ left Mecca and found refuge in the city of Yathrib, which is present-day Medina in Saudi Arabia. The Prophet's ﷺ leadership and the growing popularity of monotheism directly threatened the Meccans' economy, since Mecca was known as a center of idol worship.

To avoid a huge war, the Muslims and Meccans created the Treaty of Hudaybiyyah. On the surface, this treaty seemed like it favored the Meccans, but since it allowed for the Muslims to much more freely practice their religion, it resulted in more people coming to Islam. In reference to this treaty, the Qur'an said, "Verily we have granted you a clear victory" (48:1).

Not even two years after the Treaty of Hudaybiyyah was signed, the Meccans broke its terms, thus nullifying it. In response, the Prophet Muhammad ﷺ returned to Mecca with 10,000 of his followers and peacefully took over the city. In an act of unparalleled mercy, the Prophet ﷺ forgave all those who had spent many years abusing him and his followers.

In the last few years of his life, the Prophet ﷺ focused on protecting the Muslim borders from invasions and forming peaceful alliances with the different warring tribes of Arabia. It was not until the final year of his life, in 632, that the Prophet ﷺ embarked on his first and only *Hajj* pilgrimage in Mecca.[8] Now, more than 1,400 years after his death, the mercy, forbearance, faith, and patience that the Prophet ﷺ responded with to the changing tides of his life continuously influences and inspires the way Islam is practiced around the world.

Inspiring Stories of the Prophet ﷺ

One of the many reasons the Prophet Muhammad ﷺ has been respected and honored by Muslims and non-Muslims worldwide is due to his honesty and unique ability to find a peaceful resolution to conflicts that faced his community. There are numerous stories that document the noble characteristics of the Prophet ﷺ. The following well-known story beautifully highlights the Prophet's ﷺ ability to problem solve in a way that helped strengthen bonds between people:

> A fire had once damaged parts of the *Kaaba,* which at the time was a structure that was being used to house hundreds of idols from the various tribes that came to Mecca for pilgrimages and trade.[9]

During the renovation of the *Kaaba* the leaders of the different clans of Mecca decided to remove the sacred Black Stone *(Al-Hajaru Al-Aswad)* that was near the *Kaaba* walls until construction was finished.[10] Once the *Kaaba* walls were fixed, the tribal leaders of Mecca began to argue over who would be given the honor of returning the Black Stone to its holy place.

Before the pride and egos of the leaders escalated the conflict, an elder suggested they accept the decision of the next man to come through the precincts of the *Kaaba*. As Allah had destined, Muhammad ﷺ, who had not yet been told he was a prophet, was the first man to walk in through the gates.

After Muhammad ﷺ heard the source of their conflict he took a piece of cloth, placed the Black Stone upon it, and in order to honor every clan equally, he asked each clan leader to grab a corner of the cloth. All the clansmen unified together and took the stone toward the *Kaaba*. Then Muhammad ﷺ put the stone in its rightful place.

Even several years before publicly becoming a prophet, Muhammad ﷺ emulated an innate ability to creatively problem-solve and build unity amongst the community, while preserving the hearts of all those involved.[11] From the very beginning of his life, the Prophet Muhammad ﷺ sought ways to inspire peace and oneness among the creations of His Lord.

If you study the life of the Prophet ﷺ you will see that he was not concerned with attaining power, money, or fame, but rather his only goal was to please His loving Lord. In fact, when one of the Prophet's ﷺ followers saw his living quarters, he began to cry. When the Prophet ﷺ asked why he was crying, he said that while the kings of Persia and Rome lived in luxury and comfort, he couldn't bear that the Prophet of God ﷺ would sleep on a mat that was so rough that it left behind marks on his body. The Prophet ﷺ responded by reminding his companion that the comforts of this life meant nothing to him. Perhaps this is because his eyes were on the Hereafter, where the comforts were without end, where the beauty was without comparison, and most important, where he would be in close proximity with his Lord.[12]

Even though the Prophet ﷺ had the entire treasury of Islam under his control, he refused to take from it to satisfy even his most basic needs. He was a quiet and humble man that never deemed himself as superior to others, despite the calling God had given him. Even though Muhammad ﷺ was the highly esteemed final Prophet of God ﷻ, a leader of the Muslims, and a judge, he still milked his own goat,[13] mended the holes in his clothes, and helped his family with chores around the house.[14]

As the Qur'an says, "Certainly you have in the Messenger of Allah an excellent example for anyone whose hope is in Allah and the Final Day and remembers Allah often" (33:21). It is through the example of the Prophet ﷺ that we learn how to put the teachings of the Qur'an into practice. Many Muslims read stories of the Prophet ﷺ and follow his *sunnah* or tradition, to learn by example how to be merciful, forgiving, and kind even when people are harsh, hateful, and hurtful to you.

> One of the most profound examples of the Prophet's ﷺ compassion is illustrated in the story of an old woman who lived in his neighborhood and threw trash at him every day because she vehemently disagreed with his religious views. On one particular day, the Prophet ﷺ noticed that his neighbor was not outside as usual, waiting to harass him. When he inquired about her whereabouts and found out she was sick, he went to visit her, to see if there was anything she needed. When she saw him, she was humbled by his compassion and amazed by the gentleness of his spirit, which inspired her to become a Muslim.[15]

In another instance, when his companions asked him to curse the idolaters of Mecca, who were harassing and physically abusing the Muslims, the Prophet ﷺ replied, "Verily, I was not sent to invoke curses, but rather I was only sent as mercy."[16] Even when the Prophet ﷺ went to the city of Taif and was met with a shower of stones and profanities, he did not pray for its destruction; rather, he prayed for the people, with the hope that perhaps their offspring might grow up to believe in the message of divine love.[17]

The Prophet ﷺ was inclined to believe that the goodness that resides in the heart of all human beings could blossom at any moment if God willed it. His eyes were spiritual x-rays that saw beyond the surface. He saw the flower in the seed, the dawn in the night, and the full moon in the crescent. He saw the best in people, he saw their greatest potential, and watered that reality inside of them with the sincerity of his words and the light of his love.

The power of the Prophet Muhammad's ﷺ presence is emulated in the Qur'an; the word used in the Qur'an to describe the light of the sun is the same word used to describe the illuminating nature of Prophet ﷺ. In reference to the sun the Qur'an says, "Blessed is He who has placed in the sky great stars and placed therein a lamp (*sirajan*) and luminous moon" (25:61). In reference to the Prophet ﷺ, the Qur'an says, "And one who invites to Allah, by His permission, and an illuminating lamp (*wa-sirajan*)" (33:46). Just as the sun sets, but is not gone, the Prophet Muhammad ﷺ may have died, but the light of the message he was called to bring to this world continues to be reflected in the moonlike hearts of his most sincere followers.

Since the Prophet ﷺ is seen as fully human and not God, his humanity creates a bridge of understanding between his life and the lives of all human beings. If you have ever been an outsider, a refugee, a stranger in a land that is not your home, know that the Prophet ﷺ intimately knows how that feels, as he was exiled from his home due to his belief in one God. If you have ever lost someone you love and the grief is shattering your heart, know that the Prophet ﷺ knows how you feel, because he lost the love of his life, Khadijah, and all of his sons at a young age. If you were born an orphan or lost your parents later in life, know that the Prophet ﷺ has felt the silent weight you carry, because he lost his father before he was born and his mother died when he was six. If you have ever felt rejected by your friends or family, know that the Prophet ﷺ was verbally and physically harassed by his neighbors and close relatives. If you have ever felt in the heart of your soul that you were sent to this Earth for a purpose that those around you do not understand or support, know that the Prophet ﷺ also struggled for many years before the message of divine mercy began to be accepted.

The Prophet ﷺ knows what it feels like to be where you are, and he has reached the peaks where you seek to be. In your greatest successes and in your most devastating failures, take the Prophet Muhammad ﷺ as your guide because the example of his life is a compass that will lead you to a paradise of contentment.

The Prophet ﷺ Reminds Us Who We Are

In the Qur'an, Allah honors the Prophet Muhammad ﷺ by saying, "You are, indeed, of a sublime nature" (68:4). In esoteric commentaries, scholars have suggested that often when Allah says "you" and lovingly addresses the Prophet Muhammad ﷺ, He is also addressing the inner purity of all humankind. Every human being originated from a single soul (7:189), so when we contemplate and witness the beautiful attributes of the Prophet Muhammed ﷺ, and the prophets that came before him, we begin to see the innate beauty of our own soul. Just as you cannot crave something you have never tried, you cannot see in another person a quality you have never tasted within yourself. Like spiritual salt, the Prophet Muhammad ﷺ brings out the diverse flavors of the divine names that are hidden within the recipe of every human soul.

> As the mystics say, "The teacher kindles the light; the oil is already in the lamp."

The Qur'an says, "To every nation we sent a messenger" (16:36), because it is only through a prophet manifesting the divine word into action that we can really experience what it means to live a life in devotion to God. Just as we would not judge the performance of a sports car by a bad driver, we cannot understand Islam through the actions of a supposed Muslim who does not honor the laws of love that are at the core of the religion. The path of Islam can most completely be understood through the example of a perfect Muslim, which is none other than Prophet Muhammad ﷺ. The lives of the divinely chosen prophets of God are the most perfect commentaries on the revelations they were sent to bring humanity. In essence, the prophets act as placeholders for a higher frequency of being.

When we call upon the Prophet ﷺ and bless him, we are spiritually pulling ourselves toward a higher vibration that allows us to see what could not be seen in the darkness of ignorance. When we send blessings upon the Prophet ﷺ, we are actually engaging in an act of worship, because we are following a commandment of God. As the Qur'an says, "Allah and His angels shower blessings upon the Prophet. Oh you who believe, send blessings on him and salute him with worthy greetings of peace" (33:56). Remembering and calling upon the purity of the Prophetic Light (*Nur Muhammadi*) inspires the goodness that resides within the soul of every human being to open and blossom. When we send blessings upon the Prophet ﷺ, we are also sending blessings of peace upon ourselves, for he is a reflection of the purest and most aligned parts of our own being. After all, it is not in the criticism or shaming of our sinfulness that we are inspired to be better, but rather through the witnessing of our greatest possible potential as a human being.

The more we discover about human psychology, the more we understand the importance of having prophets to expand our limited scope of reality. This is perfectly illustrated through the modern example of the runner Roger Bannister.

> In 1954, Roger Bannister was the first recorded runner in history to run a mile in less than four minutes. Fascinatingly enough, just a few years after Bannister's historic run, over a dozen runners were recorded running a mile in less than four minutes. Banister did not just break a record—he broke the psychological barrier in people's

minds of what was physically possible.[18] Similarly, God sent prophets to Earth to break the spiritual barriers of conventional thinking, by exemplifying the possibilities of human potential through divine assistance and grace.

In addition to being compared to the sun, the Prophet Muhammad ﷺ is also symbolically known as the full moon, because he fully faced the divine sun of Truth, and was sent to illuminate the dark nights of our souls. He embodied the divine message in his gentleness, mercy, loving kindness, and forgiving nature. His actions unveiled the spirit of the scripture, his words clarified misperceptions in the understanding of revelation, his character embodied the model of worship, and he became a human example of what it means to manifest into action the truth of God's oneness. The Prophet ﷺ was sent to teach us how to purify the heart from the lower qualities of the ego, such as jealousy, envy, greed, lust, and arrogance through the practices of repentance (*tawba*) and remembrance (*dhikr*). The Prophet ﷺ taught us that what we see in the world is a reflection of what we carry within us, and so in order to transform our lives we must transform our hearts.

> *If we do good deeds but have a rotten heart, we are in a state of hypocrisy. If we have a good heart but do not do good actions, then we are in a state of illusion.*

The Prophet Muhammad ﷺ was sent to teach us how to integrate inner purification with outer obedience, so that we can reach a state of completion in our spiritual journey. As the Prophet ﷺ said himself, "I have come to complete the noble character traits."[19] The Prophet ﷺ showed us that leadership is not just about authority; it is about influencing hearts through love and leading a life worth being followed.

The Prophetic Light of Wisdom

The prophetic role of inspiring unity and peace through the light of wisdom is beautifully illustrated in the following story narrated by Rumi:

A wealthy man gave a single gold coin to four strangers, with the instruction that it should be shared amongst them. The first man, who was Persian, said, "I want *angur!*" The next was an Arab, and she said, "I want to buy *inab!*" The third man was a Turk and said, "I don't want *angur* or *inab*, I want *uzum!*" The fourth was a Greek woman who said, "I don't want any of these things, I want *stafil!*" Since none of these four strangers spoke each other's language, they started to fight.

A wise man who spoke many languages came across the four people arguing and asked if he could help. When the four strangers told him in their different languages what had happened, the wise man smiled and said, "Ahh, well, I can satisfy the desires of all four of you with one coin. Trust me and I will make your one coin seem as if it was four, and your four desires will be unified together." Rumi then tells us, "Only a person of such wisdom would know that each in his and her own language wanted the same thing: grapes. Many cultures, ideas, and religions, have many things in common, but they are not aware of it."[20]

The prophets are like the wise man; they are people chosen by God to share the profound truth that no matter what we call the object of our seeking, we are all in fact reaching for one thing: Allah. Some may call it Justice *(Al-'Adl)*, Love *(Al-Wadud)*, or Oneness *(Al-Ahad)*. Others call it Richness *(Al-Ghaniy)*, Awareness *(Al-Khabir)*, Greatness *(Al-Kabir)*, or God *(Allah)*. However, ultimately these names point to the same singular God, who manifests Himself through the face of His infinite qualities. Every prophet that has been sent since the time of Adam was sent with the singular goal of revealing that beneath the illusion of outer forms, nothing but the reflection of Allah's names exists. It is because the Prophet Muhammad ﷺ has traveled to heavenly destinations we seek to reach that he has proven to be the perfect guide to bringing us closer to God, The Most High *(Al-'Aliy)*

Prophet Muhammad ﷺ came to offer the divine message of pure monotheism in its entirety, which is why, when you affirm his prophethood, you affirm every divinely sent prophet that came before him. The path to God necessitates the need for guidance because, as finite beings, we cannot understand an infinite and eternal Creator unless He chooses to tell us who He is. Although we cannot know entirely who God is, for "There is nothing like Him" (42:11), through the example of Prophet Muhammad ﷺ, and the prophets before him, we are shown how to live our lives in relationship with God. The prophets are guides that show us how to walk *from* Allah *to* Allah *by* Allah through experiencing the divine names, that are manifested both inwardly within us and outwardly through His glorious creation.

Whereas the first part of the *shahadah* declares God's singularity, the second part confirms the validity of faith, through the confirmation of action through the guidance of the final Prophet ﷺ sent to man. When we follow the Prophet ﷺ, we are not following a mortal man, but are being led by the light of God, shining through the lamp of the Prophet's ﷺ presence. We do not worship the messenger, we worship the One who sent the message, because whereas all human beings will one day die, the light of God's message is forever. We are called to anchor our souls deep into the seabed of divine light, because when the sun of God's love rises, the dark night of despair melts away. When God unveils the illusion of separation and shows His face, nothing but the symphony of peace will resonate through the strings of existence.

> *Oh Allah, let us never forget that "There is no God but You! Highly exalted are You!" (21:87) Allah, help us to turn to You alone for help and guidance. Oh Allah, help us to worship You alone and make no distinctions between any of Your messengers. "Ash-hadu an la ilaha illa Allah Wa ash-hadu anna-Muhammad-an rasul Allah. I testify that there is no god but God. And I testify that Muhammad is the Prophet of God ﷺ." My beloved Lord, allow the light of your Prophet ﷺ to shine upon the path of truth, just as the messengers before him lit the path of truth for their people. "Our Lord! we believe*

in what You have revealed and we follow the messenger,
so write us down with those who bear witness" (3:53). In
Your unifying names I pray, Ameen.

Reflection: "La Ilaha Illa Allah"

La ilaha illa Allah is one of the most powerful sacred phrases within Islam. The following practice is a simple but profound way of becoming receptive to the blessings of this holy chant:

- Find a comfortable place to sit, with your feet grounded on the floor.
- Connect with your breath. Witness your natural pattern of breathing.
- Make the intention of turning away from all other than Allah.
- Chant *la ilaha illa Allah* 33–100 times.
- Once you feel comfortable reciting this, practice elongating the words to feel the real impact of each letter.
- Elongate the *la* and *ha* in *la ilaha* while emphasizing the *il.*
- Emphasize the *ill* in *illa Allah,* while elongating the *ah* in *Allah.*
- All together it would be pronounced as *laaaaa ILahaaaaa ILLa Allahhhhhhh.*
- Do this repetition for five minutes.
- Notice how you feel before and after this practice.

Reflection: "Connecting with the Light of the Prophet Muhammad ﷺ

The Prophet Muhammad ﷺ is more than a messenger—he carries the light of the message. When we send blessings upon the Prophet ﷺ, we join the angels in praise of his beautiful soul, step into the river of his light, and are washed of our impurities through the example of his excellence. The following practice is a direct doorway to experiencing this powerful Prophetic Light or *Nur Muhammadi:*

- Find a comfortable place to sit with your feet grounded on the floor.

- Connect with your breath. Witness your natural pattern of breathing.

- Once you feel centered and calm, ask Allah, *"Oh Allah, help me to open my heart and allow my soul to drink from the holy light of Your Prophet ﷺ."*

- Take a few more breaths allowing yourself to open more to the Prophetic Light.

- Once you feel ready, begin by repeating, *Allahumma Salli 'ala Sayyidina Muhammadin wa Aalihi wa Sabihi Wasallim,* which means *"Oh Allah! Send Your blessings upon our master Muhammad and his family and his true companions, and grant peace."*

- Repeat this phrase silently and aloud. Notice the difference.

- Contemplate on how, when you send blessings of peace upon the Prophet ﷺ, you are sending blessings upon yourself, for he is like a polished mirror—whatever you shine upon the Prophet ﷺ reflects back to you.

- Place your hand on your chest bringing your awareness to your heart, then repeat *Allahumma Salli 'ala Sayyidina Muhammadin wa Aalihi wa Sabihi Wasallim* at least 33 times.

- Take 2–3 minutes to write down any insights and feelings that come up.

- Repeat this practice whenever you feel disconnected from your true essence.

"Oh believers, remember Allah often and with a lot of remembrance, and glorify Him in the morning and evening."

QUR'AN 33:41-42

"All that is in the heavens and all that is in the earth glorifies God, The King, The Holy, The Mighty, The Wise."

QUR'AN 62:1

"Seek help in patience and prayer; and truly it is hard save for the humble-minded."

QUR'AN 2:45

7

Salat: How to Tune Into Divine Love

The Arabic word for ritual prayer is *salat,* which originates from the triliteral root *sad-lam-waw,* which means "supplication, to follow closely, connect, attach, and bind together."[1] When we pray, we unplug ourselves from the matrix of this world and connect into the divine reality of Truth (*Al-Haqq*). The *salat* is a daily body prayer that incorporates gentle, yoga-like movements with special recitations from the Qur'an, as a means of integrating mind, body, spirit, and soul in the worship of Allah. *Salat* is a charging station where five times a day, we are called to connect to the Source, recharging the battery of our spiritual hearts through the electric love of God.

Allah says, "I have not created the invisible beings and humankind except to worship Me" (51:56). The purpose of our creation is to know, love, and ultimately worship our Lord, through becoming an instrument of His unconditional love. The *salat* is like an antenna that tunes our awareness to the station of divine love that is continuously being broadcast into our universe.

Allah says in the Qur'an, "He is with you wherever you are" (57:04) and that He is closer to you than your jugular vein (50:16), so prayer is not a means of getting closer to God, but a way to remember how close we already are to His all-encompassing presence.

> *"And when My servants ask you concerning Me, then surely I*
> *am near; I answer the prayer of the supplicant when he calls*
> *on Me, so they should answer My call and believe in Me that*
> *they may walk in the right way."*
>
> QUR'AN 2:186

When we sincerely ask for God, He answers our call and unveils His proximity to us. When we turn to God, leaving our sense of self behind, we come to see that we are not separate from this universe, that God is not in some faraway future Heaven, but that everything in this creation is reaching for and reflecting God right here and now.

> *"Your task is not to seek for love, but merely to seek and find*
> *all the barriers within yourself that you have built against it."*
>
> RUMI

Just as waterwheels raise water from a flowing river toward a fertile garden, prayer pulls our consciousness from the flow of our passing thoughts toward the garden of the eternal soul. Prayer is more than physical motions; it is more than words of praise and gestures of humility. When we pray, we join the orbit of love: we flow with the rivers, sway with the trees, dance with the moon, and sing with the birds. When we pray, we join with what is and has always been, in constant praise of the Divine.

> *"Have you not considered that those in the heavens and the*
> *Earth, the sun, the moon, the stars, the mountains, the trees,*
> *the animals, and many people, all bow down to God?"*
>
> QUR'AN 22:18

Prayer is not about punishment or reward, it is about cultivating an intimate connection with God. The deep purpose of prayer is not to obtain a certain outcome; rather, it is about having an intimate conversation with your Lord.

Prayer Is for *You*

God does not need us to pray for Him, therefore our prayer is not for God, but for the protection of our own souls (45:15). If every time we committed a sin we stopped praying, no one on this Earth would pray. It is human to sin, so the faithful are not those who are perfect, but those who return to God after they have gone astray.

> *"Come, come, whoever you are. Wanderer, worshiper, lover of leaving. It doesn't matter. Ours is not a caravan of despair. Come, even if you have broken your vows a thousand times. Come, yet again, come, come."*
>
> RUMI

The *salat* is not about achieving a specific outcome; rather, it is about stepping into the waterfall of Allah's mercy, which has been and always will be pouring down upon us. We should never hold back from praying to God because we feel too imperfect, unworthy, or sinful, because although our honoring of God is limited by our fallible mortal nature, God's mercy for us is endless and infinite.

> *We do not worship God and declare His greatness because He forgets how great He is, but rather because we forget how small we are and how needy we are for His grace.*

Prayer is a divine blessing, because by its very nature it removes the veils between God and us, returning us to our natural state of love. As the Qur'an says, "Prayer prohibits immorality and wrongdoing" (29:45), because it consistently reminds us of who we are and why we are here; prayer has a way of easing our souls from the burdens of this world, by constantly turning our attention from the creation to the Creator.

Often people look at prayer in terms of what they might gain from it; but prayer is not about gain as much as it is about letting go of all that prevents you from witnessing your innate alignment with God. The *salat* shines a light on the mental idols we carry with us that we struggle with surrendering to God: whether it be obsessing about what people think of us, trying to manage our schedule for the day, thinking about how we will pay our bills, or how we can be more successful, all the distractions we experience during prayer are places in our life where God is calling us to surrender to Him. Surrendering does not mean we no longer put effort into solving the different problems of our life; rather, it means that we do not take ownership over the outcomes. It is only when we bring our awareness to what keeps us from being present with God and slowly return our consciousness to Him that we can begin to feel contentment.

> *If we pray only when we feel like it, then we are not praying*
> *for God, but for our egos to feel a certain way.*

Prayer should not be used as a means to an end, because connection and conversation with God is the whole purpose of life. *Salat* can be one of the greatest opportunities to foster patience and gratitude, because we are called to pray to God regardless of how we feel or what we are going through. We are called to be consistent in prayer, even on the days when we feel disconnected from God, because He is not disconnected from us. When we are grounded in the soil of prayer, we are able to be grateful in times of blessing, and graceful in times of difficulty and despair.

Sometimes we can get stuck focusing so much on what we are getting out of prayer that we miss out on being grateful for all the harm and negativity that prayer removes and protects us from. As the Prophet ﷺ famously asked his companions, "Tell me, if one of you had a river at your door and you washed five times a day, would any filth remain?" His companions said that no filth would remain. The Prophet ﷺ then said, "That is the likeness of the prayer; five times a day, God obliterates wrongs with it."[2]

The *salat* is the "center pole" of the tent of faith, because of how it unveils our inner idols and connects us with the Divine.[3] Prayer is like a spiritual shower that washes the dirt of forgetfulness from the spirit. It is like a flashlight, bringing to light all the hidden idols and barriers we have placed before God, that veil us from fully basking in the sun of His eternal presence, so that we can purify ourselves.

> *The distractions that arise during prayer—the fleeting thoughts, regrets of the past, and anxiety about the future— are all part of the wisdom of the prayer.*

It is important to understand that, just as when we get closer to a light source our shadows become greater, as we approach the light of God, the Devil and the voices of darkness can grow, working harder to pull us away from the Divine. However, when Allah unveils an idol or barrier we place before Him, it is not to punish or shame us, but rather as a deep mercy, because only when we become aware of an idol can we begin the process of breaking it.

Prayer is not a means of avoiding or repressing our feelings; rather, in prayer we are called to stand in the brokenness of our experience and turn to Allah in that place. God wants us to come to Him with our problems, struggles, and even our idols. God wants us to surrender to Him so that He can guide us back to who we have always been, but lost sight of in sin. The Prophet ﷺ said, "The key to Paradise is prayer"[4] because prayer connects us to God, purifies the eyes of the heart, and realigns us on the path back to the heavenly gardens that we once called home. In a sense, prayer is not a map to a place we have never been, but an unveiling of who we already are.

God Gave the *Salat* to the Prophet ﷺ

Salat is the only pillar given directly from Allah to the Prophet ﷺ without the intercession of the Angel Gabriel. It is through the divine revelation and prophetic inspiration that God speaks directly to man, and it is through prayer that we speak and relate to God, on behalf of ourselves and all other creatures on the Earth. This is why, even when we pray in solitude, we say, "You alone *we* worship; You alone *we* ask for help"

(1:5). In every moment, through everything that Allah has created, He is speaking to us, and prayer is how we reply, and show our gratitude.

> As the mystics say, "If you don't have time to remember God
> for thirty minutes, then remember Him for one hour."[5]

In other words, if you do not have time for the Creator of time, you need prayer more than you think. What a restful night's sleep does for the body, prayer does for the soul. What most people fail to understand is that when we pray we are actually taking back time's dominion over us. To understand how, consider the following: The famous physicist Albert Einstein proved with his theory of relativity that time is relative. Einstein's theory says that, as an object gets closer to the speed of light, time slows for that object.[6] A single ray of light traveling through space is in an eternally present moment with no past or future. If we were to somehow enter into a wave of light, time would stop. This is why whenever we sincerely connect to the presence of Allah, who is known as "The Light of the heavens and the earth," time begins to expand (24:35).

The Qur'an says, "A day with Allah is like a thousand years as you count them" (22:47), because the closer we get to the gravity of Allah's infinite light, the more time begins to slow down. The secret to having more time is not to rush, but rather slowing down in mindful prayer, allowing the light of God to draw you into its timeless presence. Angels are made of light, meaning they are in the present moment with their worship and praise of God. When we mindfully pray with both our bodies and our voices we are mirroring the praise of the angels in the highest celestial realms.

The more we humble our egos and turn away from the illusion of separation, the closer we get to unveiling the all-encompassing oneness of Allah. When we turn down the chaotic voices of the mind, tuning instead into the gentle presence of God in the heart, we are better able to hear the continuous stream of God's guidance. This is why the soul of the prayer is said to be in the position of prostration, because it is the only position in which the heart is elevated above the mind, reigning as the conscious king of the body. When we prostrate, the head is lower than the heart, making blood and oxygen flow to the brain more effortlessly, which research has indicated may help relieve stress and depression.[7]

When we pray in direct contact with the earth, as the prophets used to pray, we are spiritually, emotionally, and physically being healed. Dozens of scientific studies have proven the benefits of "grounding" or having physical connection with the earth. The contact of our bare feet, hands, and foreheads with the earth allows us to discharge harmful electrostatic charges we are bombarded with throughout the day while absorbing healing electrons from the earth.[8] These electrons are strong antioxidants that help neutralize and eliminate free radicals in our bodies that cause disease and inflammation.[9] World-renowned cardiologist Dr. Stephen Sinatra has said, "Grounding can restore and stabilize the bioelectrical circuitry that governs your physiology and organs, harmonize your basic biological rhythms, boost self-healing mechanisms, reduce inflammation and pain, and improve your sleep and feeling of calmness."[10]

Beyond the potential for physical healing, prostration serves as a reminder of the greatness of Allah and our humility in relationship to Him. As the Prophet Muhammad ﷺ said, "The nearest a servant comes to his Lord is when he is prostrating himself, so make supplication (in this state)."[11]

The Prophet ﷺ would sometimes prostrate long enough for 50 verses of the Qur'an to be recited.[12] When we prostrate, all the worries of the world fall from our backs, like a wave returning to the ocean of its origin, and all differences are dispelled as we enter into the oneness of God.

> *"Verily, when a servant stands to pray, his sins are placed on top of his head and shoulders. Every time he bows or prostrates, they fall away from him."*[13]
>
> PROPHET MUHAMMAD ﷺ

As the mystics have said, "One prayer to God frees you from a thousand prostrations to your ego." Just as water flows to lowlands, the humble position of prostration is a state of receptivity in which we are able to receive the infinite bounties that Allah has written for us to experience. Essentially, prayer is the opening and emptying of our hands so that we can receive and experience God holding us through His mercy and blessing us through His generosity. When we submit our egos to God the deep connection we carry with our Lord unveils itself from beneath life's distractions. An example of being connected to the presence of Allah is illustrated through the following story:

> Imam Ali was pierced in the leg by an arrow and due to the excruciating pain, nobody was able to remove it. Someone suggested that they wait until Imam Ali began to pray before removing it. When he began his *salat*, Imam Ali entered a different realm of reality, becoming so detached from his body in the presence of Allah that his companions were able to remove the arrow with ease.[14]

Imam Ali had mastered *khushoo*, or a sense of shyness, awe, and humility before the greatness of Allah. The Qur'an calls us to pray with *khushoo* and with deep surrender when it says, "Successful indeed are the believers, those who humble themselves in their prayers" (23:1-2). As the mystics say, "Prayer without presence of the Lord in the heart is not prayer at all."

The five daily prescribed outward prayers are meant to be a manifestation of the heart-based inner prayer that is continuous and unending. Sayings of the Prophet ﷺ suggest that the original command for prayer was 50 times a day, which was eventually reduced by God's mercy to five times a day.[15] Without God reducing the original order, we would have had to pray roughly every 20 minutes of our waking life, leaving almost no time for anything except prayer! The wisdom behind the original order—and the eventual reduction—is that the remembrance of God is meant to be constant and never-ending, whether we are in a state of ritual prayer or out in the world. Our relationship with God is not confined to our prayer mats because He is always speaking to us. As Rumi says, "What are you talking about! Having to earn a living doesn't stop you digging for the treasure. Don't abandon your everyday life. That's where the treasure is hidden."

*Remembrance of God is to the spirit like oxygen is to the body,
and just as we must constantly breathe to survive, it is in a
continual state of worship that our hearts thrive.*

Since as human beings we are forgetful, it is only in continuously surrendering the separations made by the ego that we are able to "bow in adoration and draw near" (96:19) to Allah's greatness, through the door of humility. The true prayer is one when our consciousness of ourselves melts into our all-encompassing awareness of Allah. The one who is remembering disappears and all that remains is the remembrance and the One remembered. The importance of being present when in prayer and remembering the Divine is beautifully exemplified through the following story:

A king was once praying deep in the forests of India when a young woman day-dreaming in the jungle walked, unbeknownst to her, right in front of him. After finishing his last prostrations, the king turned over his shoulder to yell at the women for being so careless as to distract him while he was deep in prayer.

She replied innocently that she had become so lost in passionate thoughts of her husband that she became unaware of her surroundings. She wondered how, if the king was lost in loving worship of his Beloved, someone like her could distract him. The king was amazed by her response, and instead of punishing her, gave her a bag of gold coins for teaching him such a deep lesson.

When the Qur'an says, "Tell the believing men to lower their gaze and be modest. That is purer for them; surely Allah is aware of what they do" (24:30), it is not just referring to a physical lowering, it is also referring to an internal and spiritual lowering, from anything other than Allah. In prayer, our intention is to be so immersed in Allah's beauty that we see and are aware of nothing but our Lord. When we are in this state of pure, surrendered prostration, the silent whispers that we utter into the ears of the humble earth beneath our foreheads are magnified by Allah and heard in the highest heavens.

The Secrets Behind Pre-Prayer Rituals: *Adhan* and *Wudu'*

Five times a day, we are called to return our gaze to our heavenly Lord of peace through the call to prayer, known as the *adhan*. The *adhan* is recited loudly in homes or in speakers at mosques, as a communal reminder to turn one's awareness from the outer world of passing forms toward the face of God's eternal reality. As the Indian poet Kabir says, "God hears the anklets on the feet of insects," so the loudness of the call to prayer is not for Allah, but rather as an alarm to awaken the sleeping human heart from being consumed with the world. No matter what we are doing, no matter how important it is to us, the call to prayer reminds the believer that there's something far more important than every dream, desire, and fleeting thought that we may have. Five times a day, we are held accountable for our actions, giving us the opportunity to consistently realign with the straight path of love, mercy, and faith.

The *adhan* turns our gaze from worldly desires toward a God-centered reality, reminding us that true happiness is not found in money or worldly accomplishments but in prayer and intimacy with Allah. The *adhan* reminds us that *salat* is "the highest spiritual realization of success" *(hayya ala-l-falah)*. Here the word *falah* in the *adhan* is often translated as "success or salvation," but it comes from a triliteral root word that also means to "cultivate or harvest."[16] The root of the word implies that, just as the value of sowing is actualized at harvest, the benefit and success of the day is actualized through the *cultivation* of prayer. This is why it is said that the prayer itself is the reward: five times a day, God invites us to a spiritual feast, and if we are absent it is we who miss out on the soul food.

Before we step into the holy banquet of God, we must enter a divine state of consciousness through a ritual act of purification or ablution known as *wudu'*. The Qur'an is referring to *wudu'* when it says, "Oh you who believe! When you rise up to prayer, wash your faces and your hands as far as the elbows, and wipe your heads and your feet to the ankles" (5:6). *Wudu'* consists of using water as a symbol of purifying our body from all the sins they may have committed and the idols we may have placed before God through the very blessings God has given to us. The Prophet Muhammad ﷺ confirms this claim by saying that when a believer engages in *wudu'*, the sins of his limbs are cleansed away with every last drop of water "until he emerges purified from sin."[17] The Qur'an states that everything is created from water (21:30), so when we do the *wudu'* we are symbolically washing away our existence with the water of the truth.

The act of bringing water to the body from the top of the head to the feet also serves to physically ground us, by bringing light, presence, and connection to our bodies. In fact, the word *wudu'* is closely related to the Arabic word *wadu'a*, which means "brightness and illumination," implying that when we engage in *wudu'*, we are illuminating our limbs and awakening our senses to the divine presence that is reflected everywhere.[18] The Prophet Muhammad ﷺ said, "The key to prayer is *wudu'*."[19] *Wudu'* is not just a physical purification, but also a spiritual cleansing and perfuming of the soul as preparation for entering into the King's court. *Wudu'* is like a pre-prayer meditation that step-by-step shifts our awareness from the outer world to the inner realms of the soul, cleansing the mind and heart from anything other than Allah.

Turning Toward the Kaaba

Once our senses and spirit are in alignment with God, we then turn our faces toward the direction (*qibla*) of the center of monotheism on Earth, known in the Muslim world as the *Kaaba*. The *Kaaba*, which is also known as the "House of God," is a cube-shaped structure covered in a black cloth in the holy city of Mecca. It is believed to be the first place of worship on Earth— established by Adam and Eve, then reestablished in the name of Allah by the father of monotheism, Prophet Abraham.[20] However, the *Kaaba* is not seen as the actual physical house of God, because Allah has no form and is beyond space and time. We are called to turn to a single geographical point in prayer in order to unify the community of believers. When every Muslim on Earth from every continent and country prays toward a single point, it transforms the entire Earth into one big prayer mat.

> "*The Kaaba is in the middle of the world. All faces turn toward it. Take it away, see! Each is worshipping the soul of each.*"
>
> SHAMS TABRIZI, RUMI'S SPIRITUAL GUIDE

Like the angels were commanded to bow at the feet of Adam, we do not bow to the physical form, we bow to the signature of God, to the divine fingerprints left upon every spirit of man. We bow to the fragrance of Allah's breath that brings to life everything it touches. The *Kaaba* represents the human heart. When we pray from within our hearts, all direction loses meaning as everywhere we turn becomes the face of God. The mystic Rabia Al-Adawiyya speaks to this place of inner unity when she says, "I kneel in the universal temple of my heart and I pray at the altar where walls and names do not exist." We bow to the light and love of God that is manifested in all of creation.

Once we unite the outer form of prayer with our inner presence we begin our journey into the embrace of God through the stating of our intention (*niyah*). The clarity of our intention helps align our mind, body, and soul in worship. Once we state our intention of aligning our gaze toward the Divine, we then begin the prayer by saying *Allahu Akbar*, meaning "God is the Greatest." As we say these words, we sweep our hands backwards toward our ears as a symbolic gesture of putting everything in the world behind us as we walk into the presence of our Lord.

Why Does the *Salat* Have a Set Form?

God has to tell us how to approach Him because our minds are incapable of understanding how to approach a God who transcends space and time. As mortal beings, how can we use our words to honor the holiness of a God who is beyond language, forms, and time? God sent us the Qur'an and the Prophet Muhammad ﷺ to teach us how to pray in the ways that allow us to most completely experience God's mercy and love. The guidance mapped out in the Qur'an and emulated by the Prophet ﷺ serve as a blueprint of how to foster the growth of the spirit.

> *"Truly God was gracious to the believers when He raised*
> *up among them a Messenger from themselves, to recite*
> *to them His signs and to purify them, and to teach them*
> *the Book and the wisdom, though before they were in*
> *manifest error."*
>
> QUR'AN 3:164

Every created thing has specific and necessary conditions for it to function properly. A plane requires an engine to fly, an apple tree requires sun and water to blossom, and the human soul requires remembrance of God to fully flourish. Only the One who created us can tell us how to maximize the time we have on Earth. Just as a computer requires a very specific charger, our souls require the precision of the *salat* to energize our spirits and help us actualize our full potential.

The *salat* incorporates physical movements, alongside reciting verses from the Qur'an, because in the Islamic worldview the mind, body, and soul are not separate but interconnected. Scientific studies have shown that the actions of the physical body affect our emotional states; for example, the physical act of smiling actually contributes to us feeling happier.[21] What the body does affects the soul, and what we do on a soul level affects the body.

Bringing together the different elements of prayer as the Prophet ﷺ taught us creates a synergy of power that is greater in spiritual value than the sum of the parts. This is why Muslims follow every movement that the Prophet ﷺ made—standing, bowing, prostrating, and kneeling while saying specific prayers alongside each pose within every cycle or *rakah* of the prayer.

To better understand in a modern context why *salat* has a set physical form paired with very specific prayers, consider the following: Medicine is made of very precise ingredients in exact amounts. If the ingredients of a medicinal blend are in the incorrect ratio or one ingredient is missing, the formula will significantly lose its healing effect. Similarly, in *salat*, the physical poses and the prayers combine together like precise spiritual ingredients, that holistically create a powerful medicinal blend for the soul.[22]

The Symbolism of the Postures of Prayer

As we dive deeper into the symbolic significance of the prayer postures, we can better appreciate how the *salat* both confronts and awakens the worshipper. Despite the spiritual importance of prostration, the *salat* does not begin with a posture of effacement, but rather begins in the standing position. This position is a reminder that one day we will all stand before God, and that as human beings we have the propensity to be arrogant and to position ourselves above those who are smaller in stature and status. Allah created us not to stand above the rest of creation, but to stand in humble service of all sentient beings for the sake of Allah.

As we stand and recite the holy verses from the Qur'an, the weight of revelation naturally draws us into a bowing position. We bow with our hands on our knees and our backs straight, staring at the space between our feet. Whereas when we were standing our gaze could reach as far as the horizon, when we bow we are humbly reminded that, as vast as the Earth is, we only occupy the small space beneath our feet. We are reminded that we do not own this Earth and our time upon it is short and fleeting. When we bow, we remind ourselves that the spiritual path begins exactly where we are, that all spiritual growth begins by first acknowledging and addressing our own pride, faults, and judgments. As we bow, our earthly crowns of wealth and influence fall, reminding us that everything we have is but a loan from Allah. Once we acknowledge how vulnerable and needy we are for Allah, we stand again, with a new-found humility and appreciation for our place in the universe.

Now, we stand not in arrogance, but as a servant of Allah. From this position of servitude, we then descend into the holy station of prostration. The first time we prostrate and put our head upon the earth, we are humbly reminded that we come from the very dirt we walk upon. With our heads pressed upon the ground, we are reminded that had Allah not blown His breath into us we would be nothing but dead earth—void of life and consciousness. From here, from our lowest depths, from the very soil of our humble creation, the seeds of true sincerity and faith begin to blossom.

When we rise up from the fetal position of prostration to the sitting position, we are reminded of how Allah pulled us out of the earth and gave us life. Like a seed that grows into a flower, we sit above the ground and appreciate the life we have been given. And just as every flower will eventually wilt and give her petals to the earth that once nurtured her into being, we return to the earth for our second prostration.

Where the first prostration represented our creation through the earth, the second prostration represents our return to the earth through death. Although the second prostration symbolizes the end of our earthly life, it is not the end of the *salat*. After this prostration, we then rise into the second cycle (*rakah*) of prayer by returning to the standing position. We stand again as a reminder that death is not our end, but that one day we will all be resurrected from our graves and called to stand before God to answer for the choices that we made.

Although on Earth injustice may prevail, on the Day of Judgment all wrongs will be made right. *Salat* actively confronts every illusion that this world tries to sell us as truth. When we engage in prayer and turn to God, we are simultaneously turning our backs on racism, sexism, and bigotry. Standing up for God means standing up against everything that does not honor the priceless value of human life and the holiness of the human spirit. The spirit of *salat* is not meant to be limited to the dimensions of our prayer mats. The *salat* is meant to encourage us to be more caring, to stand up against oppression with our words and our actions, and to open the path to divine love for all people who seek it.

Al-Fatiha: The Heart-Opener

Every *salat* begins with the recitation of the first chapter of the Qur'an, known as the *Al-Fatiha* or "The Opener." The *Fatiha* opens the heart to the light of guidance and healing. Its seven verses are often referred to as the "Mother of the Qur'an," and the executive summary of the entire revelation;[23] the verses of the *Fatiha* are doorways to the Divine, because they teach us not just how to seek guidance, but also how to have a relationship with God.[24]

Following the invocation of *Bismilliahi Ar-Rahman Ar-Rahim*, or the declaration of God's infinite mercy, the *Fatiha* begins with *Alhamdullilah*, which means "All praise and glory belongs to Allah." The Qur'an begins with gratitude and praise of God, because gratitude is a precursor to experiencing God. When we are grateful, our attention is on the present moment, allowing us to receive the love that God is consistently pouring upon us. The *Fatiha* is not just an integral part of every *salat*, but it teaches us the etiquette of how to pray to Allah.

The following is the translation of the *Fatiha*:

> *"In the name of Allah,*
> *The Lord of Mercy, The Bestower of Mercy.*
> *All praise and glory belongs to Allah, Lord of the worlds.*
> *The Lord of Mercy, The Bestower of Mercy.*
> *Master of the Day of Judgment.*
> *You alone we worship; You alone we ask for help.*
> *Guide us to the straight path.*
> *The way of those on whom You have bestowed Your grace,*
> *Not of those who earned Your anger nor of those who went*
> *astray."*

QUR'AN 1:1-7

The *Fatiha* opens by calling us to witness the greatness of God. The first few verses of the *Fatiha* begin with knowledge of God, while the following verse teaches us how to put that knowledge into action: "You *alone* we worship; You *alone* we ask for help" (1:5). When we understand that God *alone* is the Master of this world and the next, we are naturally inclined to turn to Him for guidance because we know that He *alone* has power over the outcome of our lives.

Only once we have voiced our gratitude, and declared our commitment to God *alone,* do we then ask Him for what we seek: "Guide us to the straight path. The way of those on whom You have bestowed Your grace, not of those who earned Your anger nor of those who went astray" (1:6-7). The *Fatiha* teaches us that the path of the spiritual seeker always begins with being with Allah. After all, it is through being present with the Divine and contemplating His countless blessings that we are inspired to worship Him. It is only after we are committed to Allah alone that we are receptive to divine guidance.

The Celestial Power of Prayer Times

As a symbol of unifying the outer with the inner, even the times for the daily prayer are determined by the celestial dance between the Earth and the sun. The Earth rotates around its axis as it orbits the sun, which causes the sun's light to manifest in our atmosphere in five distinct stages, which represent the five times for prayer. Some scholars suggest the first prayer of the day is the predawn morning prayer (*fajr*), while others suggest the first prayer of the day begins when the sun sets, with the evening prayer (*maghrib*). Since, according to the Islamic calendar, each new day begins at sundown, we will follow the opinion that the first prayer of the day is technically the evening or *maghrib* prayer.[25] Regardless of which opinion you follow, the fact that Allah specifically identified different times for prayer, is evidence that these specific times are spiritually significant.

The stages of the day symbolize the physical and spiritual stations we travel throughout our life. The day begins as the sun sets on the horizon, descending further into darkness, rising into dawn, ascending to its zenith directly overhead, and finally falling in prostration toward the same horizon where its journey began. Since the times of the five daily prayers correspond exactly with the movements of the celestial realm, the *salat* serves to align the outer and inner by turning our awareness to Allah through every change and shift we experience both physically and spiritually.

Maghrib, the evening prayer, comes in after the sun has set and the clouds undress themselves of the colorful hues of red and orange. The *maghrib* prayer is symbolic of our journey from the light of the heavens into the darkness of this world. Just as the sun prostrates on the horizon and sets, our souls prostrate to God as our egos begin to set. It is only when we prostrate into the darkness of death that we can dawn into eternal life; we must first die before we can be reborn. This is why the spiritual path begins with the death of the attachment to the ego. We must first bow in surrender to God before we can rise as a representative of His love on Earth.

Isha, the night prayer, starts when the colorful hues of the sunset sky disappear into the darkness of the night. Turning to prayer at this hour symbolizes the body fully surrendering the ego before God. When we pray at this hour, we turn our awareness from mortality to immortality, from the unreal to the Real, from what is perishing to the Eternal. This prayer symbolizes the season of death, and subsequent renewal into what will become a new birth in the light of God's presence.

Fajr, the morning prayer, is done in the deep darkness of predawn, a period of silence and stillness unlike any other point of the day. Although the word *fajr* means "dawn," it comes from the Arabic root word *infijar,* which means "to burst forth." Just as the dawn breaks the night into day, the *fajr* prayer breaks the darkness of forgetfulness with the light of awareness. The weakness of the body at this hour allows for greater witnessing by the soul, making a clear channel of conversation between the subtle divine realms and our dense world. Prayer at this time of day helps remind us of our greater purpose, anchoring us in the remembrance of God as the "dawn breathes away the darkness" (81:18) and the day unveils itself. Our spiritual path may begin in the night, but *fajr* represents the rising of the soul's light upon a new spiritual horizon.

Dhuhr, the noon prayer, comes in when the sun is directly overhead, marking the busiest part of the day, when we are most susceptible to forgetting Allah. This period of the day represents the majority of our life on Earth. It symbolizes the initial surrendering and subsequent bursting into the light of faith. This is a time of vibrant growth and energetic abundance, when the fire of our worldly desires burns brightly as we chase after our dreams with laser focus. As we enter the field of competition, our anger, arrogance, and anxiety intensify as we may become impatient with the process of seeking and striving. On the outside, we are fiercely pushing ourselves to be better than everyone else, which creates separation; on the inside, our spirit—which is intimately connected to God—is fighting to annihilate the attachment to the self and join the unity of oneness.

When we turn to God during this heightened state of awareness and movement, it redirects the powerful energies present around noon toward spiritual progress, rather than physical gain. Prayer at this point in the day reminds us that whatever we reach for is ultimately a reaching for Allah. Prayer reminds us to reflect before we act, bringing a deep sense of intentionality to our day, which helps us to ground in the presence of God, preventing the breeze of our passing desires from blowing us off the straight path.

Asr, the mid-afternoon prayer, arrives when the sun has declined toward the horizon and the length of your shadow is twice your height. The day matures as life slows down, but as we approach sunset, dormant desires of lust, greed, and jealousy tend to arise as we are pulled toward idle distractions that can derail us. Turning to Allah amidst our fleeting thoughts helps remind us that our work on this Earth is beyond material gain. Aligning our hearts to the Divine, helps to put out the fires of our egoistic desires before they jeopardize the gardens of our faith. Spiritually, this time of day represents a state of maturity and a constant moving toward the final chapter of earthly life. As the body weakens, the list of things to accomplish can feel endless, so our thoughts still churn like a water wheel in our minds. When we fall into a state of prostration during these final moments of the day, our worries fall from our shoulders as we surrender to God's all-encompassing mercy and love. Prayer during this period helps return us to the divine ark of safety, amidst the waves of our endless fears. As our anxieties around death and the unknown rock the boat of our peace, prayer brings a sense of stability and security by returning us to God, in whose presence all hearts find rest (13:28).

Since there are so many Muslims that live in so many different countries with different time zones, every second of every single day there is someone somewhere in the world prostrating in *salat*. In addition to the holy times dedicated to the ritual prayer, Muslims can also make *dua,* or prayers of supplication, at any time, in any language or form that opens their hearts and honors the holiness of God. The mystics challenge us to be more generous with our prayers by asking, "If God answered all of your prayers would it just change your life or would it change the world?"[26] In other words, we are encouraged to pray not just for ourselves, but for all of creation.

The Qur'an reminds us that those who sincerely love God do not just ritualistically pray five times a day in a set form, but also "celebrate the praises of Allah, standing, sitting, and lying down on their sides and contemplate the creation in the heavens and the earth" (3:191). Since God is consistently blessing us with life, we are called to lovingly remember Him with gratitude in every single moment of our lives.

The Mystery of Repetition and Remembrance

Just like ocean waves can over time break down massive cliffs into particles of sand, the repetitive nature of *salat* serves to crumble the mountain of our egos. Repeating our prayer in a heartfelt way is like submerging the fabric of our souls into an ocean of God-consciousness. Just as leather has to be consistently dipped into tubs of dye to retain the color, when we repetitively turn to God our spirits become wrapped in Allah's colorful qualities, permanently dyeing us with the beauty of divine grace (2:138).

Praying five times a day is not easy, but for the sincere believer it's more than just obedience. Prayer is about swimming in the current of God's generosity and immersing every atom of our souls in gratitude for the blessing of being given another day to serve God's will on Earth. We are called to sink into our utter helplessness, to become fully aware of how vulnerable we are, how desperately dependent on Allah we are for every breath we take and every beat our heart makes. The more immersed we are in God's love, the more we'll see prayer as a divine blessing, rather than on obligation.

> *The lover of God is not the one who carves out of his day time*
> *to pray, but the one who carves out of his time for worship*
> *time to work.*

Prayer is about connection and conversation with the One who created you. We are called to pray not only because we want or need something from God, but because we are grateful for all that we have already been given. Know that God always answers our prayers whether or not we find His response favorable. As Imam Ali says, "Sometimes your prayers are turned down, because you often unknowingly ask for things that are really harmful to you." God calls us to pray for what we want, but we must remember that God will always give us what we need, when we need it.

In the Qur'an Allah says, "Remember me and I will remember you" (2:152), not because Allah will forget us if we forget Him, but rather because when we magnify Allah, by association we magnify and honor ourselves as creations of Allah.

> *As the mystics say, "When we praise God, God does not*
> *become holy, we become holy!"*

It is not our prayer and worship of God that makes God love us; rather, it's God's unconditional love for us that results in our worship. We do not pray *for* the love of God, but *from* the love of God. God's power inspires and allows us to pray, and it's that same divine power that we are calling to in prayer. As Rumi says, "I am a mountain. You call, I echo."

God pursues us, through His love and mercy, which encompasses everything. As one mystic said, "For thirty years I sought God. But when

I looked carefully, I found that in reality God was the seeker and I the sought." You cannot find God, because God cannot be lost. It is we who are lost and need to be found. Prayer is God's invitation to His infinite blessings that have always existed, but our lack of awareness prevents us from experiencing.

> *"When Allah inspires your tongue to ask, know that He wants to give."*
>
> IBN ATA ALLAH AL-ISKANDARI, 13TH-CENTURY MYSTIC

Our worship of God is by God's grace. How can we give anything to the One who needs nothing, but has given us everything? It is God that moves our tongues and it is He who inspires our praise of Him. Our very act of thankfulness of God requires thankfulness for it is He who inspires it. Like the sun pulls the Earth into its orbit, Allah pulls us into worship of Him through the gravity of His love.

When we worship God from our hearts, we come to see that Allah loved us before we could ever love Him, that He prayed for us before we could ever pray to Him, and that He gave us life before He ever asked us to dedicate our lives to Him.

When we pray, we abandon everything we think we are, remove every mask we hide behind, release our grip over this fleeting world, and open our hearts to be healed by the divine love that surrounds everything and everyone. Prayer helps the soul see that its longing for all earthly manifestation is really a deep longing for God. So never let your past, your situation, or your sins make you feel unworthy of having a relationship with God.

> *God does not love you just because of who you are; He loves you because love is who He is.*

So never stop praying. Even when the pain is too much to bear, even when you have broken a thousand promises, even if all that comes out is a silent whisper that only God can hear. No matter what storms you are facing, no matter how bad you mess up, no matter how painful life becomes, the door to prayer is always open for you. After all, as Imam Ali said, "When the world pushes you to your knees, you're in the perfect position to pray."

> *My Lord, help me to honor the holiness of prayer and to turn to you in my greatest successes, my most painful failures, and every moment in between. Oh Allah, whether I am in the deepest valley or on the highest summit, "My Lord! Truly, I am in need of whatever good that You bestow on me!" (28:24) Oh Allah, help me to never lose sight of Your love and to never stop seeking Your guidance and help. In the words of Your beloved Prophet ﷺ, "Oh Allah, help me to remember You, to thank You, and to worship You in the best of manners."[27] My beloved Lord, please help me continuously align my heart to You. Oh Allah, please help me be mindful of You before, during, and after all of my prayers. Oh Allah, please be patient with me; please keep calling me back toward You; please keep opening the doors to Your mercy and keep tuning my ears to the calls of Your guidance. In Your sacred names I pray, Ameen.*

Reflection: "Overcoming Distractions During Prayer"

It is a constant battle for most people to stay mindful and focused during prayer. In fact, the *mihrab*, the semicircular niche that you find in most mosques pointing to the direction of the *Kaaba*, comes from the Arabic root word *harb*, which means "battle." In essence, when we stand in *salat* facing Mecca (*qibla*), we are in a battle between our soul and the fleeting desires of the ego. On the one hand, the *salat* gives us the opportunity, five times a day, to have an intimate conversation with our Lord, and on the other hand, the *salat* is a battlefield where we fight the distractions of the outside world. However, attentiveness and sincerity in prayer are not just achieved by trying harder, but by surrendering more deeply to Allah. The following practice helps us turn from fighting our distractions to asking Allah for help in overcoming them.

- Keep a journal with a pen next to your prayer mat.
- Every day after prayers, write down 2–3 things that distracted you in prayer. It can be anything from thinking about the tasks of the day, to obsessing over the things people said to you or you said to others, to overthinking past mistakes, to anxieties over a project or assignment you have to finish at work or school, etc.
- At the end of each day, read over this list and see if you find common themes. Make note of the patterns you see.
- Every day, intentionally pick one or two things from this list, and before every prayer place your hand on your heart and ask Allah: *"Oh Allah, Your mercy encompasses all things, You are the owner of every outcome and the best of planners. Oh Allah, please help me set aside this thought or worry as I step into Your presence."*
- It can often be helpful to incorporate the practice of *tawba* at this point.[28]
- Take a moment to briefly journal on how you feel before and after this practice.
- Use this practice whenever you notice yourself getting repeatedly distracted during prayers.

"And the likeness of those who spend their wealth, seeking to please Allah and to strengthen their souls, is as a garden, high and fertile which is hit by a downpour—so it yields its fruits in double. And [even] if it is not hit by a downpour, then a drizzle [is sufficient]. Allah sees well whatever you do."

QUR'AN 2:265

"None of you will believe until you love for your brother what you love for yourself."[1]

PROPHET MUHAMMAD ﷺ

"When you have more than you need, build a longer table, not a higher fence."

ANONYMOUS

8

ZAKAT: GIVING AS AN INSTRUMENT OF GOD

When you have in your hands what another person's soul needs, Allah is answering that person's prayer through you. When you say yes to the opportunity of serving someone in need, you are saying yes to being an instrument of God's love, compassion, generosity, and abundance. You are called by the Qur'an to "give of what you love" (3:92), for loving the creation is a manifestation of our love for the Creator. As the Prophet ﷺ said, "He has not thanked Allah who has not thanked the people."[2]

Our gratitude of Allah is not just manifested in words of praise, but also through charitable acts of service toward His creation. When the Qur'an speaks of almsgiving and charity, it uses the two following forms: *sadaqah* or recommended charity, and *zakat*, which is seen as an obligatory divine tax. The word *sadaqah* comes from the root word *sidq*, which means "to speak the truth, to be sincere, to give alms." At its most basic, *sadaqah* is the giving of a gift that is rightfully ours, with a sincere intention for the benefit of others, and for the sake of Allah alone. Unlike *zakat*, *sadaqah* is not a pillar or an obligatory act and has no conditions other than seeking to serve Allah through serving His creation.

> *"A believer who plants a tree or sows a field from which man,*
> *birds, and animals can eat is committing an act of charity."*[3]
>
> **PROPHET MUHAMMAD** ﷺ

Sadaqah is not just donating money, it is also inspiring and celebrating all acts of goodness, while forbidding what is wrong. It includes removing harmful obstructions from the road, being patient with the old, leading the blind, and listening to the unheard. The Prophet Muhammad ﷺ says in reference to *sadaqah* that even, "Your smile for your brother is charity."[4] There is *sadaqah* in giving hope to the hopeless, offering compassion to the hurt, supporting the weak, being a voice for the oppressed, and smiling and bringing joy to every heart you meet.

Spoken *Sadaqah*

The Prophet ﷺ says that even "A kind word is a form of charity."[5] The ability to speak is a gift from God, so it is important that we protect our tongue from ungodly things such as gossip, foul language, and using our words in ways that would be hurtful. As the mystics say, "Before you speak, let your words pass through three gates. At the first gate, ask yourself, 'Is it true?' at the second ask, 'Is it necessary?' and at the third gate ask, 'Is it kind?'"

We must use the gift of our speech to uplift, inspire, encourage, and guide others. The incredible power of words is profoundly illustrated through the following story:

> Two frogs were hopping through the forest when they fell down a hole in the ground. The hole was so deep that when a group of other frogs found them trying to jump out, they started screaming, "You guys, it's too deep! There's no way you can get out! Just give up trying, so you can at least die in peace!"

Hearing this, one of the frogs sat down and died from hopelessness. However, the other frog just kept jumping and pushing himself to get out. The other frogs started yelling louder, "Give up, my friend! It's no use! Give up!" But the frog pushed even harder, until suddenly a huge surge of energy pushed through him and he jumped out of the hole.

All the frogs of the forest were amazed. They hopped up to the frog who'd escaped and asked him what had motivated him to get out even as they yelled at him to give up. The frog said, "Oh! I am deaf, and at that distance I couldn't read your lips, so I thought you were encouraging me to get out!"

Words have power, which is why Imam Ali says, "Speak only when your words are more beautiful than the silence." After all, everything in existence sprouted from the vibration of the divinely uttered word "Be!" (36:82). So remember, your tongue is like a knife; it can either kill like the sword of a samurai or save like the scalpel of a surgeon.

Give Without Judgment

When God puts someone in need on our path or calls on us to give charity, it is not for us to judge who is worthy. The human inclination to judge based on outer conditions is illustrated in the following story:

The mystic Abu Jafar received divine guidance to give a large sum of money in charity to the first person he saw in the street after predawn prayers. The next day, after his morning prayers, Abu Jafar exited the mosque and offered a sum of money to the first man he saw. Afterward, his friend grabbed his arm and said, "Why did you give that man money? Do you not know he is a thief?" The confused sage went back into the mosque and prayed to God for guidance.

After a few hours of prayer, he received the guidance that after noon prayers he should go outside and again give charity to the first person he saw. After noon prayers, Abu Jafar left the mosque, and this time the first person he saw was a woman, so he respectfully offered his charity to her and headed toward his house. Then, a man stopped him and said, "Brother, why did you give that woman money? She's a prostitute!"

The holy man was distraught, and quickly went back into the mosque to repent and ask for guidance. This time he got the guidance to go out after sunset prayers and give all the money he had in his pocket to the first person he saw. Despite having doubt in his heart as to the validity of this guidance, the holy man sincerely said his prayers, walked out into the night, and gave the first person he saw all the money he had. As he turned away to walk home, yet again someone came up to him and said, "Why did you give that man money? He is rich!"

This time, the old sage ran back to the mosque, fearing that his spiritual compass was broken. He cried and prayed to God for hours, and then fell into a state between wakefulness and sleep. The Angel Gabriel came to him in a dream and asked him, "What bothers your heart, faithful lover of God?" After the man explained his dilemma to Gabriel, the angel smiled and said, "Do not judge the ones you are asked to give to. Your Lord would never ask something of you without purpose. Perhaps the thief was inspired by your kindheartedness to stop stealing; maybe your kindness gave hope to the prostitute that there was another way to make ends meet; and perhaps your generosity toward the rich man opened his heart to becoming more generous."

We never know how our actions can inspire those around us. Sometimes a little bit of light is all that a flower needs to blossom. Don't underestimate the power of your kindness.

Zakat: A Divine Tax on Your Blessings

Aside from giving charity when the need arises, Muslims that are financially capable are asked to donate at least 2.5 percent annually of their net worth, known as *zakat,* to the poor, as a means of preventing widespread poverty. Unlike *sadaqah,* *zakat* must be given specifically to one of the following eight categories of people: the poor, those who are in a state of difficulty, those who disperse the *zakat,* those whose hearts are in need of reconciliation, to free people from bondage, to help people who are in debt, to support those who are striving to establish peace in the name of God, and to those who are struggling while traveling in foreign lands.

When giving *zakat* or even *sadaqah,* the money donated must have been earned in a religiously permissible way (*halal*). Income made through selling alcohol, as interest on money loaned, gambling, or through any other impermissible means does not count toward the obligatory *zakat.* It is also important to remember that *zakat* is only obligatory after you have first provided for your own family and basic needs. It is not simply charity, but a tax on our blessings, to be given to those who are incapable of providing for themselves. *Zakat* is like a spiritual mortgage we pay for our place here on Earth.[6]

Aside from being an obligatory donation, the word *zakat* is often translated as "that which purifies." Just as the body must excrete its waste product to maintain health, *zakat* purifies us of materialism by excreting our attachments to wealth.

> *"Spend in charity for your own good. He who remains safe from his own greed will prosper."*
>
> **QUR'AN 64:16**

Greed is an enemy of gratitude and faith, which is why the Prophet ﷺ said, "I am not afraid that you will worship others along with Allah after my death, but I am afraid that you will fight with one another for worldly things."[7] When we give to others with a sincere intention, it helps to loosen our hold on our attachments to this material world.

Idealistically, *zakat* helps establish a sense of balance in society—a natural flow of giving and receiving. Just as if we only inhaled and never exhaled we would suffocate, *zakat* is in essence an exhaling of charity, to make room for the inhale of blessings. In the ancient Indian text, *Upanishads*, it profoundly says, "There is enough in the world for everyone's need; there is not enough for everyone's greed." Without giving, we would spiritually suffocate. In fact, a word often used for money in the English language is "currency," which comes from the Latin word *currere*, which means "to run the racecourse" or to flow in movement. In other words, when currency is not circulated it creates stagnation in our lives. Like a river or current, money must flow in and out of our hands or it will strangle the vibrancy of the spirit within us.

Zakat is a divine blessing from Allah, because it is through the purification of our worldly attachments that we expand and progress in our spiritual life. The less we feed our egos, the more our spirits thrive. We get closer to God not through what we have, but through what we give. Since everything that is in our hands is perishing, it is only what we give for the sake of God that we ever really keep.

This is wonderfully expressed through the following conversation between the Prophet ﷺ and his wife: After his wife had donated meat from a slaughtered sheep to charity, the Prophet ﷺ asked, "What remains of it?" She replied, "Nothing remains of it except its shoulder." The Prophet ﷺ profoundly replied, "All of it remains (in the book of Allah) except its shoulder."[8] In other words, the Prophet ﷺ was illustrating that only what we give in charity for the sake of Allah actually remains.

> *"If you gave it all away do you think God would be stingy?*
> *When you sow seeds the barn is left empty, but the ground*
> *is made rich. If you leave the seeds in the barn all you'll*
> *have is a decaying feast for the mice and beetles."*[9]
>
> RUMI

The good deeds we plant in this world do not go to waste; rather, they blossom into the eternal realm of the Hereafter. As the Qur'an says, "So whatever thing you are given, that is only a provision of this world's life, and what is with Allah is better and more lasting for those who believe and rely on their Lord" (42:36).

When we go to the grave, we do not take the money we saved; we take the currency of grace created from the money we gave away.

"Charity does not decrease wealth."[10]

PROPHET MUHAMMAD ﷺ

At the root of the word zakat we find the meaning "growth, blessing, and multiplication." When we give for the sake of Allah, we are in fact opening the doors to Allah's generosity, becoming receptive to further growth and multiplication of both our material and spiritual wealth. Allah reiterates this notion when He says, "He will replace whatever you give in alms" (34:39). Similar to how when farmers prune plants it helps them grow faster, when we give in charity we are energetically pruning our wealth to allow for greater growth (2:245).

Your *Zakat* Does Not Belong to You

To preserve the dignity of the poor, *zakat* is seen as being owned not by the giver, but by the one who is qualified to receive it. *Zakat* is not charity as much as it is repaying what we owe to the poor. It is a reminder that whatever we have acquired and earned is not owned by us, but is instead a loan from Allah. When we give charity, we are not giving to another person from ourselves; rather, Allah is the One giving to them, through us. We are not owners of our wealth, we are only divinely chosen caretakers of it. When we are in a state of true giving, there is no longer a giver and a receiver, there is only the universal love of God manifesting through our hands and deeds.

As the mystics say, "There are four dimensions to Islam: (1) What's mine is mine and what's yours is yours. (2) What's mine is yours and what's yours is also yours. (3) There's neither mine nor yours. (4) There is no longer 'me' nor 'you' only an Us."[11] So if you give charity to me, it's not really you that's giving to me—it's God who is giving to us. In receiving charity, I may experience God's name, The Provider (*Ar-Razzaq*), and as the giver of charity you may taste God's name,

The Generous (*Al-Karim*), manifesting through you in response to my need. In essence, we are just mirrors reflecting God to Himself.

There is a big difference between doing a good deed and seeing ourselves and doing a good deed and seeing only Allah. For the one who looks to the Lord with sincere seeking, charity becomes a *wudu'* or cleansing of the ego's tendency to claim ownership over the gifts given to us by Allah.

> "Do not waste your acts of charity by reminders of
> your generosity."
>
> QUR'AN 2:264

Do not take ownership of your generosity; our generosity is actually a manifestation of Allah's generosity, for it is He who gives us the means to be of service. As the twentieth-century Lebanese poet Khalil Gibran said, "There are those who give with joy, and that joy is their reward. And there are those who give with pain, and that pain is their baptism. And there are those who give and know not pain in giving, nor do they seek joy, nor give with mindfulness of virtue...Through the hands of such as these God speaks, and from behind their eyes He smiles upon the earth."[12] Allah gives us the opportunity to serve the world not because He needs us, but because our soul blossoms when we water it with service.

The Qur'an says, "If you give alms openly, it is well, and if you hide it and give it to the poor, it is better for you and will atone some of your sins, and Allah is aware of what you do" (2:271). Giving alms in private protects the reputation of those we are giving to, and protects us from seeking praise and gratitude. When we are asked by Allah to give to the poor, it is we who should be grateful for the opportunity to give. After all, if it were not for the neediness of another or the surplus of wealth that Allah blessed us with, we would not be able to reflect and experience God's qualities of generosity, compassion, and love.

It is in service to others that we express our gratitude for all that Allah has blessed us with. When we serve others, we water our seeds of compassion and kindness, allowing us to see that it is in giving to others that we ourselves blossom. As the Qur'an says, "If you do good, you do good for your own selves" (17:7). When we truly give to others, we give to ourselves, uplifting our stature in the eyes of God. As Allah says, "Oh son of Adam! Spend, and I shall spend on you."[13]

The true manifestation of *zakat* is illustrated through an extraordinary story of the beloved daughter of the Prophet ﷺ, Fatima Zahra, on her wedding day.

> As the gentle-hearted Fatima was getting ready for one of the most memorable nights of her life, a beggar knocked on her door, seeking a dress to wear. Fatima was going to give the beggar her older dress, but then she remembered the verse from the Qur'an that said, "You will never attain piety until you give of what you love" (3:92). So instead, Fatima kept the older dress for herself, and before she even got married she gave her new wedding gown to the beggar. This is an example of being a true representative of God's love and generosity, without conditions or worldly attachments.

Fatima Zahra knew that like everything else in her life, her dress belonged to Allah, so when her Lord called her to give what He had given her, she gave joyfully and without questioning.[14] Allah promises those who give freely of what they love eternal rewards and "a profit that will never perish" (35:29).

Every Atom of Giving Counts

Sometimes we may feel our capacity to give is so limited, and the world's needs are so great, that we get discouraged from even trying. When we feel too overwhelmed to try and heal the great pains of the world, we must remember that everything created originates from a humble beginning. Grains of sand over time create mountains, a microscopic sperm and egg creates a human being, and even the big bang that may have resulted in the creation of our entire universe began from the space the size of a pea. Do not underestimate what Allah can create through a sincere heart and intention, no matter how small the gesture may be. As Imam Ali famously said, "Do business with Allah and you will profit."

The Qur'an confirms this claim when it says, "The parable of those who spend their wealth in the way of God is that of a grain which grows seven ears, each bearing a hundred grains. God gives multiple increases to whomever He wills. God is The All-Bounteous, The All-Knowing" (2:261).

We are also reminded in the Qur'an that we are only asked to give according to the capacity that Allah gave to us: "Let him who has plenty spend from his plenty. And let the one whose provision is measured spend from what Allah has given Him. Allah does not charge a soul for other than what He has given. Allah will bring about ease after hardship" (65:07). It is the small steps we take today that become miles tomorrow; acts done with love and consistency create revolutions of kindness and light that overthrow the forces of darkness.

Give your money, give your time, give everything you have to give, because in your emptiness and deficiency you experience Allah's unending bounty. As the Qur'an says, "He has given you everything that you asked Him for. Had you wanted to count a single blessing of Allah, you would not have been able to do it" (14:34). After all, we give Allah what is fleeting and finite, and He rewards us with what is eternal and infinite.

> "Listen, oh drop, give yourself up without regret, and in exchange gain the ocean. Listen oh drop, bestow upon yourself this honor and in the arms of the sea be secure. Who indeed should be so fortunate? An ocean wooing a drop! In Allah's name, in Allah's name, sell and buy at once! Give a drop and take this sea full of pearls."
>
> RUMI

When we return the blessings Allah has given to us back to Him, we end up gaining more than we gave. Like a raindrop dissolving into the ocean, no matter how small our gesture of kindness may be, Allah embraces it with His generosity. In the Qur'an, Allah says, "Whoever does an atom's weight of good shall see it, and whoever does an atom's weight of evil shall see it" (99:7-8). So there is no good deed too small to make a difference. Imam Ali says, "Do not feel ashamed if the amount of charity you give is small, because to refuse the needy is an act of greater shame." This notion is beautifully depicted through the following story:

> An old man went to the beach in the morning, to walk before work. When he reached the shoreline, he found the entire beach, from the shore to the edges of the cliffs near the houses, covered with starfish. As he struggled to walk around them, he saw a boy in the distance, picking up the starfish and throwing them into the ocean. When the man reached the boy, he asked him what he was doing and the boy replied, "There was a huge storm last night, so these starfish have washed up on the beach and they cannot make it back to the ocean. I am throwing them back in the water because when the sun comes up it will get really hot and they will probably die."
>
> The old man smiled in pity at the boy as he said, "My sweet boy, there are probably a hundred thousand starfish on this beach. It's hard to think what you are doing will make any difference." The boy crouched down and picked up another starfish, petted it gently, and then threw it into the ocean, then turned to the old man and said, "Well, it sure made a difference to that one!"

There is no good deed too small for Allah to see. As Prophet Muhammad ﷺ said, "There is a reward for kindness for every living being."[15] We have never fully given to another person until we give to someone who can never repay us. We may not change the world with a small act of kindness, but the more love we consistently plant, the more fragrant our Earth becomes, through the beautiful blossoms of Allah's qualities of compassion, beauty, holiness, and mercy. As the Prophet ﷺ said, "Know that the most beloved deed to Allah is that which is done regularly even if it is small."[16]

The Science of Giving

Giving to others not only awakens and heals the spirit, but sincere generosity has been proven to have the power to transform us, both emotionally and physically. Researchers at the National Institutes of Health discovered that giving to charity stimulates the reward center of the brain, known as the mesolimbic pathway. When we give to others, our brain releases dopamine and endorphins, which help block out pain signals creating a "helper's high." Giving inspires tranquility and a sense of deep gratification.[17]

But unlike other highs, research shows that giving charitably can help us live longer, boost our mood, create more social connection, lower stress—and that giving tends to be contagious, as it often creates a positive ripple effect within our community.[18] This is why whenever we feel lost, uninspired, or failing to find purpose in our life, we are called to give to others.

> *"Those who expend their wealth night and day, secretly and in public, they shall have their reward from their Lord and they shall have no fear, nor shall they grieve."*
>
> QUR'AN 2:274

Most of our anxieties in life are rooted in overemphasis on the self. As it has been said, "Humility is not thinking less of yourself, it's thinking of yourself less."[19] When we expand our field of vision to include the bigger picture, what once felt like a huge burden can begin to dissolve.[20] This is why many Muslims give *sadaqah* when they feel stuck or are seeking guidance. When we reflect generosity, kindness, and love upon the world, we become more aware of Allah's corresponding and omnipresent divine qualities of endless generosity (*Al-Karim*), abundant kindness (*Ar-Ra'uf*), and eternal love (*Al-Wadud*).

However, our intentions matter, because as studies have shown, it is only when we give selflessly and from a place of genuinely wanting to help and connect with others that we obtain health benefits. Although human civilization advances and benefits from competition, our existence is not dependent on "survival of the fittest" as much as it is on the "survival of the kindest."[21]

To really understand the importance of connection and creating a tight-knit community, consider the following: Despite having roots that can be only five or six feet deep, redwood trees are the tallest trees in the world, growing as tall as 350 feet.[22] Redwood trees grow as tall as they do with such shallow roots because their roots interlock and weave together with neighboring trees, creating thick groves of communal support up to hundreds of feet from the base of any given tree.[23] Redwood trees do not just share nutrients, but their braided roots create a powerful defense against floods and strong winds, allowing the trees to keep growing through hundreds of years of seasonal changes. Just like Redwood trees we human beings are also interconnected; when we share our blessings with others and invest in our community, we are directly investing in our own well-being. As an ancient proverb says, "If you want to go fast, go alone; but if you want to go far, go together."

Give for God's Grace, Not for People's Praise

> "*Aim to live in this world without allowing the world to live inside of you, because when a boat sits on water, it sails perfectly, but when water enters inside the boat, it sinks.*"
>
> IMAM ALI

Zakat and *sadaqah* are ways to empty the ship of our heart from the weight of greed, attachment, and stinginess. The one who spends his wealth not for honor or praise, but rather to purify himself before God, is the one whose ship of faith will stay afloat. As Allah says, "He who spends his wealth in order to purify himself, not as payment for any favors received by anyone, but only seeking to gain the pleasure of his Lord Most High, and indeed he will eventually be satisfied" (92:18-21).

The Qur'an calls us to give solely for the sake of being a reflection of God's love on Earth. We are not called to give to others looking for praise, rather we are called to say, "We feed you for the face of Allah, we neither want a reward from you nor gratitude" (76:9). When we see all the ways that God constantly gives to us, we turn our focus from what people did to us and focus on all that Allah has done and continuously does for us. We see that giving for the sole purpose of direct reciprocity invalidates the countless blessings given to us by Allah. This notion is beautifully exemplified through the following story:

> A king who was once walking through a plantation, when he no-
> ticed an old man with a white beard on his knees planting some
> seeds. He walked over to the man and said, "My kind father, what
> are you doing?" The old man smiled innocently and said, "Hello,
> my dear majesty, I am planting tiny date palm saplings." The king
> surprisingly replied, "But, father, doesn't it take twenty to fifty years
> for date palms to bear fruit?" The old man smiled as he replied, "Yes,
> my majesty, that is correct." The confused king asked, "Will you
> ever be able to eat the dates from the trees you are planting?" The
> old man sweetly replied, "I will surely never reach the age to enjoy
> these fruits, my majesty. But I have eaten dates from trees my fathers
> planted but never tasted, and so by God's mercy I too plant for those
> who come after me to one day enjoy."
>
> The king was so touched by the old man's words that he gave him a
> bag of gold coins. The old man replied, "I have yet to even plant these
> saplings and they have already blossomed with fruits of abundance.
> What is done in the name of God is beyond seasons and time, He
> surely answers instantly!"

Give Like the Sun Gives to the Earth

Zakat reminds us that Allah is the sustainer and provider, because "To Allah belongs whatever is in the heavens and earth" (24:64). If everything is created by God and everything returns to Him, then what do we really own of this world? We are nothing more than caretakers of this Earth; we are here to both gratefully enjoy and generously share the blessings Allah has bestowed upon all people without discrimination.

If someone is worthy, in the eyes of God, of having been created, how can we say they are undeserving of our help? As the Prophet Muhammad ﷺ said, "He is not a believer whose stomach is filled while his neighbor goes hungry."[24] As Muslims, we are called to give like the sun gives to the Earth, freely and without conditions.

> *"Even after all this time the sun never says to the Earth, 'You owe me.' Look what happens with a love like that. It lights the whole sky."*
> HAFIZ, 14TH-CENTURY PERSIAN POET

All human beings and creations of Allah are like cells in a single body. As the Prophet Muhammad ﷺ said, "The surrendered ones, in their mutual love, kindness, and compassion are like the human body; where one of its parts is in agony, the entire body feels the pain, both in sleeplessness and fever."[25] This is why in the Qur'an it says if anyone unjustly takes a life, it is as if they have killed all of humanity, and "If anyone saved a life, it would be as if he saved the life of all humankind" (5:32).

Just as a stone that is dropped anywhere in a lake creates ripples that reach across the entire body of water, when one of us is suffering, that pain ripples through all of existence. As Rumi said, "The differences are just illusion and vanity. Sunlight looks slightly different on this wall than it does on that wall and a lot different on this other one but it is still one light." We are seeds planted in the soil of our shared humanity. The healthier our society and environment becomes, the quicker we will grow on the path to God.

*"When 'I' is replaced with 'we' even illness
becomes wellness."*

MALCOM X, HUMAN RIGHTS ACTIVIST

May we never look down on another person unless we are reaching out our hands to help them up. *Zakat* is seeing the money in your bank as nothing other than the manifestation of God's richness, and it is seeing the one in need as an opportunity to serve none other than God. The Prophet Muhammad ﷺ validates this claim with the narration that Allah will say on the Day of Resurrection, "Oh son of Adam, I was ill and you did not visit Me." The man will say, "Oh Lord, how could I visit You when You are the Lord of the worlds?" He will say, "Do you not know that My slave so-and-so was ill and you did not visit him? Do you not know that if you had visited him, you would have found Me with him? Oh son of Adam, I asked you for food and you did not feed Me?" He will say, "Oh Lord, how could I feed You when You are the Lord of the worlds?" He will say, "Do you not know that My slave so-and-so asked you for food and you did not feed him? Do you not know that if you had fed him, you would have found that with Me. Oh son of Adam, I asked you for water and you did not give it to Me." He will say, "Oh Lord, how could I give You water when You are the Lord of the worlds?" He will say, "My slave so-and-so asked you for water and you did not give it to him. Do you not know that if you had given him water, you would have found that with Me?"[26] Allah is reminding us that when we serve the creation we are in service of the Creator.

*"God has no need of your money, but the poor have. You
give it to the poor and God receives it."*

ST. AUGUSTINE, 4TH-CENTURY THEOLOGIAN

In homage to Allah's unconditional, all-encompassing mercy, the mystics symbolically say, "Only in embracing all can we become the arms of God." Life is a series of waves: sometimes we surf the peaks of blessing and other times we crash into the cliffs of poverty and despair.

On the darkest nights—when we feel the most broken, when we feel the most helpless, when tragedy hits and medical bills pile up, when we lose our job, when we cannot pay rent, when we cannot pay the lease on our cars, when we are about to be evicted—*zakat* and *sadaqah* become our safety net. The blessings of our brothers and sisters catch us from falling, buying us time to find a new job, pay back the bills, to pay our rent. *Zakat* and *sadaqah* preserve our dignity, preventing us from being humiliated on the days the waves are too great to weather on our own.

Zakat is a boat in the storm, a crutch that helps you until you heal, the mercy of God being manifested through the hands of humankind. It brings love to a broken heart, the dawn to someone's darkest night, a rainbow into someone's rainy day.

> *"What actions are most excellent? To gladden the heart*
> *of human beings, to feed the hungry, to help the afflicted,*
> *to lighten the sorrow of the sorrowful, and to remove the*
> *sufferings of the injured."*[27]
>
> **PROPHET MUHAMMAD** ﷺ

May Allah inspire us to give more than we think we can, helping us to trust that His generosity and richness will fill in the gaps. We might not have the means or opportunity to change the world, but if we can save one life, feed one person, or bring joy to a single heart then we have at the very least lived true to what it means to be human. As Rumi says, "Be a lamp, or a lifeboat, or a ladder. Help someone's soul heal. Walk out of your house like a shepherd."

> *Oh Allah, help me step out into this world as a mirror*
> *that reflects the faces of Your generous love. My beloved*
> *Lord, remind me that I am not the owner of the outcome,*
> *but I am responsible for my actions—so help me use my*
> *time on Earth to be in service of Your will. "God, grant*
> *me the serenity to accept the things I cannot change,*
> *courage to change the things I can, and wisdom to know*
> *the difference."*[28] *Lord, help me be a representative of Your*

kindness in how I worship, in how I speak, in how I love,
and in how I live in all the moments of my life. In Your
beautiful names I pray. Ameen.

Reflection: "Reflecting Divine Light"

When we give from ourselves, we may run out of love, mercy, and compassion, because we are finite. However, when we connect with Allah and act as a conduit of His love, we will never run out of the passion to serve the creation. We can bring kindness and love to all people at all times by intentionally connecting our heart with the Divine and allowing His light to lead the way. Try the following practice, to foster and reflect the light of God upon all of existence.

- Place your hand on your chest and bring your awareness to your heart.
- Observe the gentle rising and falling of your chest with every breath you take.
- Imagine a divine beam of light coming from above you, down through your head, and into your heart.
- As this divine light fills your heart, witness what it feels like to be receiving God's light. Breathe in the energy of the light and imagine the cells and atoms of your body drinking from the source of light until you feel fully saturated. Observe how the light spreads throughout your body, being conscious of the buzzing, vibrating, or wave-like feeling as it spreads.
- Imagine branches of light blossoming from your heart into the earth. Allow this divinely inspired inner light to expand deeper into the earth and outward, to people around you.
- Consciously send this light to your friends, parents, co-workers, brothers or sisters, a stranger walking past you, a waiter serving you at a restaurant, and even to those who have hurt or offended you. Send your light to the plants, the animals, and all living things. Allow your inner light to spread like the

morning sun, over and into the hearts of all the people you come across.

- As you consciously braid the divine light of your heart with the hearts of others, make a simple and sincere prayer to God on their behalf. Say, *"Oh Allah, I pray that You bring Your light into the heart of this person or creature, making their day joyful and fulfilling."*

- Journal or take note of what it feels like to connect with the light of Allah and to share it with others.

"It was in the month of Ramadan that the Qur'an was revealed as guidance for humankind."

QUR'AN 2:185

"Fasting blinds the body in order to open the eyes of your soul."

RUMI

9

RAMADAN: THE HOLY MONTH OF FASTING

The Qur'an was revealed to the Prophet Muhammad ﷺ in the lunar month of Ramadan on the mysterious Night of Power (*Laylatul Qadr*), said to be "greater than a thousand months" (97:3). To celebrate the miracle of the Qur'an, Muslims spend the entire month of Ramadan in a state of self-purification, abstaining from food, drinking, smoking, and sex from dawn until sundown. The word Ramadan comes from an Arabic root word *ramad*, which means "heated by the intensity of the sun" or "burning," reminding us that the purpose of Ramadan is to burn the sins that veil us from the omnipresence of God.[1]

> *Fasting is not about losing body weight; it's about losing the weight of your sins and learning to detach from the ego that weighs you down.*

The word for fasting in Arabic is *sawm*, which comes from a root word that means "self-restraint." In essence, fasting is about mastery over the self. When we are asked to restrain the ego, our addictions reveal themselves, giving us the awareness needed to break free from them. When we can no longer dull the pain of our emptiness with outer forms, we are forced to search for the root of our longing.

When we fast, we are withdrawing the resources of energy from our physical senses and redirecting our focus toward spiritual awakening. As Rumi says, "There is a hidden sweetness in the stomach's emptiness...if the soundbox is stuffed full of anything" the music of our souls could not vibrate into the world.

In the month of Ramadan we are called to use the polish of prayer, the chisel of fasting, and the cleanser of charity to break the veils of separation between us and Allah. The ultimate purpose of fasting is to remove everything between you and God through a practice of physical, emotional, and spiritual detoxification.

> "Fasting is prescribed for you as it was prescribed for those
> before you, that you might remain God-Conscious."
>
> QUR'AN 2:183

The Month of Endless Mercy

Ramadan is known as the month of mercy and love, when Allah's forgiveness descends upon the entire Earth, realigning souls from the fire of separation toward the embrace of the Divine.

> "Allah intends for you ease and does not intend for you
> hardship and wants for you to complete the period [of
> fasting] and to glorify Allah for that to which He has guided
> you; and perhaps you will be grateful."
>
> QUR'AN 2:185

The month-long fast during Ramadan is not meant to be a hardship, but to foster gratitude and thankfulness in the believer's heart, for Allah having sent human beings divine guidance through the Qur'an. During the month of Ramadan, it is believed that God rigs this month in our favor, facilitating the turn from creation to the Creator by thinning the veils between Heaven and Earth. It is said that it is in this month that the angels are sent to the Earth and the spirit of God descends to our universe, embracing the world with a divine mercy that intimately encompasses everything.

> *"When the month of Ramadan begins, the gates of Heaven*
> *are opened, the gates of Hell-fire are closed, and the devils*
> *are chained."*[2]
>
> PROPHET MUHAMMAD ﷺ

Ramadan is not only seen as a time of retreat—it is strength training for the soul. The real test of a successful Ramadan is not just in fasting every day, giving charity, and reading the Qur'an—the real test of success is who you are the week after Ramadan is finished. We're not just meant to temporarily refrain from sinful actions, but to uproot the weeds of sin and permanently break the bad habits that turn us away from Allah. It is when we train our hearts, strengthen our willpower, and return to witnessing God through our body, mind, and soul.

Fasting is not solely about hunger and thirst; it's about putting God first in every moment. As Imam Al-Ghazali says, "The merit of fasting is not in its hunger, as the merit of medicine is not in its bitterness."

> *Ramadan was not sent by Allah to imprison and chain you;*
> *it is a divine gift that is meant to inspire and change you.*

This month is an opportunity Allah gives us, to strengthen our faith and change our negative habits so that we can live from a place of higher consciousness—not for a single month, but for our entire lives. When we fast for the sake of Allah alone, we are showing Him that as much as we love to consume the pleasures of this world, our love for Him is greater. When we fast with full awareness of who we are fasting for, our hunger and thirst become acts of remembrance and worship of Allah.

The Prophet ﷺ says, "Whatever is prayed for at the time of breaking the fast is granted and never refused."[3] Perhaps this is because when we surrender everything to the Divine, we are not giving up what we have, but becoming receptive to the infinite blessings Allah has given us. Ramadan teaches us how discipline and boundaries don't restrict our freedom, but actually lay the foundation for true freedom.

Our addictions enslave us. Our attachments to our desires enslave us. Allah only calls us to let go of the things that weigh us down and prevent us from being truly free. The following story beautifully demonstrates how learning to let go and detach from our desires leads to freedom:

> In order to catch monkeys in certain Asian villages, hunters carve a hole in a coconut shell and fill the hole with peanuts. The hole is just big enough for the monkey's hand to go inside, but small enough that when the monkey makes a fist to grab the peanuts, its hand gets stuck. All the monkey has to do to escape is let go of the peanuts and pull its hand out. However, even as the hunters approach "trapped" monkeys, they do not let go of the peanuts, resulting in being caught.

When we let go of the lower desires of the self, we discover that the key to escaping our self-made prison has always been in our hands. Ramadan teaches us that the spiritual path is not so much about *doing* as it is about *non-doing*. When we surrender and let go of the desires that do not serve us, we come to see that we're floating peacefully along the river of God's decree.

Becoming Receptive to Divine Guidance

It was in a heightened state of receptivity during one of Muhammad's ﷺ retreats at the Mountain of Light (*Jabal an-Nur*), where he went to fast from the temptations of the world, that the Qur'an was revealed to him.[4] Through this early example of the Prophet ﷺ, we see that fasting from the world to cultivate God-consciousness is the foundation for receiving and understanding the divine revelation. Just as the usefulness of a bowl as a vessel comes from its emptiness, when we empty ourselves of the self and the world, we are able to be filled with Allah.

Allah is continuously pouring His loving guidance upon our seeds of faith. When we fast, we serve to remove all attachments to this world, casting out of our heart everything that prevents us from drinking from the well of Allah's mercy. The "certain number of days" (2:184) Allah has designated for us to fast is a divine prescription that helps us extinguish our sins, bringing us closer to God.

> *Just as it takes a baby nine months in the belly of its mother to develop, the moon many nights to become full, and a caterpillar weeks in a cocoon to become a butterfly, through entering the womb of Ramadan and fasting the entire month, our faith transforms.*

Fasting allows the human being to mirror the qualities of God, because when we do not eat, drink, or have sex, we are transcending our lower human qualities. Allah illustrates the high station of fasting when He says, "Fasting is for me and I shall reward it."[5] Fasting is more than just abstaining from physical desires—it is entirely transcending the self so that the seeker can stand before a singular God. The Prophet Muhammad ﷺ makes the connection between fasting and being with Allah when he says, "One who fasts has two joys: joy upon breaking the fast and joy on meeting God."[6]

> *The spiritual path is not one where we find our way to God, but rather one where we remove everything that prevents us from seeing that we're already in the divine court.*

Beneath the noise of our desires and the whispers of temptation there resides an innately good essential self (*fitra*).[7] In essence, all humans are intrinsically good, but our misperceptions of the past, our false beliefs, and our ego can prevent us from experiencing our full alignment with God. When we fast, we must face our weaknesses, the voices of temptation, and our addictions to this world. Through a temporary period of asceticism, fasting helps to weaken the hold of the ego, thus amplifying the whispering guidance of our spirit. The following profound Cherokee parable exemplifies the inner war between the ego and the spirit that fasting seeks to mediate:

> A Cherokee elder explained to his grandson, "Every person has a war inside their hearts between two wolves. The first wolf is evil and creates conflict by inspiring greed, envy, lust, arrogance, pride, hatred, and fear through overemphasis on the ego. The second wolf is good, fostering peace and unity through a state of God-consciousness." The wide-eyed grandson replied, "Who will win this battle, Grandfather?" The wise elder replied, "The one you feed."

If we think and act in ways that feed our ego, then our ego will overpower our starving spirit, but if we feed our spirit divine qualities of love and mercy, then our spirit will overcome our ego. The ego can only be truly transformed in the embrace of love and discipline. It is when we turn inward, denying the desires of the flesh to feed the spirit, that the spiritual light within us dawns, shattering the darkness of illusion and liberating us from our self-imposed prisons.

The Spiritual Stages of Fasting

The fast of Ramadan may look identical for all Muslims, but on the inside it progresses through the following three spiritual stages: an outer fast, an inner fast, and a heart-centered fast. Ramadan holistically approaches the body, mind, and soul, because in Islam the physical and spiritual realms are interwoven and intimately connected.

The three stages of fasting are not separate, but three dimensions within the singular intention of getting closer to God through disciplining the lower desires of the self through asceticism. It is only when our outer actions, the thoughts in our mind, and the state of our heart are holistically aligned to God that we experience peace and harmony in life.

The Outer Fast of the Limbs

The outer fast both lays the foundation and creates the container for the internal and heart-based fast, by weakening the physical strength of the ego. With the external, physical fast, we adhere to the minimum requirements of the fast: to not eat, drink, smoke, or engage in sexual intimacy from dawn until sunset. As the Qur'an says, "Eat and drink until the white thread of dawn becomes distinct to you from the black thread [of night]. Then complete the fast until the sunset. And do not have relations with them [your spouses] as long as you are staying for worship in the mosques. These are the limits [set by] God, so do not approach them. Thus does God make clear His ordinances to the people that they may become righteous" (2:187).

To understand why these physical restraints are necessary, we must remember that the ego is connected to the body. Just as a rainbow exists only when light and water meet, the ego is a product of the body and the spirit meeting. Since the ego depends on the body, when we weaken the body it serves to weaken the hold of egoistic desires upon us.

"The son of Adam cannot fill a vessel worse than his stomach."[8]

PROPHET MUHAMMAD ﷺ

The stomach is the fuel tank of the body: when it is full, it gives the ego the resources to power the desires of envy, lust, greed, and pride. You cannot surrender to God with the ego in charge. When we fast, we slow down the entire body, weakening the ego through exhaustion and starvation, allowing our spirit to reestablish control over the self (*nafs*). Fasting transforms the ego from an inflexible tyrant to a surrendered servant of God.

It has been scientifically proven that when we practice delaying our gratification by putting off a reward to a future date, we become better able to control our impulses.[9] When we prevent our ego from bandaging our emotions with quick fixes, we are forced to face the root of our emotional instability. Fasting helps us recalibrate and strengthen our willpower in the face of temptation, which is why it has been proven to reduce addictive behaviors. Scientific studies have shown that fasting detoxifies the organs, reduces inflammation, brings mental clarity, helps our cells purify and repair faster, and helps protect against cancer, heart disease, diabetes, depression, and many other ailments.[10] Fasting fosters a state of equilibrium in the body, so that the believer can be a stronger and a more effective instrument of God's loving will on Earth.

When we tame the ego, we create space for the power of the spirit to be enhanced. As the 6th-century Chinese philosopher Lao Tzu reminds us, "He who controls others may be powerful, but he who has mastered himself is mightier still." The purpose of Ramadan is not that we only restrain our desires, but rather that we learn to discipline them. This is why, when we break our fast, we must remain vigilant of our tendency to overeat and strive against our ego's desire to return to old patterns.

> "More caution and perhaps more restraint are necessary in
> breaking a fast than in keeping it."
>
> MAHATMA GANDHI

There is a deep healing and wisdom in mastering the art of self-restraint. The Okinawa Centenarian Study, done on the Island of Okinawa in Japan—known as the "healthiest nation in the world"—showed that the secret of the Okinawans' longevity is mainly attributed to the idea of *hara hachi bun me*, translated as "eat until you are 80 percent full."[11] This Japanese phrase beautifully mirrors the words of the Prophet ﷺ, when he said that man should fill his body with "1/3 for his food, 1/3 for his drink, and 1/3 for his breath."[12]

In essence, the purpose of Ramadan is to teach us the balance the Prophet ﷺ and the Okinawans actualized, by reflecting on our patterns of overindulgence. In Ramadan, we are reminded of what our relationship with food is meant to be. We are not meant to eat food to solely satisfy our egoistic needs, but rather we eat to honor and support our body with the energy necessary to worship God and to become vessels of His love and peace.

The Inner Fast of the Senses and Mind

The external fast is prescribed as a means of paving the way to the inner fast, where you begin to "cultivate within yourself the attributes of God."[13] The Prophet ﷺ urges us to reach past the minimum requirements of fasting when he says, "Many people who fast get nothing from their fast except hunger and thirst."[14]

> *Just as we empty our stomachs of food, we are also called to empty all of our senses from everything that does not bring us closer to Allah.*

Our senses are our connections to the world. What we see, hear, speak, touch, and where we go determine how we think, believe, and eventually act. Some scholars have described the human body as a country: the heart is the capital, surrounded by the seven gates of the stomach, eyes, ears, mouth, feet, hands, and genitals. Since the heart is the seat of God-consciousness, the believer's work is to protect these seven entrances by filtering, tuning into, and allowing to enter only that which aligns the heart to Allah.

In order for our hearts to be changed, we have to change what we feed it through the doors of our senses from the world around us. How can we say we are fasting in a state of God-consciousness if our ears are obese with gossip and idle conversation? How can we say fasting brings us closer to the best version of ourselves if our eyes rarely lower their gaze, taking this world as a buffet of all they can taste and our hands reach for temptation as if we were made just to satisfy our lowly desires? How can we say that fasting brings us closer to Allah if our feet take us to places that dishonor the holiness within us, and our mouths are dry from our fast, but we still talk behind the backs of other people?

The Prophet ﷺ says, "If anyone does not refrain from indecent talking and evil acts, Allah has no need for him to abstain from eating and drinking."[15] Fasting is not just abstaining from the world of form, but it is also about purifying all of our senses from gluttony. It is returning our whole self, both our limbs and our senses, back to Allah.

We are created to be *in* this world, but our work here is striving not to be *of* this world. Fasting from the lower self begins with resisting the ego's desire to seek praise and validation from others. Once we are able to fast from our physical desires and the expectations of others, we then have to learn how to break free from the tyranny of the mind.

> *"As water drops make a river, thoughts make character and faith."*
>
> IMAM ALI

In order to change our thought patterns and pave new pathways in our brain, we must fast from engaging in thoughts that do not serve our higher selves.[16] Scientific studies have shown that whether we visualize raising our right hand or we actually do it, it affects the same areas of the brain.[17] A study at Harvard University also showed that participants who imagined flexing their fingers for several weeks actually increased the physical strength of their fingers by 35 percent.[18] Since these studies show that thoughts affect both the development of the brain and the entire physiology of the body, we know that we need to be conscious of our thoughts, since what we think about directly affects our well-being.[19]

> *When we fast from our thoughts, we are not attempting to stop our thinking; rather, we are choosing to not consume every thought that sprouts from the soil of the ego.*

When thoughts arise, we do not judge them, analyze them, or try to change them—instead, we watch them pass by like clouds floating in the sky of our mind, and gently return our gaze back to the Divine. When we create space between our thoughts and who we *actually* are, we realize that we are not our thoughts. It is only then that we are able to let go of the self-judgment and shame associated with the ego, which often prevents us from feeling worthy of having a relationship with Allah. Once we can see that Allah is our refuge and safe haven from the grips of the ego, we can begin to turn our hearts from the fleeting creation to the eternal Creator.

The Heart-Centered Fast

While the outer fast is broken when the sun sets, the inner, heart-based fast is meant to be continuous and never-ending. This state of fasting mirrors the Prophet's ﷺ saying, "My eyes sleep but my heart remains awake."[20] When we witness Allah in everything, every action becomes prayer, every moment becomes worship, and every person, place, and thing points back to Allah.

When we are in a state of union with our Lord, even though our feet are planted on the earth, our heart is fully present with Allah in the highest heavens. To fast from all other than Allah is to turn away entirely from the creation. When we are empty of food, drink, thoughts, and all other desires, we carry only the divine breath of life that God gave to us. In this state of being, we are so empty of the self that we become a pure mirror for God on Earth.

Islam is the path of removing everything in the way of your inherent connection with God. Ramadan is a period of *muraqaba* or "observation," when God gives us the opportunity, both as individuals and as a Muslim community, to notice the thoughts and feelings within our minds and hearts that veil our witnessing of God. Allah inspires us toward this month of introspection as a means of helping us identify and break the habits that move us away from the love of God, fostering the actions that bring us closer to Him. The importance of reflection is that it helps us identify the ways in which we get in the way of experiencing God's love. Whereas worship perfumes the spirit with God-consciousness, fasting and contemplation protect us from our ego's inclination toward arrogance and lordship.

Fasting enters us into a state of humility by reminding us how quickly our body weakens: in a few short hours of abstaining from food and water, our blood slows, our energy dissipates, and our illusion of invincibility disappears. As we feel our poverty before God and experience our utter dependence upon Him, our hearts naturally are more generous to those who are in need. Our judgments of the poor are purified as we experience the heaviness of hunger. When we take the time to acknowledge the many blessings we have freely been given to by God, we start to open our eyes to the reality that billions in the world are in a perpetual state of hunger, having little hope for a meal when the sun sets. Fasting transforms our mirrors into windows, widening our vision from a state of self-centeredness to a state of being where we consider the needs of those who are far less fortunate than us.

> *"The nourishment of the body is food, while the nourishment of the soul is feeding others."*
>
> IMAM ALI

For those who have trouble completing the fast—due to illness or because they are traveling—the Qur'an exhorts them to feed a poor person for each day missed. The verse goes on to say that giving more than what is expected is much better for the state of their souls (2:184). As the Prophet Muhammad ﷺ said, "Whoever does not show mercy will not receive mercy."[21] The Prophet ﷺ reminds us that the more we emulate and reflect the qualities of God upon others, the more those qualities will blossom within our own souls.

Laylatul Qadr: The Night of Power

The spiritual culmination of Ramadan is considered *Laylatul Qadr*, "The Night of Power," which represents the anniversary of when the Qur'an was revealed. Although no one knows for certain which night of Ramadan is *Laylatul Qadr*, the Prophet Muhammad ﷺ has suggested that it is one of the odd nights of the last ten days of Ramadan.[22]

It is believed that on this night Allah's mercy and compassion is overflowing and abundant, that all sins are forgiven, that every supplication that is made is accepted, and that the Angel Gabriel and many other angels descend from the highest heavens to our world, fulfilling the decrees of God. In fact, the Prophet Muhammad ﷺ said, "Truly the angels on this night are as numerous as the pebbles upon the earth."[23] In a sense, our world becomes crowded with celestial beings that outnumber humankind innumerable times.

"Behold, We revealed the Qur'an on the Night of Power. And what will explain to you what the Night of Power is? The Night of Power is better than a thousand months. The angels and the Spirit descend therein by permission of their Lord for every matter. Peace it is until the emergence of dawn."

QUR'AN 97:1-5

Since not everyone can afford to go on the pilgrimage to Mecca known as *Hajj,* the mystics say that "*Laylatul Qadr* is when Allah brings *Hajj* to your feet." On this night, Allah opens the doors of His mercy for all people and magnifies every good action an enormous amount of times—as the Qur'an says, "*Laylatul Qadr* is better than a thousand months" (97:3). In a sense, Allah is reminding us that this one night is greater than more than 80 years of worship, which is essentially an entire human life span.

Laylatul Qadr is considered the most important night of the year because it is believed to be the night in which Allah invites us, through prayer, to have a hand in creating our destiny. On this mystical night, our free will interacts with divine will to mysteriously manifest new possibilities for the upcoming year.

As holy as this night is, Muslims are not called to only welcome *Laylatul Qadr* inside of mosques, but to be in service to humanity by protecting the environment, feeding and clothing the impoverished, and seeking forgiveness for past sins. A good heart, complemented by good actions, serves to protect us from bad outcomes, both in this life and the next.

The End Is the Beginning

The day that marks the end of Ramadan is called *Eid Al-Fitr,* which translates to mean "Festival of Breaking the Fast." The word *fitr* is correlated with the words *iftar, fitra,* and *Al-Fatir.* The word *iftar* refers to breaking one's fast, the word *fitra* refers to the innate essential goodness at the core of all people, and the word *Al-Fatir* is one of Allah's divine names, meaning, The Originator. In a sense, the purpose of Ramadan is to help us break our old patterns, actualize the *fitra* or innate goodness we already carry within us, and return to the origin of all that exists—Allah.

The purpose of Ramadan is not short-term behavior modification; Ramadan is meant to be the dawn that leads to the creation of a new day. Part of the purpose of Ramadan is to reset patterns in your life that are no longer serving you and to create new possibilities. Since as human beings we are forgetful, having a month-long period of self-reflection is a powerful way of reminding us what is most important in life.

Despite the hardships that are endured, for many Muslims, the month of Ramadan is one of the most joyful periods of the year. During Ramadan we spend more time doing what we were created to do—worshipping God, serving the poor, restraining our ego, seeking to reflect more of God's qualities of love, and being in community—which results in us being more fulfilled and content.

Only for the Sake of Allah

The following story beautifully captures how when we fast from all other than Allah, our hearts naturally open to being more compassionate and loving to all of creation.

> A mystic by the name of Mansur, who was fasting the month before Ramadan, was walking to the mosque when he passed a group of lepers who were eating leftovers from the trash. One of them invited the well-known mystic over to eat lunch with him. The mystic said, "Are you sure? I don't want to be an inconvenience to you." The man assured him that he would be honored to eat with such a famous scholar. Mansur accepted the offer and sat down with the old leper on the floor as he prepared the meal.
>
> The leper turned to his guest and said sadly, "Are you not afraid of us? We often invite the imams we see going to the mosque to break bread with us, but none of them ever do." The sweet mystic smiled softly

at the man and said, "That is because they are most likely fasting." The leper replied, "But aren't you a religious man? Aren't you God-fearing? Why then are you not fasting extra fasts before Ramadan?" The mystic smiled and said, "Yes, surely I love God, and today I have the good pleasure to eat with you."

The leper smiled and together they enjoyed a few bites of food. When the call to prayer rang, Mansur got up, lovingly embraced the leper in gratitude, and headed to the mosque for afternoon prayers. After the sun set, Mansur prayed, "Thank you Allah, for the opportunity to serve you, may you accept my fast today." A few scholars overheard Mansur's prayer and turned to him and said, "Mansur! We saw you eating with the lepers today. You are a hypocrite and a liar for trying to come across as more righteous than you are!"

Mansur turned to them humbly and said, "I may have broken my fast, but I did not break a heart. You tell me which Allah will forgive more easily: a fast we have broken out of love or a heart we have broken out of self-righteousness?"

If fasting makes someone more closed-minded and judgmental, they are not fasting for Allah but for the joy of their own ego. While fasting can detox the body and strengthen your willpower, it is through sincerity and love that the heart truly experiences God.

The true fast is the one where we become more aware of God's all-encompassing presence, which in turn helps us to be more cognizant of our behavior in all aspects of our life. The purpose of Ramadan is to help us face our own hearts in a deeper way, cultivate God-consciousness, and learn self-restraint. Ramadan is a month of forgiveness and guidance for the anxious mind, for the broken heart, and for every soul seeking to be healed. It is a time when we become intimately aware of God's witnessing of us and of our utter dependence on Him. In Ramadan we are called to fast from everything but Allah as a reminder to be present with Allah in all things.

Allah says, "Fasting is a shield,"[24] because it protects us from the fire of separation by constantly reminding us that our love for Allah is greater than our love for our desires. During Ramadan we eat less, sleep less, and worship Allah more than any other month, moving from our animalistic nature that seeks solely for worldly pleasures toward our angelic nature, which seeks solely for Allah. Ramadan is a holy time when we are given the gift of renewing our vows in our covenant with Allah. After all, it is only when we break the tomb of our mortal ego that we can be resurrected into the eternal presence of our loving God.

> *My beloved Lord, help me fast from all that does not serve me, from all that is in the way of my heart's witnessing of You. Oh Allah, as I abstain from food and water, allow my heart to fast from all hatred, jealousy, greed, and harshness. Oh Allah, I come to You prostrating, seeking Your light to guide me and Your mercy to embrace me. My Lord, help me give up every desire that prevents me from experiencing Your truth. My beloved Lord, help me fast from the lower qualities of my ego until the sun of my life sets. As Your beloved Prophet ﷺ prayed, "Allahumma innaka aafuwon tuhibu al aaffwa fa afu aanni—Allah, You are the Forgiver. You love to forgive. So forgive me."[25] Oh Allah, help me be steadfast on the spiritual path, help me be mindful of You, and help me to never lose sight of Your love, generosity, and endless mercy that encompasses every atom of existence. In Your compassionate names I pray, Ameen.*

Reflection: "Observing the Illusion"

Meditation is not the act of having no thoughts, but rather the practice of creating space between your thoughts. It's important to remember that our thoughts and emotions like the seasons will naturally change, but our deep inner essence (*fitra*) will remain the same. Buddhist nun, Pema Chödrön, profoundly says, "You are the sky. Everything else – it's just the weather." We must always remember that our thoughts, like the weather will change, but who we are, the observer of those thoughts stays the same.

In Islamic spirituality, *muraqaba* is the practice of mindfulness, "observing" or "watching over" the fleeting and constantly changing projections of the mind. Just as food and water do not disappear when we fast, but rather it is we who choose not to consume them, when we are in a state of meditation our thoughts do not disappear, we just choose to observe, rather than engage with them. With meditation we learn how to make a distinction between who we are and what we think. When we keep realigning our focus and turning our energy toward Allah, a growing peace begins to slowly blossom within us. As Rumi says, "The quieter you become, the more you are able to hear." The following practice is a great way to observe your thoughts, quiet your mind, and introduce the ancient practice of *muraqaba* into your daily life:

- Sit in a comfortable position, with your back straight and your feet firmly grounded on the floor.
- Focus on your breath. Think, as you inhale through your nose, "Breathing in," and as you exhale through your mouth think to yourself, "Breathing out."
- As you bring consciousness to your breath, notice how you start to breathe more deeply and slowly.
- As you witness your breath, if thoughts sprout in your mind, do not shut them down or resist them; simply acknowledge and observe them, as you might observe clouds passing in the sky or watching leaves float by on a flowing river; and then return your awareness to your breath.
- For 2–3 minutes, sit in a state of *muraqaba,* observing your passing thoughts, without analyzing or judging them.
- Every time you start to analyze a passing thought, it helps to gently return your awareness to your breath or the name of "Allah."
- Notice how the gentle mention of the name of Allah, resembles a natural flow of inhale and exhale of the breath.

- What is it like to shift your awareness from your constantly changing thoughts toward an eternal and unchanging God?
- Take a moment to briefly journal on how you feel after this practice.

"Complete the Hajj and minor pilgrimage (umrah) for the sake of God."

QUR'AN 2:196

"Do you want to become a pilgrim on the road of love? The first condition is that you make yourself humble as dust and ashes."

RUMI

10

Hajj: A
Pilgrimage to
God

G od calls every Muslim that is physically fit and financially capable
to journey with love to the sacred city of Mecca and participate in
the holy pilgrimage known as *Hajj* (3:97). Although you can perform an
optional pilgrimage to Mecca, known as *Umrah,* at any time of the year,
the obligatory *Hajj* pilgrimage must be done in a specific six-day period
in the twelfth month of the Islamic calendar.

Hajj represents the spirit's lifelong journey of return to God. The
Qur'an talks of our eventual return into the arms of divine mercy, but
often in the context of being through the door of death. We prepare for
Hajj as if we are preparing for our death. We must pay all our debts, write
a will, leave money for our family, and seek forgiveness from all those
whose hearts we may have hurt. The physical exertion of the practices
of *Hajj* are part of the process of purifying the soul because as the body
weakens so does the grip of the ego and materialism creating the ideal
conditions for the spirit to awaken. *Hajj* is a physical, psychological and

spiritual journey that calls us to contemplate how attached we are to this life and how ready we are for death.

The rituals of *Hajj* help facilitate a path of return to Allah by helping us gradually detach from our ego and awaken our heart. In reference to the *Hajj*, the twentieth-century scholar Gai Eaton says, "The physical journey is neither more nor less than an outward enactment of an interior journey, the journey from the periphery of our being to the center, the heart, which, for Islam, is the point at which the vertical and the horizontal meet, the point at which the Divine intersects with the human."[1] The Holy Pilgrimage is not a journey to passively worship Allah, but rather the process of dissolving into the love of Allah the way the clouds dissolve into the light of the sun.

> *Hajj is not just an outward journey, but a journey within the heart, in which we actualize all that we already are.*

The *Hajj* rituals are specifically geared toward dissolving not only the chains of our limiting ego, but the superficial borders of race, class, and gender created through culture. Before commercial flights, it took weeks, months, and even years for Muslims from all over the world to travel by boat, horse, and foot to reach the holy city of Mecca.

As a result, pilgrims would often take time after Hajj to recuperate before heading back to their lives and families, often halfway across the world. During this layover, they were given a rare opportunity to learn from and interact with Muslims of different races and cultures that they otherwise would have never met. This was a time when scholars would share their ideas, hate between cultures would be extinguished, and cultural stereotypes were broken. Since fear and bias tend to be changed not through facts or data, but rather through relationship, *Hajj* united men and women from all social classes and cultures, through worship, as brothers and sisters in faith. This unifying presence had a profound effect on the human rights activist Malcom X, who described the Hajj pilgrimage by saying, "There were tens of thousands of pilgrims, from all over the world. They were of all colors, from blue-eyed blondes to black-skinned

Africans. But we were all participating in the same ritual, displaying a spirit of unity and brotherhood that my experiences in America had led me to believe never could exist between the white and non-white."

We may look different, but the love we long for is the same. There is no hierarchy in the rituals of *Hajj*, for all human beings are equal in the eyes of God. In the Qur'an, Allah speaks about how all of humankind comes from a single soul, and so the diversity in our colors and languages is not a means of creating separation between people, but rather an opportunity to experience God's boundless creativity.

> *"Oh humankind, indeed We have created you from male and female and made you nations and tribes that you may know one another. Indeed, the most noble of you in the sight of Allah is the most righteous of you. Surely, Allah is All-Knowing and All-Aware."*
>
> QUR'AN 49:13

Religion was sent not to divide us, but to unveil to us the truth that although we may be separate fruits, we are all hanging from the same tree of life. Our skin may have been painted by God in many shades and tones, but the color of our souls is one. During *Hajj*, we walk together as one soul, back to the same divine home we left so long ago. Our shared goal of seeking intimacy with God supersedes all differences in color, culture, and socioeconomic standing.

Prophet Abraham: The Father of Monotheism

The pilgrimage of *Hajj* dates back thousands of years to the time of the Prophet Abraham. Abraham is the core bridge between the main monotheistic faiths. As Rumi says, "Jews, Christians, Muslims, we all bow down to Abraham's God." In fact, there are rituals of the *Hajj* that commemorate the greatest divine test Prophet Abraham had to endure: when God asked him to sacrifice his firstborn son, Ishmael.[2] When it comes to this story many people wonder, "How could God ask a father to kill his innocent child?"

The key to understanding the deeper dimensions of the stories in the Qur'an is to not get lost in the outward forms, but to listen to what the stories symbolically represent. The symbol of death in revelation represents not an end but a door to a different station of reality. Scholars suggest that God did not seek for Abraham to cause any physical harm to his son, but He was asking him to relinquish his attachment to anything other than Allah. God gave Abraham this infinitely difficult test as a means of breaking Abraham's heart so that everything other than God would fall out of it. Essentially, Allah was teaching Abraham how to actualize *la ilaha illa Allah* in his heart and soul. As a child, Abraham was so opposed to worshipping physical forms that he broke the idols carved by his forefathers in the temple; now in his old age Allah was asking him to break his attachment to his son in the sanctuary of his heart. God was not punishing Abraham, but reminding him not to love the gift of his son to the extent that he may lose sight of the Gift Giver.

However, this story is not just about the Prophet Abraham, but also about his son Ishmael. When the Prophet Abraham received the divine order to sacrifice Ishmael, he went to his son and said, "'My son, I have had a dream that I must sacrifice you. What do you think of this?' He replied, 'Father, fulfill whatever you are commanded to do and you will find me patient, by the will of God'" (37:102). Ishmael beautifully modeled how to truly surrender and lean into divine revelation. This represents one of the greatest examples in the Holy Qur'an of *tawakkul* or "complete trust" in God. When Ishmael heard the command of God, he obeyed without questioning, because he trusted God and knew that his Lord loved him more than any human could, including his father.

We are encouraged to love the passing fruits and flowers of this beautiful Earth, but Allah reminds us to hold these gifts in our hands instead of our hearts, as the heart of the faithful servant belongs only to God. To experience a singular God, we must strive to be empty of both the self and the worldly attachments that define us. The oneness of God is beautifully illustrated in a mythical story of an old seeker that went looking for God.

A lover of God searched for two years before finally finding where his Beloved lived. He knocked on the door and the other side answered, "Who is there?" The lover replied ecstatically, "It is me! The one who loves You more than anyone else!" The other side answered from behind the door, "You have made a mistake; this is not the house you are seeking."

The lover was distraught and confused, so he departed into the desert, praying and worshipping for years before returning again. He again knocked on the door and when the voice answered, "Who is there?" The seeker this time answered, "It is You!" At which point the door was opened for him.

When the sage first came to God's door, his ego was still at the forefront of his existence, which was veiling him from divine oneness. But when he went into the desert, with Allah's help he dissolved his attachment to his self; he sacrificed his inner Ishmael, returning as nothing but a mirror for his Lord. This is what it means to be a true and loving caretaker of this Earth, and a clear reflection of the divine qualities. This is the station of Abraham, the station of detaching from all that is not Allah. The moment Abraham surrendered to what Allah was asking of him, his heart was essentially saying "Yes, yes, I testify!" to the primordial covenant Allah made with all souls.[3]

Every time our desires are in conflict with the Qur'an, we are being asked the same question by Allah: "Am I not your Lord?" When Abraham answered in surrender and submitted his will to be enfolded in the will of God, the order came to kill a sheep instead of Ishmael as a symbol of Abraham's having sacrificed his ego before God.[4] Once Abraham and his son passed the test given to them by God, they were divinely inspired to rebuild the ancient *Kaaba* in the valley of Mecca.

The Mysteries of the *Kaaba*

Although there are no universally agreed upon prophetic narrations, some scholars and mystics have suggested that after Adam and Eve reunited on Earth, they were drawn to the valley of Mecca by the incredible scene of angels they saw circling the *Bait-ul Ma'mur* or the "Frequented House" (52:4). The *Bait-ul Ma'mur* is said to be located outside the human realm, in the seventh heaven above the *Kaaba*. Some have suggested that it was here, directly beneath the center of celestial worship, that Adam and Eve were guided to build the *Kaaba,* which was the first human-made altar of worship in the name of a singular God on Earth.[5]

> *"Indeed, the first House [of worship] established for humankind was that at Becca [another name for Mecca]— blessed and a guidance for the worlds."*
>
> QUR'AN 3:96

Time swallowed the remnants of this sacred shrine only to be resurrected thousands of years later by Prophet Abraham and his son Ishmael (2:127). Over time, the *Kaaba,* which once stood as a symbol of monotheism, became filled with tribal idols and had become a popular destination of worship for pagan pilgrims. It was not until the Prophet Muhammad ﷺ was sent that the *Kaaba* was purified of all idols and reinstated as the center of monotheism for all Muslims.

The *Kaaba* is metaphorically known by Muslims as the "House of God." It is architecturally very simple, but contains a lot of rich symbolism. The structure of the *Kaaba* is cube-shaped, so it points to north, south, east, west, below, and above while not facing in any one particular direction, reminding us that God faces all directions simultaneously.

Today, the *Kaaba* is covered in a black cloth, which wonderfully represents the endless and transcendent nature of God. Black is not the absence of color, but rather the outcome when all color is absorbed without reflection. Similarly, God unites all diversity within His singularity. The *Kaaba* is empty inside, signifying that God cannot be captured or contained in any finite form. The importance of not being too literal when conceptualizing the *Kaaba* is perfectly illustrated in a story of Mullah Nasruddin, who traveled to the holy city of Mecca for the *Hajj* pilgrimage.

After finishing his *Hajj*, the Mullah Nasruddin decided to take a short nap in the Grand Mosque. While sleeping he tossed and turned until unconsciously his feet faced toward the sacred *Kaaba*. The Mullah was rudely awakened by a group of angry Meccans, screaming at him for having his feet pointing toward the holy House of God (*Kaaba*). The Mullah replied, "Oh forgive me! I am terribly sorry for my forgetfulness! Could you please direct my feet in a direction where God is not present?" The Meccan elites were left speechless because they knew that God was present in every direction, so they left the clever Mullah alone.

The *Kaaba* deserves the utmost respect *and* we must under no circumstances fall into the trap of worshipping forms; especially not to the extent that we forget the intention and symbolism of the *Kaaba*. The Qur'an beautifully teaches us that righteousness does not come from facing a geographical direction, but is based in the sincerity behind our beliefs and actions.

> *"Righteousness is not that you turn your faces toward the east or the west, but righteousness consists of the belief in God, the Day of Judgment, the angels, the Books of God, His prophets; to give money for the love of God to relatives, orphans, the needy, the wayfarer, those who ask; to set free slaves; and to be steadfast in prayer; to pay the alms; to fulfill one's promises; and to exercise patience in poverty, in distress, and in times of war. Those are the ones who have been true, and it is those who are the righteous."*

QUR'AN 2:177

Muslims do not see the *Kaaba* as a house where God lives, but rather as a reflection of the *Bait-ul Ma'mur*, where countless celestial beings are constantly circling in a perpetual state of prayer. When we circle the *Kaaba* in worship of Allah, we are joining the entire universe in a dance of praising the Divine. Allah is seen as the central point of the circle of existence. He is the axis point by which everything rotates around—He does not move, change, or shift, for He is outside time and space.

Everything in existence is in a constant state of circumambulation. Electrons orbit the nucleus in an atom, the moon orbits the Earth, the Earth orbits the sun, and the sun orbits a black hole in the center of our galaxy. Just as a black hole pulls all surrounding matter into its orbit with its gravity, the *Kaaba* attracts the soul through the infinite gravity of divine love.

Without the divine pull of love there would be no life because matter cannot form without attraction. If the love and attraction from the electron to the nucleus or from the Earth to the sun were removed, life would cease to exist. From the microscopic to the macroscopic level, we are in a constant state of orbiting. Like 300 million sperm reaching toward a single egg, millions of pilgrims are all reaching to dissolve in the Divine, for it is our union with God that inspires life within us. Just as the nucleus is the center of an atom and a black hole is the center of our galaxy, the *Kaaba* serves as the geographical center point of a Muslim's spiritual life. Every believer's life orbits around the unified field of God-consciousness.

We circle the *Kaaba* in a counterclockwise direction, known as a circumambulation, symbolizing that our relationship with God is outside of time and space and a metaphor that the journey to God is endless. This is why we end each of our seven circumambulations exactly where we began, at the *Al-Hajaru Al-Aswad*—the mysterious black stone said to have fallen from the heavens during the time of Adam and Eve. Our journey on Earth is from God, who is our origin, to God, who is our end.

The purpose of every *Hajj* ritual is to unveil us of our attachments to this world, so we can become aware of God's proximity. As Rumi says, "Be crumbled so wild flowers will come up where you are. You have been stony for too many years. Try something different. Surrender."

Mystical Symbolism in the Rituals of Hajj

Hajj rituals provide an opportunity to contemplate our existence, in relationship with God and His entire creation. The long hours of prayer in the harsh desert climate, crowded traveling conditions between ritual sites, and clothing prohibitions remind us of our reliance on God. The pilgrimage of *Hajj* consists of many beautiful rituals, most of which are rich in symbolism. The following are some of the main rituals of *Hajj*:

Aside from meaning "pilgrimage," the word *Hajj* comes from the tri-literal root *ha-jim-jim* that means "complete intention, definite proof." A major condition of *Hajj* is making the intention (*niyah*) of leaving behind the world and everything in it, seeking solely Allah. As Rumi says, "Give your life to the One who already owns your breaths and your moments." In approaching the *Kaaba*, the pilgrims all lovingly sing the following prayer of intention, known as the *Talbiyah*: "Here I am at Your service, Oh Lord, here I am. Here I am at Your service and You have no partners. To You alone is all praise and all bounty, and to You alone is the sovereignty. You have no partners."

Alongside with setting a sincere intention, we must change from our worldly clothes and enter into a state of *ihram*. The word *ihram* refers to both a type of clothing and a state of being. As a noun, the *ihram* is a white cloth with no seams, that is void of brands and adornments of wealth, which is symbolic of stepping outside of human culture and worldly pursuits. Although the requirements for what women should wear for *Hajj* are not as specific as those for men, they are still encouraged to wear clothing that is modest and without brands, in order to preserve a uniform sense of unity. The outer unity symbolizes that every person before God is equal; there are no divisions based on wealth, race, or culture.

Hajj is the only place where king and peasant dress the same, starving artist and billionaire pray side by side, famous movie star and villager must both sleep in tents. When both women and men enter *ihram*, they are prohibited from certain activities like having sex, hunting, or cutting their hair in order to shift their focus from the desires of the ego toward pure God-consciousness. All the distinctions of the self and the egoistic "I" of each pilgrim melts away, evolving into a universal "we." Like drops in the ocean, the pilgrims blend into a single sea of white where culture, race, social status, gender, and age make no difference in the face of God. Hierarchy in the eyes of God is not based on how much wealth you have, but is based on spiritual richness, righteousness, and God-consciousness. As the pilgrim approaches the *Kaaba,* they must strip themselves of every attachment and mark of separation, emptying themselves of the world and longing to be filled with God's presence alone. The *ihram* is sometimes called the "coffin cloth," because it mirrors the *kaffan,* the white fabric Muslims are wrapped in when they are buried. When you put it on, you are in effect surrendering to God like the dead in the hands of the washer and completely submitting your will to God.

Once we have entered a state of *ihram,* we can enter into the holy city of Mecca and circle the *Kaaba* seven times. Like circling the seven rings of an atom, every time we circumambulate the *Kaaba* we are circling closer and closer to the nucleus of our own being, until we can access the spiritual essence within us, where God is most brilliantly reflected. In essence, the entire outer pilgrimage is a symbol for our inner pilgrimage to the *Kaaba* of our hearts.

One of the most symbolic practices of *Hajj* is running seven times between the hills of Safwa and Marwa. As the story goes, after waiting almost a century to have a child, Prophet Abraham was commanded by God to leave the mother of his child, Hajar, and his infant son, Ishmael, between the two hills of Safwa and Marwa, in a dry and inhabitable desert in Arabia, later to be called Mecca. Abraham was commanded to leave them exposed to the harsh elements of the Earth and to trust that Allah would protect and provide for them out of the infinite ocean of His mercy. During *Hajj,* we run between these hills as a reenactment of when Hajar ran between Safwa and Marwa, searching for water for her thirsty baby. These hills are symbolic of the earthly journey of running between God's qualities of Beauty (*Al-Jamal*) and Majesty (*Al-Jalal*), thirsty for the waters of His love and mercy. As Hajar ran seeking water, the infant Ishmael was crying and digging his heels into the desert sand. From where his baby feet struck the ground, a spring of water bubbled forth, later to be known as the miraculous Zam Zam.

The sacred well of Zam Zam has continued to provide water to the pilgrims of Mecca since before the time of Prophet Muhammad ﷺ. Symbolically, this story shows us that just as it was beneath the thirsty feet of Ishmael that the spring of Zam Zam sprang forth, it is within our pain and longing that our cure resides. As Rumi beautifully says, "Wherever a pain is, that's where the cure goes; wherever poverty is, that's where the provision goes. Wherever a difficult question is, that's where the answer goes; wherever a ship is, water goes to it. Don't seek the water; increase your thirst, so water may gush forth from above and below. Until the tender-throated infant is born, how should the milk flow from the mother's breast?"

One of the most memorable and life changing experiences of *Hajj* is praying on the plains of Arafat. It is often said that Arafat is the apex of *Hajj*. The image of millions of people dressed in practically what they will one day be buried in, coming out from every valley and crevice of the Earth, is a symbolic dress rehearsal of the Day of Judgment, when we come before God with nothing but our faith and good deeds. Although scholars disagree about where on Earth Adam and Eve were individually sent, some scholars suggest that Arafat is where Adam and Eve reunited after being cast down from the divine Garden. Other scholars say Arafat is a symbol of God's boundless forgiveness, for it was on the Mountain of Mercy (*Jabal Al-Rahma*) that Adam and Eve prayed to be forgiven for having eaten from the forbidden tree, and their prayer was accepted.[6] The word *Arafat* comes from the root word *arafa*, which means "to recognize, discover, and know," implying that this place represents a return to our origin, a coming together, a reacquaintance with who we are and where we came from. Through the reconciliation of Adam and Eve, the dual nature of man is symbolically united before the singularity of God. As Rumi says, "Although you appear in earthly form, your essence is pure consciousness. You are the fearless guardian of Divine Light. So come, return to the root of the root of your own soul."

Arafat is a powerhouse of God-consciousness, where pilgrims come to reaffirm their divine pledge of allegiance and pray for forgiveness.[7] The

Prophet Muhammad ﷺ suggests that the following is one of the best supplications to make on the day of Arafat: *La ilaha illa Allahu, wahda-hu laa shareeka lah, lahul-mulku wa lahul-hamdu, wa huwa 'alaa kulli shay'in qadeer.* Meaning, "None has the right to be worshipped except Allah, alone, without partner. To Him belongs sovereignty and all praise and He is over all things omnipotent."[8]

A symbolic practice of breaking our idols and turning to Allah is the ritual of casting stones in Mina. We cast pebble-size stones at three pillars that symbolize the three tests the Prophet Abraham faced when the order came to sacrifice his first son. Symbolically, the number three is seen as a representation of the continuous and repetitive nature of temptation. As tradition holds, the pilgrim must stone each of the three pillars symbolizing the devil seven times. This practice represents consistently turning our worldly and spiritual affairs over to Allah. We are not called to fight the darkness on our own, but to seek out the light of God and call upon Him to illuminate our path to peace. The throwing of the stones also can be seen as mirroring the station of Prophet David, who was able to kill the giant of oppression with the casting of a single stone of faith. It is not about striking the pillars with the most might, but rather gently letting go of base desires and negative patterns in your life that hinder your spiritual progress. When we face and acknowledge the places we get stuck, we can integrate a deeper awareness around what we want to change. There is a hilarious story of the comical Mullah Nasruddin that perfectly depicts our inclination to hold onto patterns that stifle our spiritual progress.

> One day, the Mullah opened his lunch bag at work and complained, "Another cheese sandwich! I am so sick of these cheese sandwiches!" Then the next day again he opened his lunch and said, "Cheese sandwich again! I am going to die from these cheese sandwiches!" Then the following day yet again the Mullah opened his bag and, lo and behold, he said, "Cheese sandwich! I hate cheese sandwiches! Oh, why, God?! Why is it always a cheese sandwich!" Finally one

of his co-workers said, "Mullah, why don't you tell your wife you don't like cheese sandwiches?" The Mullah replied, "But I don't have a wife." His co-worker confusingly asked, "Well, then, who makes these cheese sandwiches?" The Mullah then said, "Well, I do!"

This humorous and yet profound story begs us to ask ourselves, how often do we complain about patterns in our life that we weave with our own hands? The casting of stones at Mina is a symbolic act of taking responsibility for our actions. It is not only rejecting the outside influences of the Devil, but also casting out the inner voices of criticism, envy, greed, jealousy, lust, and other temptations of the ego that keep us enslaved to the world instead of aligned with Allah.

The human being's greediness and obsession with the ego is one of the reasons pilgrims are called to sacrifice an animal and donate the meat to the poor. This sacrifice symbolizes that, like the Prophet Abraham, we are willing to surrender what is most important to us in exchange for God's good pleasure. This can also be seen as symbolic of detaching from the animalistic desires of the ego. As the Qur'an says, "Pray to your Lord and sacrifice" (108:2), because everything you seek is hidden beneath the base desires of the lower self. In the divine realm, the more we give for the sake of God, the more we receive from the hands of God. As a result, this charitable contribution not only connects us with the poor, but it also serves to make our hearts more open and receptive to the blessings (*baraka*) of God.

Aside from just sacrificing an animal for the poor, pilgrims also cut or shave their hair. This sacrifice is meant to remind us of the impermanence of our physical forms in relation to the eternal nature of God, cutting our hair is also an act of sacrifice before God. Our hair symbolizes our honor, so when we shave or cut our hair we are in effect telling God, *"I place nothing above you. I sacrifice all of my superficial attachments, my reputation, and all the worldly adornments that define me in exchange for Your good pleasure."* With the cutting of the hair we reverently leave the state of *ihram*.

However, before leaving the state of *ihram*, many Muslims return to Mecca and do the "farewell circumambulation" of the *Kaaba*. Symbolically, every time we circle the Kaaba we are peeling away one of the layers of the seven heavens, with the intention of standing before God without the veils of our ego. As the Prophet ﷺ says, "Whoever performs *Hajj* and does not commit any obscenity or transgression will return [free from sins] as he was on the day his mother gave birth to him."[9] The *Hajj* is like a shortcut to unveiling and accessing the sacredness of our essential self (*fitra*). In fact, it is said that once the rituals of *Hajj* are all completed, if the pilgrim has fully surrendered to the Divine, circumambulating around the *Kaaba* will be like circling the throne of God, amongst the angels of the highest heavens.

Every Moment Is Hajj

The roads to the *Kaaba* are infinite and many, but the goal is one. Our journey on Earth is a pilgrimage from Allah to Allah. Every inhale and exhale belongs to Him. Every time you sleep you return to Allah, and every morning by His mercy you are returned to your body. *Hajj* is now. In this very moment, you are orbiting a *Kaaba* in your life. Just as the Earth spins around its own axis, we humans orbit a central point.

What is your Kaaba?

What is the thing that pulls you toward it with the strongest attraction, that you think about when your soul returns to your body in the morning? What is the thing that orbits your mind when your eyelids kiss you into sleep every night? What do you long for more than anything else? What is the center of your life? Whatever the answer is, that is your *Kaaba*.

We do not have to fall head-over-heels for something for it to become an idol before God. Whatever we place our focus on more than Allah becomes a false god, because as it occupies more of our mind it influences more of our decisions. If your world revolves around something mortal—a person that will one day die, a thing that will one day break, or a desire that will pass away—you will never find true peace, because you have attached yourself to something that is fleeting. This is why the Buddha said, "The root of all suffering is attachment." This is also why the path to God begins with detaching from all fleeting idols with *La ilaha* (there is no god), before affirming belief in the singular eternal reality of God with *illa Allah* (but God).

We have to first negate the existence of false idols within us before we can declare the singularity and perfection of Allah. *Hajj* teaches us to let go of this mortal world, so that we can hold on to an eternal God. Every act and ritual of *Hajj* is about stripping us of all that prevents us from actualizing the all-encompassing oneness of God. We do not go on *Hajj* to gain something; rather, we go on *Hajj* to let go of everything in the way of actualizing what we already are.

Hajj is about giving up our limitations and our pictures of how reality should be, to become receptive to everything that God wants to create through us. When the veils of our misperception are removed we come to find that the door to the Divine has always resided in the *Kaaba* of our own sacred hearts.

> *My beloved Lord, please open the doors of Your abundant mercy so that I may visit Your Holy House. Oh Allah, make my entire life a Hajj, a pilgrimage from all that I am to all that You are. Forgive me for my shortcomings and purify me with Your grace, so that I can become a pilgrim on the path of Your love. In the words of my beloved Prophet ﷺ, "Oh Allah, distance me from my sins just as You have distanced the east from the west. Oh Allah, purify me of my sins as a white robe is purified of filth. Oh Allah, cleanse me of my sins with snow, water, and ice."[10] Oh Allah, I lovingly await Your invitation to come visit You, both in this life and the next. I place my hope in Your mercy and place my trust in Your perfect timing. In Your generous names I pray, Ameen.*

Reflection: "What Is in the *Kaaba* of Your Heart?"

Everybody worships something. What we worship depends on where we direct our attention. When our main focus is on anything other than Allah, the object of our attention becomes an idol. The following exercise helps to identify and remove our idols.

- Grab a few pieces of paper and a pen.
- Sit in a chair or on the ground, with your back straight, and take 3 deep breaths. Make sure when you exhale you do so slowly.
- Contemplate the following questions: What do you think about most in your life? What do you worry about before you sleep? What do you think about when you wake up? What distracts you in prayer the most?
- Write down all of your answers on separate pieces of paper.
- Lay these papers around you and imagine that they are physical idols that you have placed in the *Kaaba* of your heart. What feelings come up for you in witnessing these idols?
- Take a deep inhale through your nose for 5 counts, hold your breath for 3 counts, and exhale slowly through your mouth for 8–10 counts. Pause for 2 counts and repeat. Do this 6–8 times or until you feel a sense of relaxation. (At first this may be hard to do, but after a few tries it will get easier.)
- Notice how your state may have changed. As your mind begins to quiet, one by one, pick up each paper and ask Allah, *"Oh Allah, help me let go of this idol that is not serving me so I can grasp on to You. Oh Allah, remove this wall between us, so I can witness You more clearly."*
- After each prayer you make, tear your paper idol into little pieces, as a symbolic act of letting go.
- After each idol you tear apart, recite *la ilaha illa Allah,* which means "There is no god, but God" 33–100 times.
- Be present with how you feel before and after this practice.

*"The life of this world is but comfort
of illusion."*

QUR'AN 3:185

"Our death is our wedding with eternity."

RUMI

11

THE SPIRITUAL
SECRETS OF DEATH

We are an everlasting spirit, molded from the breath of God. Our bodies are vehicles, but not who we actually are. Our bodies are made of clay and this Earth is the oven in which we are baked and glazed into divine pottery. The Earth is not our home, but a cocoon, a gestation period, where we are molded into who we were written to become.

Death is not an end, it is a transition—a metamorphosis, in which we undress our caterpillar bodies to unveil our everlasting butterfly spirits. Everything living begins with a death, a loss, or a sacrifice; it is in the compost of death that life grows and evolves. The cocoon must be torn for the butterfly to emerge, and the seed must split before a tree can sprout.

Life is dying to evolve. Death is a bridge that leads to the evolution of our consciousness, for as Allah says, "What is to come is better than what has gone by" (93:4). If you tell a baby in the darkness of the womb that there is a world of light, mountains, seas, and stars, it will find it hard to believe. Just like that baby, our understanding of reality is limited to what we have experienced in the womb of Mother Earth. And just like a baby, we too must one day leave the womb of this world for a different reality.[1]

Our bodies will one day die, but our spirits will continue living. Death is not an end, but a means to a God who has no end.

We are not stones, we are seeds; we are not buried when we die, we are planted, to rise in another time.

The idea of existence after "death" is even alluded to scientifically, through the law of conservation of energy, which states that in a closed system, energy is neither created nor destroyed. In other words, when our bodies die, the light of life within us is not destroyed, but transformed.[2] Death is a season, a winter for our spirits, which have been written to awaken in the spring of resurrection. Death is the door to eternal life, for it is only through dying that immortality can be experienced; it is only through death that we actualize the priceless value of life.

We experience loss or "little deaths" throughout our lives as a means of reminding us that nothing on this Earth is forever. Only Allah is eternal. Everything here will one day return to Him. As the Qur'an says, "And certainly, We shall test you with something of fear, hunger, loss of wealth, lives, and fruits, but give glad tidings to the patient" (2:155). We are mere sandcastles near a rising shore, and it's only a matter of time before the ocean of unity pulls us back into its embrace.

From relationships that dissolve, to friendships that end, and dreams that break, everything is constantly dying and being reborn. The atoms and cells in our bodies are constantly dying and regenerating into a new existence. Every night, the Earth dies to the day before; every time you sleep, you taste death until God resurrects you into a wakeful state.[3]

"It is He who makes the night as a robe for you and sleep as repose and makes the day a resurrection."

QUR'AN 25:47

We are constantly being re-created into a new creation. Death is intimately braided into life. Do not fall in love with this fleeting world, do not get used to its comforts, because everything here is falling apart, dissolving, and decaying with the passage of time.

*"Wash the dead and your heart will be moved, for surely an
empty body is a profound lesson."*

IMAM ALI

The Pricelessness of Time

We are veiled from the sun of reality by the clouds of our attachment
to this life. When we learn to surrender our life to God and truly make
peace with death, the light of awareness pierces our consciousness, unveiling the truth. This is profoundly depicted through the story of Alexander
the Great's death.

> When Alexander the Great became deathly ill, he called upon the
> greatest healers and doctors from across the world. He showed them
> his riches—his diamonds, gold coins, and rubies—and said that unbelievable treasures would be given to the one who could cure him.
> But no herb, pill, tincture, or potion affected his worsening condition.
> The great Alexander, the most powerful man on Earth, was dying, and
> he could do nothing to prevent it.

> When Alexander finally surrendered and accepted his fate, he called
> the viziers and noblemen of his court to a meeting and he told them
> that when he died, he had three wishes for them to fulfill. First, he
> requested that his physicians be the only ones carrying his coffin.
> Second, he asked that the path leading to his grave be beautified with
> gems and riches from his treasury. Last, he requested that his hands
> be dangling out of his coffin.

> Alexander explained: "I want my doctors to carry my coffin so that
> my people know that when the time for death comes, no earthly
> healer could prevent it. I want the road to my grave to be paved with
> diamonds and gold so that my people see that, despite all my riches,
> I cannot take any of my treasures with me; and I could not purchase
> more life than I was given, for life is priceless. Finally, I want my
> hands to dangle outside my coffin so that my people may see that, like

everyone, I came to this world with my hands closed, with nothing in them, and now when I leave this world I am leaving with my hands open, with nothing in them."

Alexander the Great saw that his endless wealth and historic successes could not save him from death. This story reminds us to be conscious of the time we have left, for time is a commodity we can never get back. We can sin and be forgiven. We can become sick and heal. We can become poor and remake our fortune. But when time passes, it can never be returned to us. It is the seeds of charity, love, knowledge, and good deeds that we plant for the sake of Allah that blossom through the seasons beyond our life. Only the good deeds we acquired come with us to the grave.

> "Wealth and children are an ornament of the life of the world. But the good deeds which endure are better in your Lord's sight for reward, and better in respect of hope."
>
> QUR'AN 18:46

Our fortune, our worldly success, our family and friends—everything that is mortal will be left behind. As one mystic profoundly said, "Every single person you love in this world will either bury you or you will bury them. There is no other way."[4]

Losing a Loved One

Truly accepting the loss of someone we deeply love is one of the hardest trials we will ever face. It is easy to get lost in shameful thoughts about the regretful things we did or did not do, or the words we said or never got the chance to say to the one who passed away. The key to walking through loss is not to get so lost in our grief and pain that we miss witnessing the loving presence of Allah that embraces us even in the moments that shatter our hearts.

Grief has a very holy purpose. Through our feelings of loss, we actualize true gratitude. When we begin to see the depth of our grief as reflecting the depth of love that we felt, the holes that a loved one's spirit once filled go from triggers of sadness and regret to altars of gratitude. The children's book character, Winnie the Pooh, beautifully illustrates this when he says, "How lucky I am to have something that makes saying good-bye so hard." May we not allow our grief for the loss of a loved one prevent us from being grateful for having had that person in our life as long as we did.

Grief is normal, and our faith is not lessened by it. After all, the Prophet Muhammad ﷺ mourned his wife and the love of his life, Khadijah, many years after she passed. Cry the tears you need to cry, but in the midst of your pain do not forget that your Lord loves you deeply and sees you fully.

> "Do not be afraid, I am with you, All Hearing and
> All Seeing."
> QUR'AN 20:46

No matter how heartbroken we feel over the loss of a loved one, we must remember that "Allah does not burden a soul beyond what it can bear" (2:286). When the weight of life seems too heavy to shoulder, it is not because God is trying to break us, but because God is trying to unveil a strength we never knew we had.

To better understand this, consider the following: there is a plant called Bakers Globe Mallow (*Iliamna baker*) that has such a hard shell, one of the only ways it can germinate is through a wildfire. As a result, for more than a hundred years this seed can lie dormant under the soil, not manifesting a single sprout. It's not until a wildfire blazes through the forest, softening and breaking the shell of its seed, that water can reach the core of the plant and germinate it. While most trees, plants, and flowers burn in fire, the Bakers Globe Mallow grows *because* of the fire.[5]

Sometimes the wildfires of pain don't just destroy what we love, they also unveil hidden seeds of beauty and strength within us that we never knew existed and were unable to manifest in conditions of ease. God sometimes tests us in order to break the shells of our hearts—creating the opportunity for us to manifest into a garden of faith. Just as an egg must break for a bird to be hatched, sometimes God has to keep breaking our hearts until a path to the light is opened.

The more we are reminded that our loved ones are gifts given to us by God, the less we will blame God when He takes them back. In its deepest sense, loss is when we give back to God what was never really ours in the first place. Having faith does not mean we don't mourn this loss, it means that despite our sadness we place our hope in God's promise that death is not an end, and that there will come a day when we'll be reunited. The Prophet Muhammad ﷺ himself reminds the lovers of God that all earthly separation is temporary, for in the end "You will be with those whom you love."[6]

Beyond just mourning for someone we have lost, we are encouraged to give in their name, because kindness and charity transcend the barriers of the grave. Doing charity in the name of a loved one not only strengthens the bond between us and them, it also invites their presence into the lives of other people, allowing their legacy to live on beyond their time on Earth. Death may separate us from physically witnessing those who have died, but the love we feel in our hearts continues to transform our souls.

> *"Goodbyes are only for those who love with their eyes. Because for those who love with heart and soul there is no such thing as separation...Death has nothing to do with going away. The sun sets. The moon sets. But they are not gone."*
>
> RUMI

A candle's flame may die when it burns to the end of its wick, but the light and heat that it gave off lives on. Like candles, our bodies may melt away with time, but the seeds of love we planted on Earth will continue to flower beyond our finite lives. The ones we have lost are like stars in the sky, despite having passed away, we continue to experience their light within our lives.

It is also important to acknowledge that, entangled with our grief for the loss of a loved one, is often fear about our own eventual departure.

Despite the pain of losing someone we love, the hidden blessing is that it is a divine reminder to live more fully, love more fiercely, and to give more freely, for any moment could be our last.

This Is Not Your Home

Your body is a vehicle that God has given you as a loan; and this world is just a bus stop along the way from God back to God. This worldly life is not forever. The impermanence of life is beautifully depicted in the following story:

> A mystic from Kufa set out on a journey to meet the spiritual master Abu Hussein for the first time. When the mystic walked into Abu Hussein's house he was surprised to find no furniture. The perplexed seeker asked the holy man, "Why does your house have no furniture?" The master smiled and ecstatically asked, "Why didn't you bring furniture with you?" The confused seeker said, "I am a traveler. What use would furniture do me?" The master laughed and said, "Ah, yes, my friend, but I too am a traveler. I will only be on this Earth for a few short days and then I will return back to my real home!"

Our real home is not one money can buy—our real home is with God. This story mirrors the words of the Prophet Muhammad ﷺ, who said, "The worldly comforts are not for me. I am like a traveler, who takes rest under a tree in the shade and then goes on his way."[7]

As one mystic profoundly stated in reference to the briefness of our journey on Earth, "When we are born, the *adhan,* or call to prayer, is recited in our ears but no prayer is performed. When we die, no *adhan* is recited, but a prayer is performed. This is because the *adhan* of your birth belongs to the prayer of your death. That's how short life is."[8]

We are not residents of our houses, countries, or even our bodies— rather, we are visitors. And just as no visitor would decorate a hotel room they were staying in for only a few days, do not waste time obsessing over the adornments of a life on Earth that you do not own; instead, decorate your spirit with good deeds, for that is the only currency that transcends time and space. Invest in what is eternal instead of this mortal life.

> *"Die before you die." Kill your attachments to the illusions of this life—your ego, your reputation, your pride, and your material possessions—because the more you let go of this world, the higher you will rise.*[9]

It is only when we kill our attachment to the mortal desires of the self that we are freed from anxiety around losing what is perishing. In essence, this is a voluntary death of illusion, where we are drawn to the light of the Divine until all separation is extinguished. This is the station of *fana fi Allah,* or dissolving the separate self into the infinite ocean of God's love. Between the death of the ego and the death of the body is when we may truly experience life. However, it is important to remember that spiritual rebirth is not an event, it is a process. We are not called to reject the blessings of our worldly life, but rather, we are reminded to not become enslaved by our love.

> *"Detachment is not that you should own nothing, but that nothing should own you."*
>
> IMAM ALI

As a wise man once prayed to God, "Oh Lord, please do not allow death to reach me before I am annihilated." He understood that if we give everything to God that death can take, including ourselves, then once death arrives there is no struggle or pain. We find lasting peace when we fully surrender to the journey of our return to the divine light of Allah that is waiting to embrace us in its mystery and mercy.

Impermanence and the Hidden Mercy of God

In Islam, the impermanence of life is not seen as a punishment, but rather as an integral part of divine mercy. The hidden mercy of death is beautifully manifested through the following ancient story of a faithful king:

A king commissioned a council of spiritual sages to come up with a motto that could remind him to be humble and grateful during the highs of life, while also inspiring patience and hope in times of sadness. After many nights of consultation, the wise men brought the king a ruby ring engraved with the words: "This too shall pass." The awareness of the impermanence of all earthly things and emotions gave the king hope that no matter how painful or difficult life became, the pain would not be forever. On the days when blessings dropped blossoms everywhere and life seemed perfect, the ring reminded the king to stay humble.

The impermanence of life and all of its dramas is our greatest source of both hope and humility. With death, we are reminded of the mercy of God—for if everything were endless, our sorrows and our pains would last forever as well.

Death begs us to anchor our happiness not on what is fleeting, but rather on Allah, whose love is eternal and unchanging. Death reminds us that the only thing that is real and unchanging is God. Everything else in existence, whether it be good or bad, will eventually perish. As the great Tibetan master Jetsun Milarepa poetically said, "The sound of thunder, although deafening, is harmless; the rainbow, despite its brilliant colors does not last; this world, though it appears pleasant, is like a dream; the pleasures of the senses, though agreeable, ultimately lead to disillusionment."[10]

When we turn our focus from our egos and mortal bodies toward the everlasting and mystical breath of God within us, like a snowflake in the sun, the fear of death slowly dissolves. Our spiritual essence cannot die, because our spirits live beyond our time on Earth. This world only breaks the shells of the seeds of who you *think* you are, so that God can manifest the tree of your true essence, which you have always carried inside of you.

The cloud does not blame nature for tearing it apart every time the Earth's flowers and fruits long for rain. Gold does not curse the fire that purifies it. A mother does not grieve the loss of her placenta once she is handed her baby. When we see that "with difficulty there is ease" (94:5), we do not mourn what is lost. As the Qur'an says, "If God finds anything good in your hearts, He will give you something better than what has been taken from you. God is All-Forgiving and All-Merciful" (8:70). Just as the winter strips the trees of dead leaves to create room for spring blossoms, God takes from us to give to us. True peace lies in never holding on to anything tighter than we hold on to God.

> *If you are tired of pain, stop getting attached to things that pass away.*
>
> ARU BARZAK, POET

Let go of what is perishing and hold on to what is real and eternal—God. After all, everything that is mortal is by its very definition a veil before an immortal God. Trust that the spirit inside of you cannot be shattered, only the mortal illusions of this world can be broken. Let the wildfires of divine decree burn every ounce of your ego until it is transformed into compost for the garden of faith that has been dying to come to life.

Death Unveils the Truth

The lovers of God throughout time have said, "This life is a dream and when we die we wake up" to see this world without its makeup.[11] Death unveils our masks; it kills only that which is false, for the truth never dies (17:81). For the ones whose will is surrendered to the will of God, who live in truth, who plant love wherever life takes them, there is no fear in death, for death is a return to The Origin of Love (*Al-Wadud*). For the ones who try the best they can to be kind, for the ones who strive to be faithful, for the ones who sincerely seek God's mercy when they sin—in death, they are met with compassion and forgiveness.

But for the tyrant, or for the one who oppresses others, or creates separation through watering the weeds of hatred, death is a source of pain. Death is the door to the Day of Judgment where God balances the scales of justice left uneven from our time on Earth. Death is the cosmic equalizer. No matter how rich, famous, or beautiful you may be, no one can escape the fate of death—everyone will experience the grave. Death reminds us that we will not be saved by our wealth, our lovers, our children, or by our own hands. Death does not discriminate by age, race, or faith. The Qur'an makes it clear that "no one knows in what land they will die" (31:34), and when the decreed time for death arrives, no one can "delay it for a single hour nor can they bring it forward" (16:61). The inevitability of death is profoundly illustrated in the following parable:

> One day, the Angel of Death manifested as a man and entered the court of Prophet Solomon. The Angel locked eyes with one of Solomon's subjects, giving him a fierce and bewildered look. When the Angel of Death left the kingdom, the subject ran up to Solomon and asked who he was. When Solomon said it was the Angel of Death, the man began to tremble as he fearfully said, "I am afraid from the way he looked at me that he will come for my soul. Please order the winds to take me far away, to the soils of India, so I can be protected." Solomon, who had been given control over the forces of nature by God, ordered the winds to take the man to India.

> The next day, when Solomon saw the Angel of Death, he asked him, "Why did you look at that man in my court so severely yesterday?" The Angel replied, "I was surprised to see him in your kingdom, because I was ordered to take his life just a few hours later, thousands of miles away in India."

This story profoundly confronts us with the fact that if we attempt to run away from death, we will only run toward it. As the Qur'an says, "Running away will not profit you if you are running away from death" (33:16), because when it is your time "Wherever you are death will overtake you even if you are in lofty towers" (4:78).

Death teaches us to hold onto only God, because the emptiness left behind by loss can only be eternally filled with the light of God's grace.

The spiritual notion of "dying before you die" is about letting go of all that is perishing to begin with, to be reborn into eternity now. The lovers of God do not fear death because they are with God now and know they will be with God when they die too.

Our entire lives, we have literally been dying to meet God.

ARU BARZAK, POET

As Rumi says, "Everyone is so afraid of death, but the real mystics just laugh: nothing tyrannizes their hearts. What strikes the oyster shell does not damage the pearl." While your body will die and be returned to the earth, which composed it, your spirit is like an everlasting pearl that will forever remain in the ocean of God's grace.

If You Fear Death, This Is Why

Fear of death is a sign that we are holding on to something other than Allah, to something whose foundation is contingent. As long as our happiness is dependent on things we cannot control, we will never experience contentment. Inner peace is dependent on our connection with God, because God alone is forever and unchanging.

The basis of Islam is surrender, because it is only through surrendering our false sense of control that we experience true freedom. In a sense, death either pushes you to fear or it pushes you to faith. When we accept that we have no control over the future and rely entirely on God, we feel peace. As the Qur'an says, "Whoever believes in his Lord will not fear loss or oppression" (72:13).

But if we turn to ourselves to manage the unknown future, we will find ourselves riddled with feelings of anxiety and despair. When we acknowledge the place within us that thinks we know better than God and gently and with compassion turn our reliance from ourselves to the Divine, we begin to feel the serenity that comes with surrender.

It is only when we lean into death while holding onto Allah that we begin to transcend our anxiety around it. But the problem is we shy away from death, cutting it out of our conversation, labeling it morbid, and calendaring it for another time as if we know how much time we have before death knocks inconveniently on our doors. We sweep death under the rug as if we will not one day be swept under the rug of the earth. Death is not just something that happens to other people. It will happen to you and me. The Prophet ﷺ tells us to think of our death and to visit graveyards,[12] because cemeteries may be places of silence but the message is loud:

We will spend more time beneath the ground than above it.

Our culture and society has taught us that death is something we must cure; but death is not something we can fix because it is not a flaw in the system that needs troubleshooting. Allah intentionally made every single one of us with death programmed into the software of His creation. Death is not an accident, it is intentional. For it is through death, that eternal life has meaning. Without separation you cannot actualize the value of connection and proximity. If we categorize death as a disease, we will end up seeing our grief as something that needs to be fixed instead of as a reminder that death is a natural part of the human condition. It is only when we turn our grief and feelings of loss to a Higher Power that a deep spiritual transformation begins.

The spiritual path is not about bypassing our feelings, but about being present with our pain and inviting the light of Allah into our wounds. Denying our pain will not help us heal. Attempting to escape our pain is like trying to outrun our shadow. Just because we are struggling with our grief it doesn't mean we are any less faithful. All the prophets of God went through hardships and deeply grieved for the losses that they felt. In the Qur'an it states that, when the Prophet Jacob lost his sons, he declared the following:

"I only complain of my suffering and my grief to Allah."

QUR'AN 12:86

Awakening in faith does not mean we become immune to pain, but that we put that pain in its rightful place—in the hands of Allah. We can always seek the help of others, but we must always begin and end the path of our healing by turning to Allah in prayer. We must be honest with how we feel because we cannot receive God's deep healing if we continuously avoid facing our pain. It is here, in the divine crucible of pain that the alchemy of the soul begins. When the sacred and mundane braid together, the separation between us and the Divine begins to dissolve. It is in this sacred landscape that the veils drop as the face of Allah begins to emerge, reflecting upon the face of all creation. From the trees to the seas, from the stars to the bees everything begins to speak of God. Even the existence of death becomes a call of return from God—a call to remember who we are and Whose we are.

You Are Going to Die...

Death is the greatest preacher we will ever meet, for it teaches us to hold tightly to only Allah, for everything is perishing save the face of God (55:26-27). When we reflect on our death, it naturally makes us prioritize what is most important in our life. The Qur'an says, "Every soul shall taste death" (29:57), but the question is, how many will truly taste the sweetness of life?

It is not death that we fear; what we fear is not living the life we know we were created to live. We are afraid of running out of time before we are able to manifest our soul's purpose. Death is the ultimate confrontation. When we think of death, we regret all the time we have lost in procrastination. When death arrives, all of our secrets, sins, and shortcomings will be manifested. We will be confronted with all the dreams we did not pursue, the repentance we did not make, and the charity we did not give.

> *"Live as long as you may, but know that one day you will die. Love whomever you wish, but know that one day you will taste separation. Do whatever you want, but know that one day, you will be held accountable."*[13]

IMAM AL-GHAZALI, 11TH-CENTURY MYSTIC

The inevitability of death confronts us and begs us to ask: Are we living each day as if it is our last? Death forces us to reflect on whether we are living a meaningful life or just trying to kill time as time kills us.

Imam Ali said, "Do for this life as if you will live forever, do for the Hereafter as if you will die tomorrow." The Prophet ﷺ tells us to meditate on death so that we fully take advantage of our limited time on Earth.[14] The Qur'an says that Allah "created death and life, to test which of you is most excellent in action. He is The All-Mighty, The All-Forgiving" (67:2).

It is death that calls us to seize the day and be "sons and daughters of the moment," living and honoring the present as a priceless blessing given to us by God. We don't get to decide when or how we will die, but we can choose how we live. In fact, in one narration, when a man asked the Prophet ﷺ when the Day of Judgment would be, the Prophet ﷺ profoundly replied by saying, "What have you prepared for it?"[15] The Prophet ﷺ was confronting the man with what really matters. In another narration the Prophet ﷺ says, "If the Final Hour comes while you have a palm sapling in your hands and it is possible to plant it before the Hour comes, you should plant it."[16]

The Qur'an describes the Day of Judgment as the day when all human beings are resurrected to face God and to be held accountable for their good and bad deeds. Similar to biblical accounts, the Qur'an describes this day with vivid imagery. The Qur'an tells us that the Earth will shake (99:1), the mountains will be like carded wool (101:5), people will be scattered like moths (101:4), the stars will fall from the sky (81:2), the oceans will boil over (81:6), the sun and moon will merge (75:9), the heavens will be rolled up like scrolls (21:104), and the dead will be summoned back to life (36:51). On this day, all of existence will bow before God alone. This is the day when the scales of justice left uneven on Earth will be balanced and God's mercy will be more abundant than we could ever imagine.

No one knows when they will die or when the Day of Judgment will come, the only thing that is in our power is how we actively choose to live the one life that Allah has given us in this very moment. Instead of worrying about when we will die, it serves us better to focus on what we can do to positively affect this world. As the eleventh-century Persian scholar Abu Sa'id Abul-Khayr said, "You were born crying and everyone around you was laughing. Strive to live in a way that when you die you are laughing and everyone around you is crying."[17]

When you become aware of how close death is to you—that tomorrow morning you might not wake up—how does that make you feel? Do you feel crippled by fear, infused with anxiety, and unable to be present? Or do you feel a surge of urgency, a divine motivation to live each day to its absolute fullest? When we trust God, accepting that our time is limited has a way of dissolving our fears, breaking our pride, and humbling us. The unknown nature of our death inspires us to apologize when we are wrong, to forgive others when they are wrong, to give freely of what we love, to not hold back our words of kindness, to be honest with our feelings, to pray with every ounce of our spirits, to not put off doing our soul's work, to see this moment as the only moment we have, to manifest God's qualities of love, mercy, compassion, and equality upon all people, without discrimination. As Rumi says, "With life as short as a half-taken breath, don't plant anything but love."

...But You Were Not Made for Death

If God created us for just this life, then there would be no death. Death is not the opposite of life—nonexistence is. Death is our evidence that we were made for more than just life. As Rumi says, "My soul is from elsewhere. I am sure of that. And I intend to end up there."

Death is not an entrance into nothingness—rather, it is the birth canal we must travel through to be born into eternal life. Similar to how we wake up from a dream by opening our eyes, when we die we do not disappear, we simply open our eyes to another reality.

> *"Death is not extinguishing the light; it is only putting out the lamp because the dawn has come."*
> RABINDRANATH TAGORE, 20TH-CENTURY INDIAN POET

As the Qur'an says, "And you see the earth barren, but when We send down upon it rain, it stirs and swells and brings forth of every kind a beautiful herbage" (22:5). Just as dead winter seeds are resurrected every spring, death is not our end, but the next season of our spiritual growth. As Sheikh Sidi Muhammad Al-Jamal beautifully says, "Listen to the sound of death, which in reality is the song of eternal life." Do not grieve leaving behind what you love of this world, because this realm is only a fragrance of the world to come.

> *"The value of this world compared to that of the Hereafter is like what your finger brings from the sea when you put it in and then take it out."[18]*
>
> **PROPHET MUHAMMAD** ﷺ

Through death you go from scent to taste, from form to essence, from objects of love to The Origin of Love (*Al-Wadud*). When we die, our consciousness does not cease to exist, but instead it becomes purified and unveiled. This allows us to see the truth as it is, instead of how we imagine or interpret it to be. When you die, you do not lose what you love—you become a part of it.

For the faithful lovers of God, their death date is seen as a celebration—the heavenly homecoming. When we die in a state of God-consciousness, the last of the veils between us and God dissolve and we witness the face of God's beauty and love. Death is not the great unknown, because we are not going somewhere unfamiliar, but rather returning to our origin. We are like waves returning to the same eternal ocean that once inspired us to rise.

> *"To God we belong and to Him we shall return."*
>
> **QUR'AN 2:156**

When we are surrendered to God's will, death becomes our ultimate liberation. A faithful death is an escape from the limiting cage of the ego, where the spirit bird is finally free to expand its wings into the embrace of God. Death is not the end—rather, it is the beginning of forever.

Oh Allah, I pray that You help me remember that my
time on this Earth is short and that any day could be
my last. Allah, help me live every moment of my life in
service to You and to those who are oppressed, needy,
poor, and hopeless. My Lord, help me to apologize
when I wrong others, to return what was entrusted
with me, and to always be humble enough to take
accountability for my mistakes. Oh Lord, I pray that
my awareness of my impermanence inspires me to be
more kind, generous, and forgiving to all people who
are suffering and in need of love. Allah, remind me
that this life is not the only life I have been given. Help
me remember that my real life begins whenever you
decide for me to leave this body behind. Oh Allah,
"You are the Creator of the heavens and the earth. You
are my Guardian in this world and in the life to come.
Make me die as one who has submitted to Your will
and unite me with the righteous ones" (12:101). In Your
eternal names I pray, Ameen.

Reflection: "Contemplating Death"

When contemplating death, we receive a deeper understanding of how we want to live. The following practice helps remind us of what we truly value in life and calls us to live life consciously.

- Lay down on the ground, with your hands overlapping on your stomach.
- Close your eyes and imagine that you are taking your final breaths of earthly life.
- Notice what comes up for you.
- Do you have any regrets in this moment? How do you wish you would have spent your time and resources? What risks do you regret not taking? Is there something you wish you would have said to someone you love? How could you have

showed up differently with your loved ones? What amends would you like to have made? What dreams would you have pursued? What would you have wanted to say to Allah? How could you have been closer to Allah?

- Write down your answers and be conscious of the feelings that come up for you.
- Make the intention of doing these things today, instead of waiting for a tomorrow that may never come.

"The way to Heaven is within. Shake the wings of love for when love's wings have become strong, there is no need to trouble about a ladder."

RUMI

12

THE MYSTERIES OF HEAVEN AND HELL

Allah says in the Qur'an, "We have created everything in pairs" (51:49), because all experience of existence depends on its relationship with its opposite. Without an inner there can be no outer, without yin there is no yang, without the feminine there is no masculine. What does light mean without darkness? What is Heaven without Hell? If there is no contrast our eyes cannot see and if there are no sound waves our ears cannot hear because the understanding of the mind is dependent on relationship, relativity, and association. The duality of creation is required for the human being to be able to have an experience of God's qualities reflected in the created world, and through that experience to fall in love with Him.

Since the fruits of love cannot blossom through coercion, God gave us the freedom of choice so that the reality of love could exist. In its most basic sense, Hell is a byproduct of our free will, because once Allah gave us the freedom to choose to love Him, He also had to allow for the possibility of our choosing to turn away from Him.

Although it is true that what we sow in this life we reap in the next, if we reduce the existence of the Afterlife to just punishment and reward, we will miss the soul of the message. Heaven and Hell are not only physical manifestations, they are also states of being that reflect what it feels like for the spirit to be close to or distant from the Divine. In essence, Heaven and Hell are like mirrors that reflect back to us our soul's relationship with God.

The Deeper Dimensions of Heaven and Hell

Heaven and Hell are not just physical destinations; they are also metaphysical realities. We cannot only speak literally about Heaven and Hell, because they are realities that transcend what we as humans have collectively experienced with our senses. This is why alongside verses of the Qur'an and sayings of the Prophet ﷺ, stories, poetry, and symbolism can be vital in experiencing the deeper truths of the Afterlife. The following is one of the most insightful and metaphorical stories regarding Heaven and Hell:

> One day a man was praying to God and sincerely asked, "God, what's the difference between Heaven and Hell?" That night, God came to the worshipper in his dream and said, "Come with Me, I am going to show you why Heaven is different from Hell."

> God first took the man to Hell, showing him a table with an incredible feast with aromas so pleasing to the scent that the man couldn't help but salivate at the sight of it. The man saw that the people around the table had spoons attached to their hands that had handles longer than their arms. The people were both thin and angry, because the spoon handle was too long for anyone to be able to feed themselves. The man watching turned to God and said, "Hell must be the place where we witness the bounties of Your glory, but we are unable to take part in it." God said, "Now let me take you to Heaven."

When God opened the second door, the man was shocked to see the exact same table, the exact same feast of food, the same delicious aromas, and the same long spoons. The confused man looked at God and said, "How can Heaven and Hell be the same?" God said, "Keep watching." The man returned his gaze to the table and noticed that the people of Heaven looked full, healthy, and happy. He watched as each person in Heaven filled their spoon with all the things they longed to eat and fed the ones next to them. One after another, spoon after spoon, the people of Heaven gave away what they loved to one another.

God said to the man, "Heaven and Hell are realties made based on the consciousness of the ones who live in them. Those who reflect my qualities of generosity, love, kindness, and compassion make every place into Heaven. And for the ones who are arrogant, self-centered, angry, and prideful, they will transform even Heaven into Hell."

In other words, God gives us the ability to experience heavenly attributes based on the qualities we water in the garden of our soul. While some people are like butterflies who come out during the day, seeking the sun's light and the fragrance of flowers, others are like moths who come out at night, seeking the darkness and the burning flame of fire.

In the Hereafter, God facilitates us toward whatever we are seeking. The next life is formed from this life; our gardens in Paradise are sowed with the good deeds we plant on Earth. The Qur'an says that you "Eat and drink joyfully for what you did in the days gone by" (69:24). If you lived in separation, rejection, and hatred of God, then Allah will bring you a reality that mirrors the life you chose to live on Earth. Hell is a state of separation, where the human being is veiled from the all-encompassing mercy of Allah. On the other hand, in Heaven, you are completely dissolved in the ocean of divine love and peace.

"Don't search for Heaven and Hell in the future. Both are now present. Whenever we manage to love without

expectations, calculations, negotiations, we are indeed in Heaven. Whenever we fight and hate, we are in Hell.”

SHAMS TABRIZI, RUMI'S SPIRITUAL GUIDE

Our purpose on Earth is not just to reach for Heaven, but rather to sincerely get to know, love, and worship God. Ultimately, if we really want to see where our place is with God, we must look at where we place God in our life. If the only reason we worship God is to seek a reward, then our relationship with God becomes transactional and we miss the entire purpose of being created. If we worship God solely for the reward of Heaven, then Heaven becomes a veil or an idol before God's presence.

God never says in the Qur'an that we were created solely to seek for Heaven or Hell. Rather, the Qur'an constantly reminds us that we were created to worship God, to overcome our egos, and to polish our hearts until we are able to see the loving face of God reflected in everything and everyone. As the mystic poet Rabia Al-Adawiyya profoundly once said, "Oh God! If I worship You in fear of Hell, burn me in Hell; and if I worship You in hope of Paradise, exclude me from Paradise; but if I worship You for Your own sake, do not withhold Your everlasting beauty."

The Qur'an promises believers "beautiful mansions in gardens of everlasting bliss," but then says that beyond all material rewards, "the greatest bliss is the good pleasure of Allah. That is the supreme triumph" (9:72). The mystics say that if God unveiled His face in the center of Hell, the fires would transform into a garden of joy; and if God veiled His presence in the heart of Heaven, the endless pleasures of Paradise would lose all meaning. The beauty of Heaven comes solely from proximity of the creation to the Creator.

Mystical Symbols and Metaphors

Heaven is a place where you are wrapped in the physical manifestations of Allah's qualities. This is a realm where you are covered in the shade of Allah's kindness, living in palaces of His glory, enjoying the gardens of His generosity, drinking from the rivers of His mercy, wrapped in the silk of His beauty, reclining on couches of His peace, drinking the wine of His love,[1] swimming in fountains of His truth, surrounded by majestic trees of His greatness, eating dates of His generosity and pomegranates of His wisdom. Above all else, the Prophet Muhammad ﷺ says that in Heaven "you will see your Lord just as you see the full moon."[2] Heaven is the realm where the unseen becomes manifest, where the qualities of God come to life, where no anxiety, depression, or grief can enter, because everything you seek is given to you before there is even the longing to ask.

The Qur'an declares that, "To those who have said, 'God is our Lord,' and who have remained steadfast to their belief, the angels will descend saying, 'Do not be afraid or grieved. Receive the glad news of the Paradise which was promised to you'" (41:30). In reference to this eternal realm of Paradise, our loving Lord says, "I have prepared for My righteous servants what no eye has seen, what no ear has heard, and what no heart has conceived."[3]

In Heaven, we will be a new creation; we will be made in a form completely unknown to us, in a world completely different than what the intellect can imagine. We may seek finite successes, but God seeks for us eternal rewards in a forever Paradise.

> *"You want worldly gains but Allah wants the life of the Hereafter for you. Allah is All-Mighty, All-Wise."*
>
> QUR'AN 8:67

God's generosity is too vast to fit into a finite world like ours. In order for us to experience God's infinite mercy more completely, we need an infinite eternal realm like Paradise.

When God describes Paradise, He mentions that there are four special rivers: "rivers of water incorruptible; rivers of milk of which the taste never changes; rivers of wine, a joy to those who drink; and rivers of honey pure and clear. In it there are for them all kinds of fruits; and forgiveness from their Lord" (47:15). Some have said that water, milk, honey, and wine represent the four kinds of knowledge: natural, spiritual, intellectual, and sensual.[4]

More esoterically inclined scholars have suggested that wine is a symbol for the spiritual seeker metaphorically intoxicated on divine love. Milk represents the return to the *fitra* or primordial essence, where we are called to be with God like a child is with their mother. Honey is a reminder that we should taste the sweetness of spirituality in experience, not just in words and discourse. Lastly, water represents humility, as water naturally flows downward. The mystics say that when we can be humble, live our faith in practice, foster a sense of childlikeness, and become intoxicated with the love of God, then no matter where we are, that place becomes a reflection of Heaven on Earth.[5]

While Heaven is about eternal proximity to God and unity, Hell is an expression of utmost separation. Think of someone you love more than anyone on this Earth. Now imagine them being sent out into space, to a place you can never reach. How would that feel? Feel the roaring voices of despair in your mind (23:106), feel the endless pit of pain and longing (25:22), watch as the smoke of anxiety steals your breath, feel the boiling of burning despair (44:46), the butterflies made of razor blades in your stomach (44:45), watch how you fall into a hopeless abyss, with no refuge or safe place to rest (7:50).

The pain of separation from what we love is the very description of Hell. Hell is a state of being in which our consciousness is not just furthest from God, but also furthest from the truth of who God created us to become. It is a perpetual state of regret for time lost, for potential wasted, for losing the chance to be reunited with The Source of Peace (*As-Salam*). The punishments of Hell symbolically represent the agony of what it feels like for the divinely inspired spirit that is intimately connected with God to experience separation from the source of its existence.

> *Heaven is when the veils of separation between you and God*
> *are removed, and you are placed in direct witnessing of Him.*

Imam Ali describes Heaven as being only two steps away: the first step is stepping on your ego's ruling desires, and the second step is stepping into Heaven.[6] Some say that what the fires of Hell actually burn is the separate will of man and all resistance to God's supreme will of peace, love, justice, and freedom.[7] In Heaven, you are fully aligned with who you are, living with perfect awareness of your spiritual nature. The rewards promised to the lovers of God in Heaven are a manifestation of the transcendent joy that is felt by the spirit as it returns into the embrace of the loving Lord that once molded it into being. As the Qur'an says, "The blessed future belongs to those who are God-conscious" (7:128).

We Put Ourselves in the Fire

In the Islamic worldview, every single human being is seen as innately good, with a primordial essence (*fitra*) that is spiritually aligned with the Divine. Since faith is an intrinsic part of what it means to be human, turning away from godly qualities of compassion, forbearance, kindness, mercy, love, and unity is turning away from our divinely aligned spirits. Heaven is seen as a destination for all human beings, while Hell is seen as the realm for those who began as humans, but eventually rejected their true humanity, through living a life of hatred, selfishness, and separation.

Interestingly, the word for "Devil" in Arabic is *Shaytan*, which comes from the root word *shatana*, which in one context can mean "to take people away from or distance people." In other words, the Devil's goal is to create isolation, separation, and arrogance by watering the weeds of the ego. The more we plant seeds of pride, envy, greed, and lust in the fertile soil of our humanity, the less light will reach our hearts. Everything we do in this life for the sake of God is sowed in the field of the Hereafter to be harvested on the Day of Judgment.

> "*Whoever does an atom's weight of good shall see it, and whoever does an atom's weight of evil shall see it.*"
>
> **QUR'AN 99:7-8**

Allah does not subject us to Hell; rather, he gives us the freedom to choose to live in separation from or in intimate relationship with Him. As the Qur'an says, "God does not wrong the people in any way, but the people wrong their own selves" (10:44). It is our free will that creates the possibility of hell, therefore, nowhere in the Qur'an does it say that the animals or plants of this world will be in Hell because they live by instinct not by free choice. It is we who light the fires of Hell with the flames of our actions.

Human beings have been given the freedom of choice, perhaps because we cannot know and fully experience God's mercy, forgiveness, or compassion if we never make mistakes. In one sense, evil functions to create the contrast necessary for an experience of goodness. To create a moral world in which good exists, then evil must exist as well. Just as cold is an absence of heat, and darkness is an absence of light, evil is not attributed to God, as it is the outcome of turning away from God.

The Qur'an says, "Whatever reaches to you of good, is from Allah, but whatever befalls you of evil, is from yourself" (4:79). In other words, evil is a veil created by human misperception. As the Qur'an says, "Oh you who have believed, protect yourselves and your families from a fire whose fuel is people and stones" (66:6). Here God is seemingly telling us that it is *we* who light the fires of Hell with the flames of our actions. "Surely you and what you worship besides Allah are the firewood of Hell" (21:98). Hell is not just a place we go, but also a state of being we carry inside of us.

> There is a mythical story of a seeker who once met a wandering mystic and asked him, "Oh lover of God, where are you coming from?" The mystic replied, "I just came back from Hell." The man looked horrified at the reply, but nonetheless listened intently as the mystic continued, "I needed some fire, and I thought Hell would be the best place to get some. But when I got to the gates and asked the angel in charge to spare me some flames he said, 'There is no fire here.' I confusingly asked him, 'But isn't Hell supposed to be the storehouse of fire and flames?' The angel replied, 'Hell doesn't have fire of its own—each person who comes here comes with their own fire!'"[8]

In a way, we put ourselves in the fire, by closing our eyes to the everlasting light of God's mercy. When we turn away from the light of God, the petals of our heart close and wither from the pain of distance from The Source of Life (*Al-Hayy*). Heaven is not just an earthly summit or destination we reach for—Heaven is a place where we are in full witness of God. It is a reality made for the people who submit their will to be enfolded in the will of God.

> *"Paradise will be brought near to the God-conscious, no longer will it be distant."*
>
> QUR'AN 50:31

Hell, on the other hand, is a place made for those who seek a life independent of God, submitting to their own will, living and dying for their own desires, turning away from a God-centered life in exchange for an ego-conscious one. If you want to be independent from God in this world, the next life will also mirror that separation from the Divine. God does not wrong you in the Hereafter, rather as the Qur'an says, "You will only be recompensed for what you did" (66:7).

If you are asking for there to be no Hell, you are asking for God to take away your freedom of choice.[9] If you are asking for the freedom to choose, but with no consequence for your choices, then you are asking for a God who is not just. As the Qur'an rhetorically asks, "Shall We then treat those who have surrendered as We treat the criminals? What is the matter with you? How foolishly you judge!" (68:35-36).

The existence of Heaven and Hell serve to balance the scales of injustice left uneven from our time on Earth. The fact that Allah chose to create a moral universe, honoring us with the freedom of choice, places us in a rank unparalleled in creation. As human beings, we can be in a station higher than the angels, because our worship is from free will—but our station can also be lower than the animals, when we make the choice to live and die by our desires.

If you are asking for Heaven to include the self-centered, you are asking for Heaven to be something it is not. The light cannot make room for darkness, because when the light arrives all darkness vanishes. God does not bar people from Heaven, but rather it is people themselves who choose to live in a reality that contradicts heavenly qualities.

God does not close His doors on those who seek to be guided, but if we choose to go left when the navigation system of revelation says go right then we will not reach our intended destination. If we choose to ignore God's directions and get lost, it is not God's fault but our own choices that led us astray. If we want to turn away from God's guidance to live by our own will, then it is we who are being narrow—rejecting a loving God who gave us infinite ways to seek Him, in exchange for living a self-centered life.

God will not force us to follow the path that He has lovingly paved for us. However, since God loves us, He will keep reminding us through the words of scripture, people we meet, places we go, and the circumstances we face that true peace can only be found in relationship with Him. The Qur'an constantly reminds us that even if we take 100 billion steps away from Allah, the door of return to Him is always open for us. Allah makes it clear that there is no sin that will ever be too big or too bad to forgive.

> "Oh My servants, you sin by day and by night, and I
> forgive all sins. Therefore, seek forgiveness from Me and
> I will forgive you."[10]
>
> ALLAH

We must not forget that Heaven and Hell were both made for sinners: Hell was created for the ignorantly arrogant sinner while Heaven was created for the regretfully repentant sinner. The Qur'an constantly emphasizes Allah's mercy, to show us that our loving Lord wants us to return to the Heaven of our origin. In fact, there is a narration that when the Prophet ﷺ saw a woman breast feeding a child he asked his companions, "Do you think this woman could throw her child in the fire?" His companions replied, "No, not if she is able to stop it." The Prophet ﷺ said, "Allah is more merciful to His servants than a mother is to her child."[11] Allah does not judge us based on the standards of our culture or society, but based on His everlasting and infinite mercy that encompasses everything in existence.

We Cannot Predict the Eternal Destination of Others

We do not have the knowledge of who will go to Heaven or Hell, because we are judged based on the state of our hearts and no one can see our hearts except God. The Qur'an says on the Day of Judgment our wealth and our children will not save us, the one who will benefit is "the one who comes to Allah with a sound heart" (26:88-89). In fact, the Qur'an warns us against even speculating about the station of others when it says, "Oh you who believe! Avoid suspicion, for surely suspicion in some cases is a sin" (49:12). The Prophet ﷺ also warns against labeling people by saying, "No one accuses another of being a disbeliever but it reflects back on him if the other is not."[12]

The Qur'an says, "Of knowledge we have given you but little" (17:85) so how could we judge anyone based on our limited vision of reality? Of course, the Qur'an calls us to inspire people toward righteousness and belief, but Allah is the only one worthy of judging us. The Qur'an says, "What will explain to you what the Day of Judgment is? The Day when no soul will be able to do anything for another; on that Day, command will belong to God" (82:18-19). The emphasis in this verse is that the command belongs to God and not to us.

The eternal destination of others has no effect on how Muslims are called to treat the creation of God. Our love, respect, and honor toward others should not be contingent on someone's faith or belief system, but on *our* faith. Since we believe every single person was created by God and is continuously sustained by Him, the life of every human being is infinitely priceless, regardless of what they believe or seek in this life and the next.

God's Mercy Encompasses All Things

In the Qur'an, Allah says, "My Mercy encompasses all things" (7:156), which means the mercy of God is not void in Hell. Out of His divine mercy, God embraces the sinful seeker in the fires of Hell, for the purpose of purifying and refining his soul, so that it may be filtered through the gates of Heaven. As Rumi says, "The blows against the carpet are not against the carpet but against the dirt on it."

Interestingly, the word for "light" in Arabic is *nur*, which shares the same root as the Arabic word for "fire," which is *nar*. Some scholars have poetically implied that the illuminating element of divine light manifests in Heaven, awakening the eyes of the heart to the many mysteries and miracles of God. On the other hand, the heat associated with light descends to Hell, in order to purify the souls of humankind, like a flame purifies a needle.[13]

While the majority of traditional scholars say that for some Hell will be an eternal, unending reality of separation from God, there are some linguists that see the word "forever" as meaning "atemporal" or beyond the concept of time. Since, in seventh-century Arabia, people used numbers as approximations, instead of implying that Hell would consist of an infinite number of days, it could very well have meant that Hell is beyond our understanding of time. Even some prominent classical scholars have suggested that the souls that go to Hell will eventually become purified and all of humanity will enter Heaven.[14] In the end, only God knows what He intended; however, we must not forget that Allah's mercy embraces all things, including Hell.

While the Qur'an makes it very clear that Heaven and Hell are actual places, some people are inclined toward rejecting the existence of Hell. However, when we refuse to fully accept the reality of Hell, we are unable to fully receive the gift of God's mercy. It's important to remember that Heaven is not filled with perfect people, but rather with sinners, who repented and were forgiven by God. If you consider the emphasis made on God's mercy, forgiveness, and compassion in Islam, it almost makes you think that Hell is harder to get into than Heaven!

Allah says that He rewards a good deed from 10 to 700 times; He says even the thought of a good deed is counted as a good deed, and an evil thought not committed is counted as a good deed. Furthermore, a sin committed, if repented, is counted as a good deed.[15] Do you see how Allah sways the scales in your favor? Now think of how the Prophet ﷺ

said that all the mercy on Earth equates just to 1 percent of Allah's mercy, while the other 99 percent is saved for the Day of Judgment.[16] Although our actions will be weighed and the state of our hearts will be judged, we cannot achieve or obtain Heaven solely through our actions because we can never worship God as He deserves.

Since an eternal Heaven cannot be purchased through finite actions, Heaven is not something you earn; rather, it is something you learn to receive. As the Prophet ﷺ himself said, "None of you will enter Paradise because of his deeds alone." He was then asked by his companions, "Not even you, oh Messenger of Allah?" And the Prophet ﷺ said, "Not even me, unless Allah covers me with His grace and mercy."[17] This is why believers are never proud of their obedience, for they see that it is because of Allah's love for them that they are drawn to Him, not through their own effort. After all, it is not we who call to God in prayer—it is He who calls us toward Himself through our hearts' longing.

We may not understand from our limited human perspective how divine mercy and justice will consider the infinite variables at play in each person's life, but we are reminded constantly throughout the Qur'an that on the Day of Judgment no one will be dealt with unjustly "even to the extent of the hair on the pit of a date" (4:49). After all, as one mystic said, "Allah is not looking for a reason to put you in Hell, but through His mercy He is looking to put you in the eternal gardens of His everlasting love."[18]

My beloved Lord, turn my seedling heart toward Your light, nourish the soil of my soul with the water of Your mercy, and help me grow toward Your presence in all that I do, both in this life and beyond. "Our Lord, give us the best of this life and the best of the Hereafter and guard us from the torment of the Fire" (2:201). My Lord, quench the fires of separation between us and embrace me with Your love. Oh Allah, sow the seeds of Your beauty within me and help foster the garden of My faith, until I become a reflection of Heaven on Earth. "My Lord! Build for me near You a house in the Garden" (66:11). Oh Allah, show me how to soften my heart, so that Your light can reach the hidden corners of my soul. Oh Allah, be the dawn of hope in my darkest moments. My Lord, unveil me of myself and help me see who I truly am. Allah, help me transcend my ego, polish my heart, and become a pure mirror for You on this Earth. "Our Lord! In You we put our trust, and to You we turn in repentance, and to You is the final Return" (60:4). In Your forgiving names I pray, Ameen.

Reflection: "Reflecting Heaven on Earth"

Heaven is a realm where God's qualities such as love, mercy, compassion, and kindness are perfectly manifested, without being obscured by the veils of the human ego. This is why the more we polish the mirrors of our hearts and reflect the divine qualities of Allah, the more we begin to channel Heaven on Earth. The following practice is a powerful way of intentionally stepping into a heavenly state of mind in the here and now:

- Every morning when you wake up, say the following prayer in your own words: *"Oh Allah, help me to be kind with my words, to be merciful with my thoughts, and to be a reflection of You with every step I take. Oh Allah, allow my eyes to see only You, unveil my ears to hear only Your praises, and help me use my hands as a means of healing for Your world and creation. Oh Allah, bring Your light into my mind, so that my intellect can be used in service of You. Oh Allah, expand my heart to be inclusive of all of Your creatures at all times and in all places. Ameen."*

- Once you have made this prayer, select a small wearable object, such as a ring, watch, or even just a string you can tie around your wrist, serving as a reminder of this prayer. Alternatively, you might set a timer on your watch or phone every hour, as a gentle reminder to realign to your intention.

- Each time you notice your chosen item or your timer goes off, take a moment to return to your breath. Breathe in deeply 3 times, inhaling through your nose and exhaling through your mouth.

- Ask Allah for help with your intention of speaking kinder words to yourself and others, being more merciful with your thoughts and judgments, and being more compassionate and loving when it comes to your actions.

- Every time you are reminded of this prayer, say, "*Alhamdullilah*, thank you Allah for keeping my heart in alignment with Your qualities." If you find that you have fallen short of your intention, let yourself feel grateful to Allah for bringing you awareness, and gently return your attention to Allah and to your breath.

- Make the intention of incorporating this short practice into your daily life, as a means of helping you consistently align with the divine qualities of Allah.

*"Stop acting so small.
You are the universe
in ecstatic motion."*

RUMI

You Are Loved

The Creator of the cosmos blew His spirit into you, planting His secrets of divine love in the depths of your soul. The God of existence chose *you*, over all of His creation, to be a representative of His loving grace. You were created by Allah for Allah. You were neither created to please others nor to fit the mold shaped by your culture and society. You were made to know yourself, to know God, to love God, and to worship Him with your whole heart. You were created to seek and praise Allah, to swim in His ocean of mercy, and to discover the spiritual gems hidden in the depths of your soul. While God does not need us to praise Him, our worship of God unveils the truth of who we are and who we were created to become. Like a bud that turns to the sun as it blooms, unveiling its hidden fragrance, it is through turning to the light of Allah that your true essence blossoms.

You Matter

The Creator of the universe has intentionally chosen to create you from the light of His eternal love and mercy. Your value is based on the One whose breath gave you life. You are not this body that will one day break; you are the soul that is everlasting. As Rumi says, "You think of yourself as a citizen of the universe. You think you belong to this world of dust and matter. Out of this dust you have created a personal image, and have forgotten about the essence of your true origin."

Why do you allow people to dictate your worth, when the
eternal origin of all of existence—Allah— has declared that
your life is more sacred than language can grasp?

Allah loves you infinitely more than you can calculate. You are worthy. You matter. This entire world was created for you to unveil the treasure you already carry inside and it is through worship and submission to Allah that you may actualize this.

God Loves You Unconditionally

Do not forget that since God is independent of His creations, His qualities of love and mercy are unaffected by our actions. When we sin, God does not love us less; rather, it is our sins that veil us from being receptive to Allah's eternal and infinite love. God's love for us never changes—it is our experience of His love that changes.

The pillars and principles within Islam are like polishing cloths that wipe away the dirt of sin, forgetfulness, and temptations, to unveil the pricelessness of your true face. When you realize that you matter because God chose you, you will no longer run in circles, looking for validation from the world.

God's love is unconditional and priceless so it cannot be purchased; however, our good deeds are important because they allow us to experience the love God has always been pouring upon us. Just as a boat must open its sails to be moved by the wind, we must open our hands and our hearts in prayer and surrender, to be moved by the breeze of God's overflowing love.

You Already Have Everything You Need

You are a microcosm of the macrocosm. You are a reflection of the entire universe, held in the embrace of clay. God is not in some faraway

Heaven, He is with you in this very moment, no matter who you are or what you have done. Nothing is void of Him. Everything that has life is a reflection of His life. Everything that has an existence is a reflection of His oneness. As the fifteenth-century Indian poet Kabir said, "I laugh when I hear that the fish in the water is thirsty." You already contain the very thing you are seeking. The path of Islam provides the framework to remove your limiting beliefs so that you are able to receive the love of God.

The names of Allah are already planted in the soil of your heart. Our work is to get out of the way of ourselves, by surrendering to Allah and allowing the light of His love and the rains of revelations and mercy to water our spirits. Heaven is not just a place we reach through death; it is a place we water inside ourselves. To live a life that is *inspired* is to live a life *in spirit,* in connection with your true essence and purpose in life. We are not called to only serve God for the sake of attaining a future Heaven—we are called to become a reflection of Heaven on Earth, by becoming a pure vessel of God's loving qualities.

You Have a Divine Purpose

God purposely created you to know, love, and worship Him. This entire visible world is a reflection of His infinite faces. God is not hiding in the *Kaaba,* a church, or a temple. God is reflected everywhere and in everything.

He has created you as a reflection of His qualities of beauty and majesty. He has sent you to this Earth to worship Him, to know yourself, to protect the sacredness of life, to serve the helpless, to take care of this holy land, and to love all people with your whole soul. God fills the pitcher of your life with the water of blessings, so that you may generously water the thirsty hearts you encounter.

Through Him, you are called to be a hand to the fallen, a crutch for the broken, a healing presence for the sick. You are not called to share the good news of God's unconditional love and mercy only to the faithful.

You are called to step out of your comfort zone and into the
valleys of the hopeless, like a lighthouse illuminating the
dark corners of the Earth.

The Qur'an says, "Struggle in the way of God with your wealth and your souls" (61:11). But do not share your faith with the singular goal of convincing people to believe what you believe. Become an embodiment of your faith, to remind people that God loves them. Call people to divine love, and let God decide what path they are meant to walk. We all cry the same tears, bleed the same blood, feel the same grief, so why should you discriminate based on faith whom you comfort in a time of need?

The purpose of Islam is to be a face of surrender to God's loving will on Earth for all people. The principles of Islam teach us to be messengers of peace—to be like water, gentle enough to wash away tears and strong enough to drown hatred. To be Muslim is to protect the weak, the orphan, the beggar, the disabled of all races and cultures. To be Muslim is not to be color-blind, but to see the differences between people and to celebrate that diversity as a product of the free will that God chose to give us.

"And of His signs is the creation of the heavens and the
earth and the diversity of your languages and your colors.
Indeed, in that are signs for those of knowledge."

QUR'AN 30:22

We are all creations of God, so how could one person be less worthy than the next when the same God took the same breath to create both of them? Let go of these outer differences and dive into the breath of divinity within this single soul we both carry.

We are many in the one. We are countless fruits in a single seed. We are a drop that carries all of the oceans, and you are you but you are also me. Show me where I end and you begin, but do not point to our skin. I love you wherever you are, whoever you are. How can I not love what love Himself made? How can I not love what *is* love? You are love, because love can only come from love.

*Do you understand who you are? You are a reflection of
God's love.*

Like snowflakes, we all come in different shapes, with a unique mission on Earth. No matter what your calling is, this world is depending on
you. Existence is a puzzle; without you in it, it would be incomplete. Now
is the time for you to step into all that you know you can be, but have been
afraid to become.

> *God is speaking to you when He says, "Do not be afraid.
> I am with you" (20:46). God is speaking to you when
> He says, "I created you for Myself" (20:41). God did not
> promise you that the path to goodness would always be
> easy, but the Qur'an did say, "Allah is with those who
> patiently persevere" (8:46).*

You will be tempted, troubled, and tested with trials, but with Allah by
your side you will be triumphant. As the Prophet ﷺ beautifully reminds
us, "Be mindful of Allah, and He will take care of you. Be mindful of
Allah, and you shall find Him at your side. If you ask, ask of Allah. If
you seek help, seek help from Allah. Know that if the whole world were
to gather together to benefit you, they would not be able to benefit you,
except with that which Allah has already prescribed for you. And if the
whole world were to gather together to harm you, they would not be able
to harm you, except with that which Allah had already prescribed for you.
The pens have been lifted and the pages are dry."[1]

Allah has written a perfect love story between you and Him.
Everything you face, every mountain you summit, every sea you cross,
and every desert you walk through was put in front of you as a means for
you to get to know yourself and your Lord. Every pleasure and pain, every
success and failure, and every up and down is from Allah. Everything you
witness is a calling for you to return to Him.

Allah has been waiting for you. He has always been right here, closer
than your jugular vein, closer than the breath in your lungs, closer than
the words on your tongue. God is here with you. Return to Him.

> *"Oh you soul at peace! Come back to your Lord well-pleased,*
> *well-pleasing."*
>
> QUR'AN 89:27-28

You matter to Allah and He loves you unconditionally. You were created intentionally, with a divine purpose. The seeds have been planted for you to blossom into who Allah created you to be. So return to your Lord, no matter how long you have been lost. No matter what you have done or said, Allah is waiting to embrace you with His forgiveness and love. Return to Him. Let Him love you and heal you and remind you that you are worthy. Let him show you that you are more than enough and that in His eyes you are perfect, because He never makes mistakes. Return to Him and let Him part the clouds of your grief and show you the brilliant sun you carry deep inside. Let Him unveil the gems that are hidden within your soul. Return to Him and let Him pour peace into every crevice and crack of your heart. Every time you go astray, return to Him. Every time you fall short, return to Him. Allah is waiting for you. Return to His ocean of love and let Him embrace you with the healing waves of His endless mercy.

> *Alhamdullilah. "All praise and gratitude due to Allah, Lord of all worlds" (1:2). Alhamdullilah, all praise to Allah, the God of the universe, the Lord of love, the face of mercy, and the Creator of all that is and ever will be. Oh Allah, thank You for giving us the opportunity to know, love, and worship You. Thank You for reaching out to us, for speaking to us, for sending messengers for us, and for loving us infinitely more than we could ever imagine. "Oh Allah, You are The Source of Peace and from You comes all peace so Allah encompass me with Your peace."[2] My beloved Lord, in Your name I pray for all those who are suffering in the world to find the peace they so desperately seek. I pray for the heartbroken, the depressed, the hungry, the sick, the oppressed, the grieving, the outcast, those who live in war-torn countries, those who are being unjustly evicted from their homes, and for all those*

who have lost something they cannot get back. Oh Allah, rain Your love upon this Earth, fix what is broken, mend what is torn, and bring a lasting peace to this world. Oh Allah, help me become a representative of Your divine love and healing for all people without discrimination. Oh Allah, make my soul generous and my tongue kind. Oh Allah, make my faith strong and my heart soft. Oh Allah, make my mind pure and my actions sincere. My beloved Lord, help me to be steadfast on the straight path and to become a faithful servant in service of You and Your creation. In Your beautiful, majestic, and loving names I pray, Ameen.

APPENDIX

Prayer of Light

Oh Allah!
Place light in my heart
And light in my tongue
And light in my hearing
And light in my seeing
And light from above me
And light from below me
And light on my right
And light on my left
And light ahead of me
And light behind me
Place light in my soul
Magnify for me light
And amplify for me light
Make for me light
And make me light
Oh Allah! Grant me light
And place light in my nerves
And light in my body
And light in my blood
And light in my hair
And light in my skin
Increase me in light
Increase me in light
Increase me in light
Grant me light upon light![1]

PROPHET MUHAMMAD ﷺ

THE 99 DIVINE NAMES OF ALLAH

Allah . . . . The Great Name

1. *Ar-Rahman* . . . . The Most Merciful, The Lord of Mercy
2. *Ar-Rahim* . . . . The Specifically Merciful, The Bestower of Mercy
3. *Al-Malik* . . . . The Eternal Lord, The King
4. *Al-Quddus* . . . . The Most Holy, The Most Pure
5. *As-Salam* . . . . The Source of Peace
6. *Al-Mu'min* . . . . The Source of Faith, The Remover of Fear
7. *Al-Muhaymin* . . . . The Guardian, The Preserver of Safety
8. *Al-'Aziz* . . . . The Mighty, The Honorable
9. *Al-Jabbar* . . . . The All-Compelling, The Restorer
10. *Al-Mutakabbir* . . . . The Dominant One, The Greatest
11. *Al-Khaliq* . . . . The Creator
12. *Al-Bari'* . . . . The Evolver, The Maker from nothing
13. *Al-Musawwir* . . . . The Shaper of Beauty, The Fashioner
14. *Al-Ghaffar* . . . . The All-Forgiving, The Continually Forgiving
15. *Al-Qahhar* . . . . The Prevailer, The Conqueror
16. *Al-Wahhab* . . . . The Supreme Bestower, The Giver of Gifts
17. *Ar-Razzaq* . . . . The Provider, The Sustainer

18. *Al-Fattah* . . . . The Opener, The One Who Reveals
19. *Al-'Alim* . . . . The All-Knowing, The Omniscient
20. *Al-Qabid* . . . . The Constrictor, The Withholder
21. *Al-Basit* . . . . The Expander, The Releaser
22. *Al-Khafid* . . . . The Humbler, The One Who Softens
23. *Ar-Rafi'* . . . . The Uplifter, The Exalter
24. *Al-Mu'izz* . . . . The Honorer, The Strengthener
25. *Al-Mudhil* . . . . The Dishonorer, The One Who Humiliates
26. *As-Sami'* . . . . The All-Hearing
27. *Al-Basir* . . . . The All-Seeing, The All-Perceiving
28. *Al-Hakam* . . . . The Judge
29. *Al-'Adl* . . . . The Just
30. *Al-Latif* . . . . The Subtle, The Refined
31. *Al-Khabir* . . . . The All-Aware, The Knower of Reality
32. *Al-Halim* . . . . The Clement, The Gentle
33. *Al-'Azim* . . . . The Magnificent
34. *Al-Ghaffur* . . . . The Great Forgiver, The Hider of Faults
35. *Ash-Shakur* . . . . The Most Grateful, The Appreciative
36. *Al-'Aliy* . . . . The Most High, The Sublime
37. *Al-Kabir* . . . . The Greatest
38. *Al-Hafiz* . . . . The Guardian, The Preserver
39. *Al-Muqit* . . . . The Sustainer, The Nourisher
40. *Al-Hasib* . . . . The Accountant, The Reckoner
41. *Al-Jalil* . . . . The Majestic, The Glorious One
42. *Al-Karim* . . . . The Generous, The Bountiful One
43. *Ar-Raqib* . . . . The Watchful
44. *Al-Mujib* . . . . The Responsive, The Answerer of Prayers
45. *Al-Wasi'* . . . . The All-Embracing, The Boundless
46. *Al-Hakim* . . . . The Perfectly Wise
47. *Al-Wadud* . . . . The Most Loving, The Origin of Love
48. *Al-Majid* . . . . The Glorious, The Magnificent
49. *Al-Ba'ith* . . . . The Awakener, The Resurrector
50. *Ash-Shahid* . . . . The Witness, The Testifier

51. *Al-Haqq* .... The Truth, The Reality
52. *Al-Wakil* .... The Trustee, The Advocate
53. *Al-Qawiy* .... The Supremely Strong
54. *Al-Matin* .... The Firm, The Resolute, The Unshakable
55. *Al-Waliy* .... The Protecting Friend, The Loving Defender
56. *Al-Hamid* .... The Praiseworthy
57. *Al-Muhsi* .... The Appraiser, The One Who Records
58. *Al-Mubdi'* .... The Originator, The Initiator
59. *Al-Mu'id* .... The Restorer, The Reviver
60. *Al-Muhyi* .... The Giver of Life
61. *Al-Mumit* .... The Taker of Life
62. *Al-Hayy* .... The Living
63. *Al-Qayyum* .... The Self-Subsisting
64. *Al-Wajid* .... The Finder, The All-Perceiving
65. *Al-Majid* .... The Glorious, The Noble
66. *Al-Wahid* .... The One, The Manifestation of Unity
67. *Al-Ahad* .... The One and Only, The Indivisible
68. *As-Samad* .... The Eternal, The Satisfier of All Needs
69. *Al-Qadir* .... The All-Powerful, The All-Capable
70. *Al-Muqtadir* .... The All-Authoritative
71. *Al-Muqaddim* .... The Expediter, The One Who Accelerates
72. *Al-Mu'akhkhir* .... The Postponer, The Delayer
73. *Al-Awwal* .... The First, The Pre-Existing
74. *Al-Akhir* .... The Last, The End, The Ultimate
75. *Az-Zahir* .... The Manifest, The Revealed
76. *Al-Batin* .... The Hidden, The Invisible, The Inward
77. *Al-Wali* .... The Governor, The Patron
78. *Al-Muta'ali* .... The Extremely Exalted One, The Supreme
79. *Al-Barr* .... The Source of Goodness
80. *At-Tawwab* .... The Acceptor of Repentance
81. *Al-Muntaqim* .... The Avenger, The One Who Repays Justly
82. *Al-'Afuw* .... The Eraser of Sins, The Pardoner
83. *Ar-Ra'uf* .... The Most Kind, The Clement

84. *Malik al-Mulk*............ The Lord of the Worlds, The Owner of All

85. *Dhul-Jalali Wal-Ikram*............... The Lord of Majesty and Honor

86. *Al-Muqsit*............................. The Most Equitable, The Just

87. *Al-Jami'*..................... The Gatherer, The Uniter, The Collector

88. *Al-Ghaniy* .... The Rich, The Self-Sufficient

89. *Al-Mughni*...................... The Enricher, The Fulfiller of Needs

90. *Al-Mani'*................. The Preventer, The One Who Averts Harm

91. *Ad-Darr* .... The Corrector, The Afflicter

92. *An-Nafi'* .... The Creator of Good, The Beneficial

93. *An-Nur* .... The Light, The Illuminator

94. *Al-Hadi*.. The Guide, The Leader

95. *Al-Badi'*....................... The Originator, The Absolute Cause

96. *Al-Baqi* .... The Eternal, The Ever-Present

97. *Al-Warith*... The Inheritor of All

98. *Ar-Rashid*............... The Guide, The Appointer of the Right Path

99. *As-Sabur*... The Most Patient

*The divine names of Allah are multifaceted and can never be perfectly translated with a single phrase or word. Throughout the book, the same divine name may be translated differently, reflecting the depth and multitude of meanings encompassed within the same name. The list above is a collection of translations inspired by the following references:

- *Divine Names: The 99 Healing Names of the One Love,* by Rosina-Fawzia Al-Rawi
- *The Most Beautiful Names,* by Tosun Bayrak al-Jerrahi al-Halveti

SUGGESTED READING

There are dozens of incredible books I would recommend for further study, but if I had to just pick a few that would facilitate a deepening of your understanding of Islam, it would be the following:

- *The Qur'an* by Allah. If you can already read Arabic then you can buy any Qur'an you find, because they are all exactly the same (the only differences being font style and size).
- *The Holy Qur'an in Today's English,* by Yahiya Emerick. This is one of my favorite translations of the Qur'an. It is written in easy-to-read, present-day English and includes many footnotes for further study and contemplation.
- *The Study Quran,* edited by Seyyed Hossein Nasr. This book is fantastic for those who are searching for a diverse collection of commentary on Qur'anic verses. This is one of the only books I have ever seen in English that incorporates a wide variety of theological opinions from Sunni, Shia, and Sufi scholars in a holistic way. There are also a multitude of essays in the appendix on various topics that are incredibly insightful.
- *Muhammad: A Prophet for Our Time,* by Karen Armstrong. I genuinely think this is one of the best books written in English

about the Prophet Muhammad's ﷺ life. The author does a fantastic job painting a picture of seventh-century Arabia, and consequently helping readers appreciate the historical context in which the Qur'an was revealed. She also wonderfully articulates the compassion, kindness, and spiritual station of the Prophet ﷺ, through countless stories and beautifully chosen Hadiths.

- *He Who Knows Himself, Knows His Lord,* by Shaykh Muhammad al-Jamal Rifa'i. This book was written by one of the greatest spiritual masters of our time. For serious seekers, this book can be life-changing, because it specifically advises you on the blind spots on the spiritual path and how to overcome them. I would classify this book as an advanced read that takes patience and dedication to fully understand and integrate.

- *Jewels of Remembrance: A Daybook of Spiritual Guidance Containing 365 Selections from the Wisdom of Mevlana Jalaluddin,* by Camille Adams Helminski and Kabir Helminski. This is one of my favorite collections of poetry from Rumi in the English language. It is inspiring, uplifting, and easy to read while still being very insightful and profound.

- *Vision of Islam,* by Sachiko Murata and William Chittick. Although this book is written more like a textbook on Islam, it is still very engaging and insightful. The authors do an incredible job mixing exoteric and esoteric perspectives alongside Qur'an and Hadith.

- *Spiritual Gems of Islam: Insights and Practices from the Qur'an, Hadith, Rumi, and Muslim Teaching Stories to Enlighten the Heart and Mind,* by Imam Jamal Rahman. This is one of the most light-hearted, yet deeply insightful and inspirational books on Islam that I have ever read. It is a mix of Qur'anic verses, poetry, and mystical stories. It is an absolute gem!

- *Divine Names: The 99 Healing Names of the One Love,* by Rosina-Fawzia Al-Rawi. For a deep dive into some of the spiritual secrets hidden within the divine names of Allah, this is a great book.

Notes

1   Collection: Tirmidhi

2   "The Sunni-Shia Divide." Council on Foreign Relations. www.cfr.org/interactives/sunni-shia-divide#!/sunni-shia-divide.

3   It's interesting to consider that in medieval toxicology the word "tolerant" refers to how much foreign and poisonous substance the body can consume before it is subjected to death. Linguistically speaking, being tolerant implies simply suffering through people's differing perspectives, instead of making space to learn from the diversity of peoples cultures, colors, and theological views.

Chapter 1—Allah: The Origin of Love

1   Shah-Kazemi, Reza. *Common Ground between Islam and Buddhism.* Louisville, KY: Fons Vitae, 2011.

2   Gagnon, Steve. "Questions and Answers." *It's Elemental—The Element Californium,* education.jlab.org/qa/how-much-of-an-atom-is-empty-space.html.

3   The Prophet Muhammad ﷺ said, "Verily, the hearts of the children of Adam, all of them, are between the two fingers of The Merciful as one heart. He directs them wherever he wills." Then, the Prophet ﷺ said, "Oh Allah, the director of the hearts, direct our hearts to your obedience." (Collection: Muslim)

4   The Qur'an says, "Indeed, Allah does not forgive association with Him, but He forgives what is less than that for whom He wills. And he who

associates others with Allah has certainly gone far astray" (4:116). *Shirk* or making partners with Allah is still forgivable if you repent and Allah accepts your forgiveness. This distinction is important because some people incorrectly think that certain sins such as *shirk* can never be forgiven, which is not what this verse is saying. The fact that *all* sins are forgivable through repentance is clearly articulated in the following verse: "Oh My servants who have transgressed against their souls! Do not despair of the mercy of Allah. Indeed, Allah forgives *all* sins. Indeed, it is He who is The Forgiving, The Merciful" (39:53).

5   Anonymous

6   The Prophet Muhammad ﷺ said, "God has seventy thousand veils of light and darkness; if He were to remove them, the radiant splendors of His Face would burn up whoever (or 'whatever creature') was reached by His Gaze." (Collection: Ibn Majah. Source: Morris, James Winston (2005). *The Reflective Heart: Discovering Spiritual Intelligence in 'Ibn Arabi's Meccan Illuminations.* Louisville: Fons Vitae. p. 115.)

7   The reason we have consciousness is because of God. It is because of Allah that we see, hear, touch, feel, smell, or taste. Although Allah created our sense perceptions, He is closer to us than anything we could ever experience. Similar to how the iris in our eyes is so close to us that we cannot perceive it and yet we see because of it, God is so close to us that we cannot witness Him directly, but our ability to witness is because of His proximity and love for us.

8   An example of God reiterating His oneness after using the word "We" is illustrated in the following verse: As the Qur'an says, "And We have not sent you but as a mercy to the worlds. Say: It is only revealed to me that your Allah is one Allah; will you then submit?" (21:107-108)

9   This narration is considered a *Hadith Qudsi*. This type of narration is different than a *Hadith Nabawi* or a general saying from the Prophet ﷺ, because the chain of transmission of a *Hadith Qudsi* goes directly back to God instead of the chain of narrators ending with the Prophet Muhammad ﷺ. However, a *Hadith Qudsi* is different from a verse of the Qur'an. Whereas a *Hadith Qudsi* is a saying in which the meaning is sent from God but the words are formulated by the Prophet ﷺ, the Qur'an comprises of God's exact speech, both in meaning and wording.

10   Allah introduces Himself with *Bismillahi Ar-Rahman Ar-Rahim*, which is
     known as the *Basmala*, in every chapter of the Qur'an except for chapter
     9, which is *At-Tawba*. However, in verse 27:30 there is an additional
     Basmala.

11   This is because it is in the form of the *ism fa'il* or "active participle."

12   Khan, Nouman Ali. "The Word Ar-Rahman." 2014.

13   Collection: Muslim

14   There are some scholars that argue that God's love is conditional. They
     suggest that God's love is given only to those who "deserve it." They
     point out that the Qur'an very clearly states who God loves and does not
     love. They say the Qur'an says that Allah only loves the patient (3:146),
     those who repent and who purify themselves (2:222), those who are just
     (60:8), who do good (2:195), who are God-conscious (3:76), who follow
     the Prophet ﷺ (3:31), who rely upon Allah (3:159), who are humble,
     grateful, faithful, and remember Allah often. They then point out that the
     Qur'an states that Allah does not love the ungrateful sinner (2:276), those
     who spread corruption (5:64), the transgressors (2:190), the oppressors
     (3:140), the treacherous sinners (4:107), those who are proud and boastful
     (4:36), the arrogant (16:23), the extravagant (7:31), and so on. Although
     at first the evidence may suggest that God's love is conditional, the
     Qur'an then confronts us with the verse where Allah clearly states, "My
     mercy encompasses all things" (7:156). Allah does not say My mercy
     (*Ar-Rahman*) encompasses only the faithful or those who obey Me. Allah
     says, "My mercy encompasses *all* things." As previously mentioned, the
     word *Rahman* translated in English as "mercy" also means compassion,
     love, and kindness. If Allah's *Rahman* encompasses everything, then it
     must encompass with love and compassion even the ungrateful sinners,
     oppressors, and arrogant tyrants. However, it is important to point out
     that justice and accountability still exist. The distinction here is that those
     that live a life in opposition to what God has dictated become veiled
     and unable to receive God's unconditional love. To better understand
     this, consider the following example: If I go thirty feet underground into
     a solid, concrete basement with no windows, I would be in complete
     darkness. From this place I could no longer experience the light of the
     sun because I would be veiled from it. However, just because I am in a

place where I cannot experience the sun, it doesn't mean the sun stopped shining. In a similar way, God never stops loving us, but when we are unkind, ungrateful, or tyrannical we become veiled from experiencing God's love. It is not God who oppresses us, but we who oppress ourselves by veiling the eyes of our hearts through insincerity and sin, rendering us unable to witness God's all-encompassing love.

15   Collection: Muslim

16   "Verse (3:32)—Word by Word." *The Quranic Arabic Corpus: Word by Word Grammar, Syntax and Morphology of the Holy Quran*, corpus. quran.com/wordbyword.jsp?chapter=3&verse=32# (3:32:1). *The Qur'an says in reference to things that Allah does not like, *la yuhibbu,* which literally means "does not love."

17   The Qur'an refers to God becoming angry, but this righteous anger is not separate from His mercy (*Ar-Rahman*). To better understand this, consider the following example: When a parent yells at a child for running into oncoming traffic, it is because they love their child. The yelling parent wants to protect their child, not hurt them. In a deeper sense, God's anger is not a manifestation of His hatred but rather a louder expression of His mercy. Sometimes God has to symbolically yell at us, to prevent us from running into the oncoming traffic of greed, lust, envy, etc.

18   Meyer, Wali Ali., and Bilal Hyde. *Physicians of the Heart: A Sufi View of the Ninety-Nine Names of Allah.* Sufi Ruhaniat International, 2012.

19   Collection: Bukhari

20   Collection: Tirmidhi

21   Hawking, Stephen. "The Beginning of Time." www.hawking.org.uk/the-beginning-of-time.html.

22   To better understand the significance of 120 decimal places, consider the following: In the number 2.1, the number 1 is in the first decimal place. In the number 2.0000001, the number 1 is in the seventh decimal place. Now imagine how precise a number would have to be that for 120 decimal places each number would have to be perfect.

23   Hawking, Stephen. *A Brief History of Time.* Bantam Books, 2017.

24   Good evidence for this is how the known laws of science seem to collapse in the world of quantum physics.

25   Asking who created God only leads to then asking who created who
     created God, and then who created who created who created God, and
     on and on ad infinitum. In other words, infinite regress begins with a
     creation and infinitely goes back without end. If you went back infinitely,
     the universe could never have come into existence, because by definition
     you cannot traverse the distance of infinity. This is why Islamic theology
     posits that God is eternal and uncreated, because otherwise you would
     run into the problem of infinite regress and this world would have never
     been created.

26   The word *Jalal* comes from the same root as the word *Al-Jalil*. Both of
     these names mean "majesty, sublimity, and greatness." *Jalal* is generally
     used to explain the category of the majestic names of God, while *Al-Jalil* is
     usually the name used in the 99 divine names lists for "The Majestic One."
     Jalal is also included in the 99 divine names as part of the name *Dhul-
     Jalali-wal-Ikram*, which means "The Possessor of Majesty and Honor."

27   As the Qur'an says, "We will show them Our signs in the horizons and
     within themselves until it becomes clear to them that this is the truth"
     (41:53).

28   Collection: Bukhari, Muslim

Chapter 2—Who Are You?

1   Collection: Muslim. This hadith is alluding to the fact that Allah always
     intended to create human beings with the gift of free will. Since our
     fallibility is a product of our free will, if we didn't make mistakes God
     would create a creation that did because it is in our fallibility that we are
     able to fully experience and taste God's mercy and forgiveness.

2   Collection: Bukhari, Muslim

3   God sent us to this world as His representative on Earth (2:30). Part of
     our purpose is to take care of the Earth and to reflect God's qualities upon
     all of creation. Since Heaven is a realm where God is apparent, when we
     reflect God's names on Earth we become a reflection of Heaven on Earth.

4   Safi, Omid. *Radical Love: Teachings from the Islamic Mystical Tradition.*
     Yale University Press, 2018, p. 33.

5   As previously mentioned, the Prophet Muhammad ﷺ said, "Allah does
     not look at your appearance or wealth, but rather he looks at your hearts
     and actions." (Collection: Muslim)

6   Collection: Abu Dawud, Tirmidhi

7   *The American Heritage Dictionary*. Houghton Mifflin Harcourt, 2012.

8   The Prophet Muhammad ﷺ reiterates the high station of women when
      he says, "Your Heaven lies under the feet of your mother." (Collection:
      Ahmad, Nasai)

9   Leaman, Oliver. *The Qur'an: An Encyclopedia*. Routledge, 2010.

10   Some scholars have suggested that Iblis was an angel because he was
      worshipping amongst the angels. These scholars often cite the following
      verse as evidence: "And (remember) when We said to the angels:
      'Prostrate yourselves unto Adam.' So they prostrated themselves except
      Iblis (Satan)..." (18:50). However, the evidence that Iblis was a jinn is
      overwhelmingly stronger considering the same verse continues to say,
      "...He was one of the jinn; he disobeyed the command of his Lord"
      (18:50). Iblis himself says in reference to Adam, "I am better than him.
      You created me from fire and created him from clay" (7:12). The Qur'an
      further validates that Iblis is a jinn by clarifying, "And the jinn He created
      from a smokeless flame of fire" (55:15). Not to mention the Prophet ﷺ
      said, "The angels were created from light, the jinn were created from
      smokeless fire and Adam was created from that which has been described
      to you." (Collection: Muslim, Ahmad, Al-Bayhaqi)

11   Fun fact: The English word "genie" is derived from the Arabic word *jinn*.

12   Wheeler, Brannon M. *Prophets in the Quran: An Introduction to the
      Quran and Muslim Exegesis*. Continuum, 2002.

13   The Qur'an says, "And Adam and his wife ate of it, and their private parts
      became apparent to them, and they began to fasten over themselves from
      the leaves of Paradise. And Adam disobeyed his Lord, so he went astray.
      Then his Lord chose him, and turned to him with forgiveness and gave
      him guidance" (20:121-122).

14   The following is an excerpt from *Chapter 11 - The Spiritual Secrets of
      Death*: "The Qur'an describes the Day of Judgment as the day when all
      human beings are resurrected to face God and to be held accountable
      for their good and bad deeds. Similar to biblical accounts, the Qur'an
      describes this day with vivid imagery. The Qur'an tells us that the Earth
      will shake (99:1), the mountains will be like carded wool (101:5), people
      will be scattered like moths (101:4), the stars will fall from the sky (81:2),

the oceans will boil over (81:6), the sun and moon will merge (75:9), the heavens will be rolled up like scrolls (21:104), and the dead will be summoned back to life (36:51). On this day, all of existence will bow before God alone. This is the day when the scales of justice left uneven on Earth will be balanced and God's mercy will be more abundant than we could ever imagine."

15   Allah is *Ash-Shakur* or The Most Grateful in response to the good deeds we perform. Allah's gratitude is manifested in the form of generosity, forgiveness, and the bestowal of blessings upon His creation.

16   Collection: Bukhari

17   Collection: Bukhari

18   The word *kufr* is often translated as "disbelief," but it not only means "to cover the truth," but also linguistically can be translated as "the rejection of a blessing."

19   Collection: Muslim

20   As previously mentioned: "In Arabic the word for a human being is *insan,* which is derived from *nisyan* which means 'forgetfulness.'"

21   For more on the practice of *tawba*, refer to Chapter 5.

22   Collection: Muslim

23   Bin Younis, Imam. "Question and Answer." 2017, California.

24   There is not one particular author attributed to this saying, but many have used it as a tool of explaining the deeper dimensions of the ego (*nafs*). This saying is also known to be widely used in twelve-step addiction programs.

25   It is important to point out that since in Heaven we will be living as new creations in a new reality we may no longer be subject to the same rules as our worldly life. It is said those that enter Heaven will be blessed with directly experiencing God without the same veils as we experienced on Earth. As the Qur'an says, "On that day some faces will be bright, looking at their Lord" (75:22-23). The Prophet Muhammad ﷺ also said, "Verily, you will see your Lord just as you see the full moon." (Collection: Tirmidhi)

26   The Qur'an makes it very clear that human beings were created as representatives of God on Earth, before Adam and Eve even ate from the fruit of the forbidden tree. As the Qur'an says, "I will create a vicegerent on Earth" (2:30).

27   Collection: Bukhari, Muslim

28   This has been attributed to the Prophet Muhammad ﷺ, Imam Ali, and many others throughout history.

29   Collection: Muslim

30   Collection: Bukhari. A companion of the Prophet ﷺ once asked him, "Which people are tested the most severely?" The Prophet ﷺ answered, "They are the prophets, then the next best, then the next best. A man is tried according to his religion. If he is firm in his religion, his trials will be more severe. If he is weak in his religion, he is tried according to his strength in religion. The servant will continue to be tried until he is left walking upon the earth without any sin." (Collection: Tirmidhi)

31   Some people incorrectly translate *jihad* as "Holy War." If you translated "Holy War" into Arabic it would literally be translated as *al-harb al-muqaddasah,* which is not found in the Qur'an or Hadiths.

32   Muhammad Ibn Talāl Ghāzī ibn, et al. *War and Peace in Islam the Uses and Abuses of Jihad.* The Islamic Texts Society, 2013.

33   Collection: Abu Dawud

34   Collection: Ahmad

35   Collection: Bukhari, Muslim

36   Formica, Michael J. "The Longest Distance in the World Is From the Head to the Heart." *Psychology Today.* www.psychologytoday.com/us/blog/enlightened-living/200808/the-longest-distance-in-the-world-is-the-head-the-heart.

37   Monastra, Yahya. "Theology: Intelligence (in Arabic)." *Sharia Law and Women.* www.mwcoalition.org/id49.html.

38   Collection: Bukhari

39   Wells, Diana. "24 Fun Facts About the Heart." Healthline Media. January 23, 2019. www.healthline.com/health/fun-facts-about-the-heart#1.

40   Yusuf, Hamza. "The Ethereal Essence of Our Hearts." 2016.

41   Collection: Al-Darimi, according to Al-Haytami Al-Makki

42   "The Energetic Heart Is Unfolding." HeartMath Institute. March 25, 2015. www.heartmath.org/articles-of-the-heart/science-of-the-heart/the-energetic-heart-is-unfolding/.

43   The Prophet ﷺ said, "Righteousness is that about which the soul feels tranquil and the heart feels tranquil, and sin is what creates restlessness in the soul and moves to and fro in the breast." (Collection: Al-Darimi,

according to Al-Haytami Al-Makki) The Prophet ﷺ also has said, "Righteousness is good character, and sin is that which wavers in your heart and which you do not want people to know about." (Collection: Muslim)

44   Allah refers to the word "heart" in the Qur'an with the following two words: *qalb* and *fu'ad*. The word *fu'ad* comes from the verb *fa'ada*, which can mean "burning, a flame, or roasting." The Qur'an generally refers to the heart as *fu'ad* when the human being is fired up with emotions and "in the heat of the moment"—when the heart is highly emotional, whether it be extremely happy, sad, fearful, angry, regretful, lustful, or frustrated. In other words, *fu'ad* is used in all intense emotional situations, while *qalb* is used in a more general sense. The word *qalb* comes from the word *taqalub*, which means "to change, shift, turn." This is a reference to both the physical heart, which turns and shifts as it contracts and expands, and to the spiritual heart, which is constantly turning toward and away from Allah. The Qur'an uses the word *sadr* not for the heart but for the chest. The word *sadr* is used when Allah is speaking about our secrets, motives, and intentions, which cannot be known or seen (17:36, 28:10, 7:179, 22:46).

45   Collection: Tirmidhi

46   For more on the practice of *tawba,* refer to Chapter 5.

47   Collection: Bukhari

48   Macdonell, Arthur A. *A Sanskrit Grammar for Students.* Oxford University Press, 3rd edition, 1927.

49   Refer to Appendix: "The 99 Divine Names of Allah"

50   Chittick, William C. *The Inner Journey: Views from the Islamic Tradition.* Morning Light Press, 2007.

51   Borenstein, Seth. "Titanic's Legacy: A Fascination with Disasters." NBCNews.com, NBCUniversal News Group, April 1, 2012. www.nbcnews.com/id/46916279/ns/technology_and_science-science/t/titanics-legacy-fascination-disasters/.

52   The word "Ubuntu" comes from the Zulu phrase "Umuntu ngumuntu ngabantu." Ifejika, Nkem. "The Question: What Does Ubuntu Really Mean?" *The Guardian*, Guardian News and Media. September 28, 2006. www.theguardian.com/theguardian/2006/sep/29/features11.g2.

53   Anonymous

54   Collection: Bukhari

55   Collection: Bukhari, Muslim, Abu Dawud, Ahmad

56   Peterson, Eugene H. *The Message: The Bible in Contemporary Language.*
     NavPress, 2017.

57   Some sources ascribe this story to the Persian poet Attar of Nishapur.

58   Collection: Tirmidhi

Chapter 3—The Mysterious World of the Qur'an

1   Collection: Ahmad

2   Forrin, Noah D., and Colin M. Macleod. "This Time It's Personal: The
     Memory Benefit of Hearing Oneself." *Memory*, vol. 26, no. 4, 2017, pp.
     574–579. Doi:10.1080/09658211.2017.1383434.

3   The moon does not generate light, rather it reflects a small percentage of
     the sun's light, which bounces off of its surface.

4   The Qur'an says, "Truly, this Qur'an has been sent down by the Lord of
     the worlds: The Trustworthy Spirit [Angel Gabriel] brought it down to
     your heart [Prophet], so that you could bring warning in plain Arabic
     language" (26:192-195).

5   Practicing Muslims repeat *Bismillahi Ar-Rahman Ar-Rahim* over a dozen
     times in a single day, just in the ritual prayer (*salat*). *Bismillah* is also
     often invoked before eating, leaving or entering a house, and pretty much
     any and all other actions throughout the day. As a result, some linguists
     have suggested that the word *Bismillah* is the most repeated word in any
     language on Earth.

6   The Qur'an may be strict about certain rules and prohibitions, but how
     we share the deeper teachings of Divine Law (*shari'a*) must always be with
     mercy and love. We are not called to shame or judge people. We are called
     by the Qur'an to advise and enjoin people toward goodness, but we must
     always remember that judgment belongs to God alone.

7   Khan, Nouman Ali. "Alif Lam Mim." 2012.

8   Naik , Zakir. "What Is the Meaning of Alif Laam Meem?" 2011.

9   Collection: Tirmidhi

10   Zakariya, Abu. *The Eternal Challenge: A Journey through the Miraculous
     Qur'an.* One Reason, 2015.

11   Although the more circulated version of the Hadith is the narration of the
       Prophet ﷺ saying, "I am leaving behind two things, which if you hold
       fast to, you will never go astray: the Book of Allah and my *sunnah*," you
       actually do not find this narration in any of the six Sunni books of sound
       Hadith or in Shia and Sufi sources. Of course, the *sunnah* or examples
       left behind from the Prophet ﷺ are both priceless and timeless, but in
       regard to this narration what you find repeatedly in the books of Hadith
       followed by the majority of Muslims (*Sunnis*) and minority of Muslims
       (*Shias*) is the Prophet Muhammad ﷺ having said I leave behind "The
       Book of Allah and my household." It naturally made most sense to quote
       the most authentic version of the Hadith, which is often called the Hadith
       al-Thaqalayn. (Collection: Sahih Muslim, Sahih Tirmidhi, Al-Kafi).

12   The *ahlul bayt* is seen by some as consisting of Imam Ali, the Prophet's
       ﷺ daughter Fatima Zahra, and the Prophet's ﷺ two sons, Hussein and
       Hassan, and their descendants. "Aisha reported that the Prophet ﷺ went
       out one morning wearing a striped cloak of the black camel's hair that
       there came Hassan ibn Ali. He wrapped him under it, then came Hussain
       and he wrapped him under it along with the other one (Hasan). Then came
       Fatima and he took her under it, then came Ali and he also took him under
       it and then said: "Allah only desires to take away any uncleanliness from
       you, Oh people of the household, and purify you (thorough purifying)."
       (Collection: Muslim) Some scholars include the Prophet's ﷺ wives into
       this category as well, citing the verse 33:33 as evidence for their claim.

13   Collection: Bukhari, Muslim

14   Anonymous

15   It is important to point out that there is nothing wrong with reading the
       Qur'an literally, so long as we take into account the historical context
       of the verses. Nonetheless, it is important to understand that Allah uses
       symbolism and many metaphors throughout the text that cannot always
       be understood in the literal context. In order to have a more complete
       understanding of revelation, we must approach the text both literally and
       esoterically.

16   Shari'ati, Ali. *On the Sociology of Islam*. Algorithm, 2017.

17   Scholars have said that some verses of the Qur'an, in reference to nature,
       are purposefully vague so people of all intellectual capabilities can

experience God's signs to the level of their understanding.

18   Collection: Abu Dawud

19   Hixon, Lex. *The Heart of the Qur'an: An Introduction to Islamic Spirituality.* 2nd ed., The Theosophical Publishing House, 2003.

20   In Arabic the word *kun* is made of two letters. It begins with the letter *kaaf,* which gives you the *K* sound. On the *kaaf* there is a small vowel by the name of *damma,* which gives you the *U* sound. Then the word ends with the letter *nun,* which gives you the *N* sound. Looking at the sacred sound code of the word *kun,* it can imaginatively be said that the power of the *K* pushed the entire universe into creation with a bang, with a burst of light. The sound of *U* expanded space, scattering everything into distances where each atom would have the chance to flourish and blossom. The *N,* with its resonance and vibration, is the energy of light that moves so quickly that it creates the illusion of form. (This is based on the teachings of sacred sound theory, which is an ancient study of sound and vibration.)

21   Collection: Bukhari

22   Koberlein, Brian. "How Are Energy and Matter the Same?" *Universe Today,* December 23, 2015. www.universetoday.com/116615/ how-are-energy-and-matter-the-same/.

23   "Scientist Proves DNA Can Be Reprogrammed by Words and Frequencies." *Collective Evolution,* August 27, 2013. www.collective-evolution.com/2011/09/02/ scientist-prove-dna-can-be-reprogrammed-by-words-and-frequencies/.

24   The Arabic word used for "sign" is *ayah,* which is the same word used to refer to a "verse" of the Qur'an. Just as the words of the Qur'an point to God, the world in and of itself is also an *ayah* or sign of God's creative power.

25   Safi, Omid. "The Sufi Tradition—Literary and Cultural Dimensions." Bayan Claremont. February 11, 2019, Claremont.

26   The Arabic word *surah* refers to a portion or chapter of the Qur'an.

27   The Prophet Muhammad ﷺ said, "Each child is born in a state of fitra" or the natural inclination to believe in the oneness of God. (Collection: Sahih Muslim, Sahih Bukhari) As the Qur'an says, "So direct your face toward the religion, inclining to truth. [Adhere to] the *fitra* of Allah upon which He has created [all] people. No change should there be in the creation of Allah.

That is the correct religion, but most of the people do not know" (30:30).

28   Paul, Annie Murphy. "Why We Remember Song Lyrics So Well."
       Psychology Today, Sussex Publishers. www.psychologytoday.com/us/
       blog/how-be-brilliant/201206/why-we-remember-song-lyrics-so-well.

29   "Memory and Mnemonic Devices." *Psych Central*, July 17, 2016.
       psychcentral.com/lib/memory-and-mnemonic-devices/.

30   Graham, William Albert. *Beyond the Written Word: Oral Aspects of
       Scripture in the History of Religion*. Cambridge University Press, 2001.

31   Collection: Tabarani

32   Nasr, Seyyed Hossein. *Ideals and Realities of Islam*. The Islamic Texts
       Society, 2006.)

33   Khan, Nouman Ali. "Miracle Word Count." 2014.

34   Since the Qur'an is seen as the final revelation that will be sent to
       humankind, the protection of this revelation is taken up by God Himself.
       As Allah says, "We have sent down the Qur'an, and We will be its
       guardian" (15:9).

35   The Qur'an says, "And we have revealed to you the Scripture in truth,
       confirming the scripture that came before it, and guarding it in safety:
       So judge between them by what Allah has revealed, and follow not their
       vain desires, diverging from the truth that has come to you. To each
       among you we have prescribed a law and an open way. If Allah had so
       willed, He would have made you a single people, but (His plan is) to
       test you in what He has given you: So strive as in a race in all virtues. To
       Allah is your return altogether. It is He that will show you the truth of
       the matters in which you dispute" (5:48).

36   The Prophet ﷺ said, "Seeking knowledge is mandatory for every
       Muslim." (Collection: Ibn Majah) The Prophet also ﷺ said, "Asking for
       knowledge is mandatory for each man and woman." (Collection: Bahar
       Al-Anwar)

37   Collection: Darimi

38   Arnett, Patricia. "How the Atmosphere Protects the Earth." *Sciencing*,
       April 24 2017. sciencing.com/atmosphere-protects-earth-6933411.html.

39   There are numerous free resources online that offer access to recordings
       of the Qur'an. If you are looking for websites that incorporate Qur'anic
       Arabic alongside the English translation, transliteration, and a recording

of each verse, you can use Corpus.Quran.com or Quran.com. If you are looking just for the recording, you can look up any verse or chapter of the Qur'an on most public video or audio streaming sites, such as YouTube, followed by the name of a famous reciter. You can try out one of the following popular reciters: Abdul Basit, Mishary Alafasy, or Sharifah Khasif Fadzilah.

Chapter 4—The Spiritual Dimensions of Islam

1   Paying our debt to God is not a one-time event; it is a process and intention we continuously strive for even though we will never fully achieve it because we can never worship God as He deserves to be worshipped.

2   As previously mentioned: "The innate alignment with the Divine that resides at the heart of being human is often called "the primordial essence" or referred to in Arabic as the *fitra*. The word *fitra* comes from a root word meaning "to split or bring forth." This implies that our work on this Earth is to split the shell of our ego and *bring forth* the divine seeds God has already planted in the garden of our spirits through the generosity of His love.

3   Sakaamini, Ahmad, and Ihsan Alexander Torabi. "Hajj and the Journey to The Divine." Soulofislamradio.com, February 7, 2019. www.soulofislamradio.com/blog/hajj-and-the-journey-to-the-Divine.

4   Collection: Bukhari, Muslim

5   Redd, Nola Taylor. "Earth's Stabilizing Moon May Be Unique Within Universe." Space.com, July 29, 2011. www.space.com/12464-earth-moon-unique-solar-system-universe.html.

6   Collection: Tirmidhi

7   Collection: Muslim

8   Anonymous

9   White, Mark D. "The Wisdom of Wei Wu Wei: Letting Good Things Happen." *Psychology Today*, Sussex Publishers, July 9, 2011. www.psychologytoday.com/us/blog/maybe-its-just-me/201107/the-wisdom-wei-wu-wei-letting-good-things-happen.

10   Collection: Muslim

11   This saying has been quoted by many. Some have attributed it to the Prophet Muhammad ﷺ, while others have attributed to Abdullah Bin

Mas'ud.

12   Collection: Tirmidhi

13   When our beliefs are tested, the conditions are created for faith or *iman* to blossom.

14   Each person's *iman* is connected to their actions, sincerity, belief in the unseen and the decrees of God. As the Qur'an says, "And for all people are levels according to what they do (their actions)" (46:19).

15   Collection: Daraqutni

16   Collection: Bukhari

17   This saying has also been attributed to Imam Ali

18   Collection: Bukhari, Muslim

19   When someone dies their body no longer has a will of its own. The mortician who is washing a dead body has full control over it. We are called to be like the dead in the hands of God, letting Him move us as He wills.

20   It is interesting to note that in the original Farsi of this poem Rumi uses the word *kufr,* which is translated here as "wrongdoing" and *iman*, which is translated here as "rightdoing." The literal translation of this poem would be closer to "Out beyond ideas of disbelief (*kufr*) and faith (*iman*)..." (Rumi Jalal-ad-Din, and Coleman Barks. *The Essential Rumi.* Harper, 2010.)

21   Since when we experience being in the presence of God we are able to truly worship Him, it is through surrender that we truly establish a relationship with the Divine. The phrase "knowledge *of* God" implies that we have an experience of God that transcends the mind's understanding. This type of knowledge cannot be learned, it can only be given to us by Allah Himself. We become more receptive to receiving this type of wisdom when we align our heart and soul to Allah through the practices of prayer (*salat*), repentance (*tawba*), and remembrance (*dhikr*).

Chapter 5—Tawba: Repent and Return to Unity

1   This narration is considered a *Hadith Qudsi.* This type of narration is different than a *Hadith Nabawi* or a general saying from the Prophet ﷺ, because the chain of transmission of a *Hadith Qudsi* goes directly back to God instead of the chain of narrators ending with the Prophet Muhammad ﷺ. However, a *Hadith Qudsi* is different from a verse of the

Qur'an. Whereas a *Hadith Qudsi* is a saying in which the meaning is sent from God but the words are formulated by the Prophet ﷺ, the Qur'an comprises of God's exact speech, both in meaning and wording.

2   As the Qur'an says, "God would not punish them while you (Muhammad) were among them nor while they were asking for forgiveness" (8:33).

3   This is a reference to the primordial essence of purity and goodness (*fitra*) at the heart of every human being.

4   Collection: Ahmad

5   Covey, Stephen R. *How to Develop Your Personal Mission Statement.* GABAL, 2010.

6   Collection: Bukhari

7   Doyle, John Sean. "Resilience, Growth, and Kintsukuroi." *Psychology Today*, Sussex Publishers, October 3, 2015. www.psychologytoday.com/us/blog/luminous-things/201510/resilience-growth-kintsukuroi.

8   Collection: Bukhari, Muslim

9   Collection: Bukhari, Muslim

10   King, Martin Luther. "Love Your Enemies." November 17, 1957, Dexter Baptist Church, Dexter Baptist Church.

11   Collection: Bukhari

12   Collection: Tirmidhi

13   Although a few scholars differ in opinion, this quote is commonly attributed to Imam Ali.

14   Collection: Abu Dawud

15   Collection: Abu Dawud, Tirmidhi

16   Collection: Bukhari

Chapter 6—Shahadah: The Ecstasy of Oneness

1   As previously stated: "The Qur'an reminds us of a realm where God planted the seeds of faith, love, and unity in the fertile hearts of all humankind, known as the Covenant of Alast. In a pre-eternal realm, before this world as we know it, every soul that would one day manifest into an earthly form was asked by Allah, "Am I not your Lord?" This soup of souls vibrated into a symphony of affirmation as every single being replied, "Yes, yes, we testify" to the singularity of God. As a result of this covenant, it can be said that at the soul level every person, regardless of

conscious belief, is fully aligned with the Divine." (7:172)

2   Collection: Muslim

3   A wife of the Prophet Muhammad ﷺ described him by saying, "Verily, the character of the Prophet of Allah was the Qur'an." (Collection: Muslim)

4   This narration is considered a *Hadith Qudsi*. This type of narration is different than a *Hadith Nabawi* or a general saying from the Prophet ﷺ, because the chain of transmission of a *Hadith Qudsi* goes directly back to God instead of the chain of narrators ending with the Prophet Muhammad ﷺ. However, a *Hadith Qudsi* is different from a verse of the Qur'an. Whereas a *Hadith Qudsi* is a saying in which the meaning is sent from God but the words are formulated by the Prophet ﷺ, the Qur'an comprises of God's exact speech, both in meaning and wording. (Collection: Bukhari)

5   As the Qur'an says, "Indeed, those who pledge allegiance to you, [Muhammad]—they are actually pledging allegiance to Allah. The hand of Allah is over their hands. So he who breaks his word only breaks it to the detriment of himself. And he who fulfills that which he has promised Allah— He will give him a great reward" (48:10).

6   Whereas Prophet Moses descended from Abraham's second son, Prophet Isaac, the Prophet Muhammad ﷺ is a descendent of Abraham's elder son, Prophet Ishmael.

7   Collection: Bukhari

8   The Prophet ﷺ and his companions set out for *Hajj* once before, but the Meccans would not let them inside the precincts of the city of Mecca. This was the same year the Prophet ﷺ signed the Treaty of Hudaybiyyah.

9   Before the Prophet Muhammad ﷺ shared the message of Islam in Mecca, the *Kaaba* was used as a center for idol worship in Arabia. Today the *Kaaba* is known as the "House of God" and is considered the holiest place on Earth for Muslims.

10   The *Al-Hajaru Al-Aswad* is a mysterious black stone that is said to have fallen from the heavens. Some scholars suggest it fell during the time of Adam and Eve and that it was later found by Prophet Abraham and his son Ishmael.

11   A'zami Muhammad Mustafa. *The History of the Qur'ānic Text: From Revelation to Compilation: A Comparative Study with the Old and New Testaments*. Al-Qalam Pub., 2011.

12 Collection: Bukhari, Muslim

13 Collection: Ahmad

14 Collection: Bukhari

15 Arbil, Majd. "The Compassion of the Prophet Towards Those Who Abused Him." *IslamiCity*, June 26, 2018. www.islamicity.org/8645/the-compassion-of-the-prophet-towards-those-who-abused-him/.

16 Collection: Muslim

17 Collection: Bukhari, Muslim. The mercy and patience of the chosen prophets of God are beyond our comprehension. One of the companions of the Prophet 🌼 reported the following narration: "I remember seeing the Messenger of Allah, peace and blessings be upon him, tell the story of a prophet who was beaten by his people and he wiped the blood from his face, saying, 'My Lord, forgive my people for they do not know.'" (Collection: Bukhari, Muslim)

18 Taylor, Bill. "What Breaking the Four-Minute Mile Taught Us About the Limits of Conventional Thinking." *Harvard Business Review*, April 10, 2018. hbr.org/2018/03/what-breaking-the-4-minute-mile-taught-us-about-the-limits-of-conventional-thinking.

19 Collection: Ahmad

20 This story is a rendition based on a translation from the following book: Nicholson, Reynold Alleyne. *The Mathnawi*. E.J. Brill Luzac & Co., 1925.

Chapter 7—Salat: How to Tune Into Divine Love

1 Some scholars have suggested that the word *salat* comes from the root word *salla*, which means "supplication." Others have said the word *salat* comes from the root word *silla,* which means "to connect, attach, and bind together." Both of these perspectives are honored when we note that the word *salat* also comes from the triliteral root *sad-lam-waw,* which can mean "prayer, supplication, blessing, magnify, bring forth, follow closely, walk/follow behind closely, to remain attached." The element of connection is at the core of supplication and prayer. It is also said that in a horse race, when one horse follows the horse in front of it so closely that its head is practically attached to the first horse's body, that second horse is called *Al-Mussalli.* In essence, since *salat* means to supplicate to God, the root can linguistically be seen as attaching and closely being connected with God.

2 Collection: Bukhari, Muslim

3 As the great eighth-century thinker Imam Muhammad Al-Baqir said, "The prayer is the pillar of religion and its parable is that of the prop of a tent—when the prop remains upright, the pegs and ropes remain straight and upright, but when the prop bends or breaks, neither the pegs nor ropes remain straight." (Biharul Anwar)

4 Collection: Tirmidhi

5 This is a popular teaching that is found across different spiritual traditions, which is why it has not been attributed to a single author.

6 Redd, Nola Taylor. "Einstein's Theory of General Relativity." Space.com, November 8, 2017. www.space.com/17661-theory-general-relativity.html.

7 Alban, Deane. "How to Increase Blood Flow to the Brain." *Be Brain Fit*, June 24, 2018. bebrainfit.com/increase-blood-flow-brain/.

8 Ober, Clinton, et al. *Earthing: The Most Important Health Discovery Ever!* Basic Health Publications, 2014.

9 Chevalier, Gaétan, et al. "Earthing: Health Implications of Reconnecting the Human Body to the Earth's Surface Electrons." *Journal of Environmental and Public Health.* www.ncbi.nlm.nih.gov/pmc/articles/PMC3265077/.

10 "Dr. Stephen Sinatra Talks About Grounding Benefits." Mercola.com. www.articles.mercola.com/sites/articles/archive/2013/08/04/barefoot-grounding-effect.aspx.

11 Collection: Muslim

12 Collection: Bukhari

13 Collection: Ibn Hibban

14 Hilyat al-Abrar, Vol. 1, pp. 321.

15 Collection: Bukhari

16 The word *falah* comes from the triliteral root *fa-lam-ha,* which means "to prosper, be successful, attain, plough, cultivate." The word *falah* shares the same root as the word *fellah* or "farmer." Again, this reiterates the notion that whatever we plant in this life we harvest in the next.

17 Collection: Muslim

18 Yusuf, Hamza. "Islam on Demand." 2011.

19 Collection: Tirmidhi

20 "Indeed, the first House [of worship] established for humankind was that at Becca [another name for Mecca]—blessed and a guidance for the worlds"

(3:96).

21   Goleman, Daniel. "A Feel-Good Theory: A Smile Affects Mood." *The New York Times*, July 18, 1989. www.nytimes.com/1989/07/18/science/a-feel-good-theory-a-smile-affects-mood.html.

22   Pronouncing Qur'anic Arabic properly is important, but Allah is merciful toward those who are not as proficient in Arabic. As the Prophet Muhammad ﷺ said, "Verily the one who recites the Qur'an beautifully, smoothly, and precisely, he will be in the company of the noble and obedient angels. And as for the one who recites with difficulty, stammering or stumbling through its verses, then he will have twice that reward." (Collection: Bukhari, Muslim)

23   The Prophet Muhammad ﷺ said, "The chapter commencing with 'All praises and thanks are due to Allah the Lord of the Worlds' is the Mother of the Qur'an, the Mother of the Book, the Seven Oft Repeated Verses and the Great Qur'an." (Collection: Tirmidhi)

24   The Prophet ﷺ narrated that, "Allah Almighty said: I have divided prayer between Myself and My servant into two halves, and My servant shall have what he has asked for. When the servant says 'all praise and glory belongs to Allah, the Lord of the worlds,' Allah says: My servant has praised me. When he says 'the Lord of Mercy, the Bestower of Mercy,' Allah says: My servant has exalted me. When he says 'the Master of the Day of Judgment,' Allah says: My servant has glorified me and my servant has submitted to me. When he says 'You alone we worship, You alone we ask for help,' Allah says: This is between Me and My servant, and My servant will have what he has asked for. When he says 'guide us to the straight path, the way of those whom You have bestowed Your grace, not of those who earned Your anger nor of those who went astray,' Allah says: This is for My servant, and My servant will have what he has asked for." (Collection: Muslim)

25   There is an ongoing debate about when the first prayer of the day is. Some scholars have said the first prayer is *maghrib*, while others believe it is *fajr*. This debate spills over into the verse that says, "Pay due attention to your prayers, especially the middle prayer and stand up while praying, in obedience to God." (2:238). Those who suggest *maghrib* is the first prayer see the middle prayer as *fajr*, while those who say *fajr* is the first prayer see the middle prayer as *asr*. There are also scholars who suggest that the

"middle prayer" is *dhuhr* because it is in the middle of the day.

26 Anonymous

27 Collection: Abu-Dawud, An-Nasa'i

28 For more on the practice of *tawba,* refer to Chapter 5.

Chapter 8—Zakat: Giving as an Instrument of God

1 Collection: Bukhari, Muslim

2 Collection: Abu Dawud

3 Collection: Muslim

4 Collection: Tirmidhi

5 Collection: Bukhari, Muslim

6 This insight is inspired by the following words from boxer Muhammad Ali: "Service to others is the rent you pay for your room here on Earth."

7 Collection: Bukhari

8 Collection: Tirmidhi

9 The original translation was "mice and weevils." Since most people don't know that a weevil is a type of beetle, I substituted the word "weevils" with "beetles."

10 Collection: Muslim

11 Safi, Omid. *Radical Love: Teachings from the Islamic Mystical Tradition.* Yale University Press, 2018.

12 Gibran, Kahlil. *The Prophet.* VIVI Books, 2016.

13 Collection: Bukhari

14 Collection: Al-Asfouri, in his book *Nuzhat al-Majalis,* on the authority of Ibn al-Tawous.

15 Collection: Muslim

16 Collection: Bukhari, Muslim

17 Bea, Scott. "Why Giving Is Good for Your Health." *Health Essentials from Cleveland Clinic,* January 30, 2018. health.clevelandclinic.org/why-giving-is-good-for-your-health/.

18 Suttie, Jill, and Jason Marsh. "5 Ways Giving Is Good for You." *Greater Good,* December 13, 2010, greatergood.berkeley.edu/article/item/5_ways_giving_is_good_for_you.

19 This quote is Pastor Rick Warren's rendition of a saying from C.S. Lewis.

20 Swalin, Rachel. "4 Health Benefits of Being Generous." Health.com, December 2, 2014. www.health.com/stress/

giving-tuesday-health-benefits-of-generosity.

21   Waters, Lea, et al. "Why Giving Is Good for the Soul." *Pursuit*, The
      University of Melbourne, July 23, 2018. pursuit.unimelb.edu.au/articles/
      why-giving-is-good-for-the-soul.

22   "Exploring the Eel River Valley." *Logging Industry*. sunnyfortuna.com/
      explore/redwoods_and_water.htm.

23   "About Coast Redwoods." CA State Parks. www.parks.
      ca.gov/?page_id=22257.

24   Collection: Al-Kubra, Ibn Abbas

25   Collection: Bukhari, Muslim

26   This narration is considered a *Hadith Qudsi*. This type of narration is
      different than a *Hadith Nabawi* or a general saying from the Prophet
      ﷺ, because the chain of transmission of a *Hadith Qudsi* goes directly
      back to God instead of the chain of narrators ending with the Prophet
      Muhammad ﷺ. However, a *Hadith Qudsi* is different from a verse of the
      Qur'an. Whereas a *Hadith Qudsi* is a saying in which the meaning is sent
      from God but the words are formulated by the Prophet ﷺ, the Qur'an
      comprises of God's exact speech, both in meaning and wording.

27   Collection: Bukhari

28   This is famously known as the Serenity Prayer. It was written by Christian
      theologian Reinhold Niebuhr.

Chapter 9—Ramadan: The Holy Month of Fasting

1   Imam Qurtubi said, "It (this month) was named Ramadan because it
      burns the sins of people with righteous deeds."

2   Collection: Bukhari

3   Collection: Tirmidhi

4   Since materialism and worshipping the world are often cited in Islamic
      theology as one of the roots of evil, when we fast we intentionally seek to
      turn our awareness from this fleeting creation to the eternal Creator. There
      is also a Hadith that is from Bayhaqi's Shu'ab al-Iman and traced back to
      al-Hasan al-Basri, who said the Prophet ﷺ had said, "Love of this world is
      the root of all evil." In some narrations this is also attributed to Jesus. The
      idea that the love of the world distracts the heart from worship is not seen
      as a new or revolutionary concept in Islam, but also exists in Judaism and

Christianity.

5   Collection: Muslim

6   Collection: Bukhari, Muslim, Malik, Tirmidhi, An-Nasa'i, Ibn Majah

7   As previously mentioned: "The innate alignment with the Divine that
      resides at the heart of being human is often called 'the primordial essence'
      or referred to in Arabic as the *fitra*. The word *fitra* comes from a root word
      meaning 'to split or bring forth.' This implies that our work on this Earth is
      to split the shell of our ego and *bring forth* the divine seeds God has already
      planted in the garden of our spirits through the generosity of His love."

8   Collection: Tirmidhi

9   Group, Dr. Edward. "20 Health Benefits of Fasting for Whole Body Wellness."
      Dr. Group's Healthy Living Articles, Global Healing Center, Inc, June 13, 2017.
      www.globalhealingcenter.com/natural-health/health-benefits-of-fasting/.

10   Whiteman, Honor. "Fasting: Health Benefits and Risks." *Medical News Today*,
      MediLexicon International, July 27, 2015. www.medicalnewstoday.com/
      articles/295914.php.

11   Stibich, Mark. "Hara Hachi Bu: The Japanese Secret to Longevity."
      Verywell Health, October 19, 2017. www.verywellhealth.com/
      hara-hachi-bu-the-okinawans-secret-to-longevity-2224043.

12   Collection: Tirmidhi

13   This narration is considered a *Hadith Qudsi*. This type of narration is
      different than a *Hadith Nabawi* or a general saying from the Prophet ﷺ,
      because the chain of transmission of a *Hadith Qudsi* goes directly back to
      God instead of the chain of narrators ending with the Prophet Muhammad
      ﷺ. However, a *Hadith Qudsi* is different from a verse of the Qur'an. Whereas
      a *Hadith Qudsi* is a saying in which the meaning is sent from God but the
      words are formulated by the Prophet ﷺ, the Qur'an comprises of God's
      exact speech, both in meaning and wording.

14   Collection: Abu Huraira, Darimi

15   Collection: Bukhari

16   Adams, AJ. "Seeing Is Believing: The Power of Visualization." *Psychology
      Today*, Sussex Publishers. www.psychologytoday.com/us/blog/
      flourish/200912/seeing-is-believing-the-power-visualization.

17   Lohr, Jim. "Can Visualizing Your Body Doing Something Help You Learn
      to Do It Better?" *Scientific American*. www.scientificamerican.com/article/

can-visualizing-your-body-doing-something-help-you-learn-to-do-it-better/.

18   B., Zoe. "Harvard Research—How Thoughts Affect Your Brain." *Simple Life Strategies*, 2013. simplelifestrategies.com/harvard-research/.

19   Pillay, Srinivasan. "The Science of Visualization: Maximizing Your Brain's Potential During the Recession." The Huffington Post. www.huffingtonpost.com/srinivasan-pillay/the-science-of-visualizat_b_171340.html.

20   Collection: Bukhari

21   Collection: Bukhari

22   The Prophet Muhammad ﷺ said, "Search for the Night of Qadr in the odd nights of the last ten days of Ramadan." (Collection: Bukhari)

23   Collection: Ahmad

24   Collection: Bukhari, Muslim

25   Collection: Tirmidhi

Chapter 10—Hajj: A Pilgrimage to God

1   Chittick, William C. *The Inner Journey: Views from the Islamic Tradition.* Morning Light Press, 2007. *Note: This quote is not saying that we become God, rather that through surrender we bypass the veils of arrogance in order to experience God.

2   Jews and Christians believe Prophet Abraham was called by God to sacrifice the first son he had from his wife Sara by the name of Isaac.

3   As previously mentioned: "The Qur'an reminds us of a realm where God planted the seeds of faith, love, and unity in the fertile hearts of all humankind, known as the Covenant of Alast. In a pre-eternal realm, before this world as we know it, every soul that would one day manifest into an earthly form was asked by Allah, 'Am I not your Lord?' This soup of souls vibrated into a symphony of affirmation as every single being replied, 'Yes, yes, we testify' to the singularity of God. As a result of this covenant, it can be said that at the soul level every person, regardless of conscious belief, is fully aligned with the Divine" (7:172).

4   Some scholars believe it was a ram that was sacrificed.

5   Anwaar, Amna. "All You Need to Know about Bait-Ul Ma'mur." *IslamicFinder*, July 21, 2017. www.islamicfinder.org/news/all-you-need-to-know-about-bait-ul-mamur/.

6   Some more mystically inclined scholars have even suggested that Arafat is where all the souls that would one day manifest into earthly bodies made the pre-eternal Covenant of Alast, where they declared that God's Lordship and Supremacy is above all of creation.

7   The Prophet Muhammad ﷺ said, "There is no day upon which Allah frees more of his servants from the Hellfire than the day of Arafat." (Collection: Muslim)

8   Collection: Tirmidhi

9   Collection: Bukhari

10   Collection: Bukhari, Muslim, Abu Dawud, An-Nasa'i

Chapter 11—The Spiritual Secrets of Death

1   As Rumi says, "Have you ever seen a seed fall upon the earth and not rise with new life? Why should you doubt the rise of a seed named human?"

2   Tuckerman , Mark E. "Law of Conservation of Energy." New York University. www.nyu.edu/classes/tuckerman/adv.chem/lectures/lecture_2/node4.html.

3   "It is He, who takes your souls by night (when you are asleep), and has knowledge of all that you have done by day" (6:60).

4   Anonymous

5   Poore, Jennifer. "These Flowers Only Bloom After Forest Fires." *Redding Record Searchlight*, June 2, 2017. www. redding.com/story/life/home-garden/2017/06/02/ these-flowers-only-bloom-after-forest-fires/364114001/.

6   Collection: Bukhari

7   Collection: Tirmidhi

8   Anonymous

9   The phrase "Die before you die" has been attributed to the Prophet Muhammad ﷺ, Imam Ali, and many mystics of different traditions.

10   Ricard, Matthieu. *On the Path to Enlightenment: Heart Advice from the Great Tibetan Masters.* Shambhala, 2013.

11   This quote is often attributed to Imam Ali.

12   In reference to death the Prophet Muhammad ﷺ said, "Remember frequently the thing that cuts off pleasures." (Collection: Tirmidhi)

13   Al-Ghazali, Abu Hamid. Dear Beloved Son— Ayyuhal Walad. Lulu.com, 2015.

14   Collection: Tirmidhi

15   Collection: Bukhari

16   Collection: Al-Albani

17   This quote has also been attributed to Prophet Muhammad ﷺ, Imam Ali, and found in Native American traditions as well.

18   Collection: Muslim, Ahmad

Chapter 12—The Mysteries of Heaven and Hell

1   This is a metaphorical reference to Qur'an 52:23.

2   Collection: Tirmidhi

3   Collection: Tirmidhi. The Qur'an reiterates the point that the rewards of Paradise are unlike anything man has ever known when it says, "No person knows what is kept hidden for them of delights of the eye as a reward for what they used to do" (32:17).

4   Quraeshi, Samina, et al. *Sacred Spaces: A Journey with the Sufis of the Indus.* Peabody Museum of Archaeology and Ethnology, 2009.

5   Safi, Omid. "The Sufi Tradition—Literary and Cultural Dimensions." Bayan Claremont, February 11, 2019, Claremont.

6   Vakil, Mohammed Ali, and Mohammed Arif Vakil. *40 Sufi Comics.* Sufi Studios, 2012.

7   Some scholars suggest that Hell, for some, is not an eternal destination, but a place of purification.

8   Some have attributed this story to Mullah Nasruddin. This story strongly correlates with Qur'an verses 66:6 and 21:98

9   The moment God gave us free will, He had to allow for the possibility that we could turn away from Him. Our free will creates duality, and that duality necessitates two ultimate destinations: one toward the light and one away from the light. If we want to eliminate Hell and only have Heaven, then we must also eliminate all the possible choices that would lead us to Hell. If God only allowed us to choose the path to Heaven, then we could not manifest our free will, because we would only have one option, with no freedom to deny that choice.

10   This narration is considered a *Hadith Qudsi.* This type of narration is different than a *Hadith Nabawi* or a general saying from the Prophet ﷺ, because the chain of transmission of a *Hadith Qudsi* goes directly back to

God instead of the chain of narrators ending with the Prophet Muhammad ﷺ. However, a *Hadith Qudsi* is different from a verse of the Qur'an. Whereas a *Hadith Qudsi* is a saying in which the meaning is sent from God but the words are formulated by the Prophet ﷺ, the Qur'an comprises of God's exact speech, both in meaning and wording.(Collection: Muslim)

11   Collection: Bukhari

12   Collection: Bukhari

13   Al-Rawi, Rosina Fawzia. *Divine Names: The 99 Healing Names of the One Love*. Olive Branch Press, 2015.

14   Khalil, Mohammad Hassan. *Islam and the Fate of Others the Salvation Question*. Oxford University Press, 2012.

15   The Prophet Muhammad ﷺ said, "Verily, Allah has recorded good and bad deeds and He made them clear. Whoever intends to perform a good deed but does not do it, then Allah will record it as a complete good deed. If he intends to do it and does so, then Allah, The Exalted will record it as ten good deeds up to seven hundred times as much or even more. If he intends to do a bad deed and does not do it, then Allah will record for him one complete good deed. If he does it then Allah will record for him a single bad deed." (Collection: Bukhari)

16   Collection: Bukhari

17   Collection: Bukhari, Muslim

18   Anonymous

You Are Love

1   Collection: Tirmidhi

2   A traditional Islamic prayer

Appendix

1   Collection: Muslim

BIBLIOGRAPHY

Al-'Arabi Ibn, et al. *101 Diamonds from the Oral Tradition of the Glorious Messenger Muhammad Mishkat Al-Anwar: A Collection of Hadith.* Pir Press, 2002.

Al-Ghazali, Abu Hamid. *The Alchemy of Happiness.* WLC, 2009.

Al-Husayn Sharif al-Radi Muhammad ibn, et al. *Nahjul Balagha.* Peermahomed Ebrahim Trust, 1972.

Al-Husayn Sharif al-Radi Muhammad ibn, and Thomas F. Cleary. *Living and Dying with Grace: Counsels of Hadrat 'Alī.* Shambhala, 1996.

Ali, Abdullah Yusuf. *The Meaning of the Holy Qur'ān: Explanatory English Translation, Commentary, and Comprehensive Index.* Amana Publications, 2016.

"Al-Qur'an Al-Kareem." *Al-Qur'an Al-Kareem.* quran.com.

Al-Rawi, Rosina Fawzia. *Divine Names: The 99 Healing Names of the One Love.* Olive Branch Press, 2015.

Ananda, Maitreya. *The Dhammapada.* Parallax Press, 2001.

Armstrong, Karen. *Muhammad Prophet of Our Time.* HarperPress, 2006.

Asad, Muhammad, and Ahmed Moustafa. *The Message of the Qur'ān: the Full Account of the Revealed Arabic Text Accompanied by Parallel Transliteration.* Book Foundation, 2012.

A'zami, Muhammad Mustafa. *The History of the Qur'ānic Text: From Revelation to Compilation: A Comparative Study with the Old and New Testaments.* Al-Qalam Pub., 2011.

Barks, Coleman, and Michael Green. *The Illuminated Prayer: The Five-Times Prayer of the Sufis as Revealed by Jellaludin Rumi and Bawa Muhaiyaddeen.* Ballantine Wellspring, 2000.

Bayrak, Tosun. *The Most Beautiful Names.* Threshold Books, 1985.

Berg, Yehudah. *Satan: An Autobiography.* Kabbalah Centre, 2016.

Bly, Robert, and Kabir. *Kabir: Ecstatic Poems.* Beacon Press, 2004.

Bradshaw, John. *Healing the Shame That Binds You.* Health Communications, Inc., 2005.

Bucaille, Maurice. *The Bible, the Qur'an, and Science: The Holy Scriptures Examined in the Light of Modern Knowledge.* Tahrike Tarsile Qur'an, 2014.

Chittick, William C. *The Inner Journey: Views from the Islamic Tradition.* Morning Light Press, 2007.

Cleary, Thomas, and Bukari Muhammad. *The Wisdom of the Prophet: Sayings of Muhammad.* Shambhala, 2002.

Coelho, Paulo. *The Alchemist.* HarperCollins Publishers, 1993.

Coelho, Paulo, and Margaret Jull Costa. *Warrior of the Light: A Manual.* HarperCollins, 2011.

"Du'aa of Light." *Authentic Dua and Dhikr.* authentic-dua.com/2011/12/10/duaa-of-light-noor, June 10, 2016.

Easwaran, Eknath. *The Bhagavad Gita.* 2nd ed., Nilgiri Press, 2007.

Easwaran, Eknath. *The Upanishads.* 2nd ed., Jaico Pub. House, 2010.

Fadiman, James, and Robert Frager. *Essential Sufism: Selections from the Saints and Sages.* Gulshan Books, 2009.

Freke, Timothy. *The Heart of Islam.* Godsfield, 2002.

Gibran, Khalil. *Prophet.* Arcturus Publishing LTD, 2017.

Glassel, Cyril. *The New Encyclopedia of Islam: A Revised Edition of the Concise Encyclopedia of Islam.* Altamira, 2002.

Goss, Phil. *Jung: A Complete Introduction: Teach Yourself.* Hodder and Stoughton General Div, 2015.

"Hadith Collection." Hadith Qudsi—Hadith Collection. www.hadithcollection.com/hadith-qudsi.html.

"Hadith of the Day." hadithoftheday.com.

Harvey, Andrew, and Eryk Hanut. *Perfume of the Desert: Inspirations from Sufi Wisdom.* Theosophical Publishing House, 1999.

Hawking, Stephen. *A Brief History of Time.* Bantam Books, 2017.

Hixon, Lex. *The Heart of the Qur'an: An Introduction to Islamic Spirituality.* 2nd ed., The Theosophical Publishing House, 2003.

Holy Bible. New Living Translation. Tyndale House, 2005.

"Humility in the Quran and Sunnah." *Faith in Allah.* abuaminaelias.com/humility-in-the-quran-and-sunnah/.

Ibn 'Ata Allah, Ahmad ibn Muhammad, et al. *Ibn 'Ata' Illah: The Book of Wisdom, and Kwaja Abdullah Ansari: Intimate Conversations.* Paulist Press, 1978.

Irving, Thomas Ballantine., et al. *The Qur'ān: Basic Teachings.* Da'awah Academy, International Islamic University, 1994.

Jaffer, Tahir Ridha. "Ghurar Al-Hikam Wa Durar Al-Kalim, Exalted Aphorisms And Pearls Of Speech." *Al-Islam.org.* www.al-islam.org/ghurar-al-hikam-wa-durar-al-kalim-exalted-aphorisms-and-pearls-speech.

Khalil, Mohammad Hassan. *Islam and the Fate of Others the Salvation Question.* Oxford University Press, 2012.

Khan, Nouman Ali. *Revive Your Heart: Putting Life in Perspective.* Kube Publishing Ltd, 2017.

Khan, Nouman Ali, and Sharif Randhawa. *Divine Speech.* Bayyinah Publications, 2016.

Kidwai, Abdur Raheem. *Daily Wisdom: Sayings of the Prophet Muhammad.* Kube, 2010.

Kidwai, Abdur Raheem. *Daily Wisdom: Selections from the Holy Qur'an.* Kube, 2011.

Kidwai, Abdur Raheem. *The Qur'an: Essential Teachings.* Islamic Foundation Limited, 2015.

Ladinsky, Daniel James. *Love Poems from God: Twelve Sacred Voices from the East and West.* Penguin Compass, 2002.

Leaman, Oliver. *The Qur'an: An Encyclopedia.* Routledge, 2010.

Lewis, Clive S. *The Problem of Pain.* HarperCollins, 2014.

Lewis, C. S. *The Great Divorce.* Collins, 2012.

Lings, Martin. *Muhammad: His Life Based on the Earliest Sources.* Islamic Texts Society, 2007.

Mazrui, Shaykh al-Amin Ali. *The Content of Character: Ethical Sayings of the Prophet Muhammad.* Sandala, 2005.

Meyer, Wali Ali., and Bilal Hyde. *Physicians of the Heart: A Sufi View of the Ninety-Nine Names of Allah.* Sufi Ruhaniat International, 2012.

Mogahed, Yasmin. *Reclaim Your Heart: Personal Insights on Breaking Free from Life's Shackles.* FB Publishing, 2015.

Muhammad Ibn Talal Ghazi ibn, et al. *War and Peace in Islam: The Uses and Abuses of Jihad.* The Islamic Texts Society, 2013.

Murata, Sachiko, and William C. Chittick. *The Vision of Islam.* Gulshan Books Kashmir, 2015.

Nasr, Seyyed Hossein. *The Garden of Truth: The Vision and Promise of Sufism, Islam's Mystical Tradition.* HarperOne, 2008.

Nasr, Seyyed Hossein. *Islamic Spirituality: Foundations.* Crossroad, 1987.

Nasr, Seyyed Hossein. *The Study Quran: A New Translation and Commentary.* HarperOne, an Imprint of HarperCollins Publishers, 2017.

Nepo, Mark. *The Book of Awakening.* Conari Press, 2000.

Nguyen, Martin. *Modern Muslim Theology: Engaging God and the World with Faith and Imagination.* Rowman & Littlefield, 2019.

Nicholson, Reynold Alleyne. *The Mathnawi.* E.J. Brill Luzac & Co., 1925.

Peterson, Eugene H. *The Message: The Bible in Contemporary Language.* NavPress, 2017.

Power, Carla. *If the Oceans Were Ink: An Unlikely Friendship and a Journey to the Heart of the Qur'an.* Henry Holt and Company, 2015.

Rahman, Fazlur, and Ebrahim Moosa. *Major Themes of the Qur'ān.* The University of Chicago Press, 2013.

Rahman, Jamal. *The Fragrance of Faith: The Enlightened Heart of Islam.* Book Foundation, 2006.

Rahman, Jamal. *Spiritual Gems of Islam: Insights, Practices from the Qur'an, Hadith, Rumi, and Muslim Teaching Stories to Enlighten the Heart and Mind.* SkyLight Paths Publishing, 2014.

Rahman, Jamal, et al. *Out of Darkness into Light: Spiritual Guidance in the Quran with Reflections from Jewish and Christian Sources.* Morehouse Pub., 2009.

Ricard, Matthieu. *On the Path to Enlightenment: Heart Advice from the Great Tibetan Masters.* Shambhala, 2013.

Rifa'i, Muhammad al-Jamal. *Conversations in the Zawiyah.* Sidi Muhammad Press, 1999.

Rifa'i, Muhammad al-Jamal. *The Deeper Meaning behind the Pillars of Islam.* Sidi Muhammad Press, 1996.

Rifa'i, Muhammad al-Jamal. *He Who Knows Himself Knows His Lord.* Sidi Muhammad Press, 2007.

Rifaʿi, Muhammad al-Jamal. *Music of the Soul: Sufi Teachings*. Sidi Muhammad Press, 1997.

Rifaʿi, Muhammad al-Jamal. *The Path of Allah Most High*. Sidi Muhammad Press, 1997.

Rifaʿi, Muhammad al-Jamal. *The Reality of Imagination*. Sidi Muhammad Press, 1999.

Robinson, Neal. *Discovering the Qurʾan: A Contemporary Approach to a Veiled Text*. Georgetown University Press, 2004.

Rubin, David C. *Memory in Oral Traditions: The Cognitive Psychology of Epic, Ballads, and Counting-out Rhymes*. Oxford University Press, 1998.

Rumi Jalal al-Din, et al. *The Illustrated Rumi: A Treasury of Wisdom from the Poet of the Soul*. HarperOne, 2010.

Rumi Jalal al-Din, et al. *Jewels of Remembrance: A Daybook of Spiritual Guidance: Containing 365 Selections from the Wisdom of Rumi*. Shambhala, 2000.

Rumi Jalal al-Din, and Coleman Barks. *The Essential Rumi*. HarperOne, 2004.

Rumi Jalal al-Din, and Jonathan Star. *Rumi: In the Arms of the Beloved*. Jeremy P. Tarcher/Penguin, 2009.

Safi, Omid. *Radical Love: Teachings from the Islamic Mystical Tradition*. Yale University Press, 2018.

Shafak, Elif. *The Forty Rules of Love*. Penguin Books, 2015.

Shah, Idries. *The Pleasantries of the Incredible Mulla Nasrudin*. ISF Publishing, 2015.

Shah-Kazemi, Reza. *Common Ground between Islam and Buddhism*. Louisville, KY: Fons Vitae, 2011.

Shariʾati, Ali. *Hajj: Reflections on Its Rituals*. ABJAD, 1992.

Shariʾati, Ali. *On the Sociology of Islam*. Algorithm, 2017.

Sultan, Sohaib. *The Qurʾan and Sayings of Prophet Muhammad: Selections Annotated and Explained*. SkyLight Paths Pub., 2012.

Tarsin, Asad, and Shaykh Hamza. Yusuf. *Being Muslim: A Practical Guide*. Sandala Inc., 2015.

"The Quranic Arabic Corpus - Word by Word Grammar, Syntax and Morphology of the Holy Quran." corpus.quran.com.

The University of Spiritual Healing and Sufism. *A Drop in the Ocean of Love: Ancient Wisdom for Living a Divinely-Guided Life*. DPWN Publishing, 2017.

Tolstoy, Leo. *War and Peace*. Walter Scott Pub. Co., 1920.

Vakil, Mohammed Ali, and Mohammed Arif Vakil. *40 Sufi Comics*. CreateSpace Independent Publishing Platform, 2011.

Walker, Brian Browne. *The Tao Te Ching of Lao Tzu*. St. Martin's Press, 1995.

Warren, Rick. *The Purpose Driven Life*. Zondervan, 2006.

Watts, Alan. *The Wisdom of Insecurity: A Message for an Age of Anxiety*. Vintage Books, 2011.

Wheeler, Brannon M. *Prophets in the Quran: An Introduction to the Quran and Muslim Exegesis*. Continuum, 2002.

X, Malcolm, et al. *The Autobiography of Malcolm X*. Ballantine Books, 1999.

Yusaf, Mamoon. *Inside the Soul of Islam: A Unique View into the love, Beauty, and Wisdom of Islam for Spiritual Seekers of All Faiths*. Hay House, Inc., 2017.

Zakariya, Abu. *The Eternal Challenge: A Journey through the Miraculous Qur'an*. One Reason, 2015.

ABOUT THE AUTHOR

A. HELWA believes that every single person on Earth is deeply loved by the Divine. She is a writer who has inspired hundreds of thousands of readers through her passionate, poetic, and love-based approach to spirituality. Her popular blog @quranquotesdaily, was established while obtaining her Masters in Divinity, as a means of helping others overcome personal and spiritual struggles on their journey of experiencing divine love.

With over 15 years of experience writing and speaking on Islam and spiritual development, A. Helwa draws from her personal experiences and traditional sources to help her readers access 'Divine love in everyday life.'

When A. Helwa is not reading at coffee shops, she can be found climbing mountains, camping in deserts, hiking jungles, or reading about black holes. Learn more about her work and how to approach the Divine through love at www.SecretsofDivineLove.com.